The Renaissance Literature Handbook

Literature and Culture Handbooks

General Editors: Philip Tew and Steven Barfield

Literature and Culture Handbooks are an innovative series of guides to major periods, topics and authors in British and American literature and culture. Designed to provide a comprehensive, one-stop resource for literature students, each handbook provides the essential information and guidance needed from the beginning of a course through to developing more advanced knowledge and skills.

The Eighteenth-Century Literature Handbook
Edited by Gary Day and Bridge Keegan

The Medieval British Literature Handbook
Edited by Daniel T. Kline

The Modernism Handbook
Edited by Philip Tew and Alex Murray

The Post-war British Literature Handbook
Edited by Katharine Cockin and Jago Morrison

The Seventeenth-Century Literature Handbook
Edited by Robert C. Evans and Eric J. Sterling

The Shakespeare Handbook
Edited by Andrew Hiscock and Stephen Longstaffe

The Victorian Literature Handbook
Edited by Alexandra Warwick and Martin Willis

The Renaissance Literature Handbook

Edited by

Susan Bruce

and

Rebecca Steinberger

continuum

Continuum

The Tower Building
11 York Road
London SE1 7NX

80 Maiden Lane, Suite 704
New York
NY 10038

www.continuumbooks.com

British Library Cataloguing-in-Publication Data
A catalogue record for this book is available from the British Library.

ISBN: 978-0-8264-9499-3 (hardback)
        978-0-8264-9500-6 (paperback)

Library of Congress Cataloging-in-Publication Data
A catalog record for this book is available from the Library of Congress

Typeset by RefineCatch Limited, Bungay, Suffolk
Printed and bound in Great Britain by The MPG Books Group

Contents

Detailed Table of Contents

General Editors' Introduction

The Continuum's *Literature and Culture Handbooks* series aims to support both students new to an area of study and those at a more advanced stage, offering guidance with regard to the major periods, topics and authors relevant to the study of various aspects of British and American literature and culture. The series is designed with an international audience in mind, based on research into today's students in a global educational setting. Each volume is concerned with either a particular historical phase or an even more specific context, such as a major author study. All of the chosen areas represent established subject matter for literary study in schools, colleges and universities; all are both widely taught and are the subjects of ongoing research and scholarship. Each handbook provides a comprehensive, one-stop resource for literature students, offering essential information and guidance needed at the beginning of a course through to more advanced knowledge and skills for the student more familiar with the particular topic. These volumes reflect current academic research and scholarship, teaching methods and strategies, and also provide an outline of essential historical contexts. Written in clear language by leading internationally-acknowledged academics, each book provides the following:

- Introduction to authors, texts, historical and cultural contexts
- Guides to key critics, concepts and topics
- Introduction to critical approaches, changes in the canon and new conceptual and theoretical issues, such as gender and ethnicity
- Case studies in reading literary, theoretical and critical texts
- Annotated bibliography (including selected websites), timeline and a glossary of useful critical terms.

This student-friendly series as a whole has drawn its inspiration and structure largely from the latest principles of text book design employed in other disciplines and subjects, creating an unusual and distinctive approach for the undergraduate arts and humanities field. This structure is designed to be user-friendly and it is intended that the layout can be easily navigated, with various points of cross-reference. Such clarity and straightforward approach should help students understand the material and in so doing guide them through the increasing academic difficulty of complex, critical and theoretical approaches to Literary Studies. These handbooks serve as gateways to the particular field that is explored.

All volumes make use of a 'progressive learning strategy', rather than the traditional chronological approach to the subject under discussion so that they might relate more closely to the learning process of the student. This means that the particular volume offers material that will aid the student to approach the period or topic confidently in the classroom for the very first time (for example, glossaries, historical context, key topics and critics), as well as material that helps the student develop more advanced skills (learning how to respond actively to selected primary texts and analyse and engage with modern critical arguments in relation to such texts). Each volume includes a specially commissioned new critical essay by a leading authority in the field discussing current debates and contexts. The progression in the contents mirrors the progress of the undergraduate student from beginner to a more advanced level. Each volume is aimed primarily at undergraduate students, intending to offer itself as both a guide and a reference text that will reflect the advances in academic studies in its subject matter, useful to both students and staff (the latter may find the appendix on pedagogy particularly helpful).

We realize that students in the twenty-first century are faced with numerous challenges and demands; it is our intention that the Handbook series should empower its readers to become effective and efficient in their studies.

Philip Tew & Steven Barfield

Introduction

Susan Bruce

<table>
<tr><td colspan="2" align="center">**Chapter Overview**</td></tr>
<tr><td>Introduction</td><td align="right">1</td></tr>
<tr><td>Renaissance Timeline: 1485 to 1639</td><td align="right">12</td></tr>
</table>

> Thou, that mak'st gaine thy end, and wisely well,
> Call'st a Book good, or bad, as it doth sell,
> Use mine so, too: I give thee leave. But crave
> For the lucks sake, it thus much favour have,
> To lie upon thy stall, till it be sought;
> Not offer'd, as it made sute to be bought;
> Nor have my title-leafe on posts, or walls,
> Or in cleft-sticks, advanced to make calls
> For termers, or some clerck-like serving-man,
> Who scarce can spell th' hard names: whose Knight less can.
> If, without these vile Arts, it will not sell,
> Send it to *Bucklers-bury*, there 'twill well.[1]

It may seem something of a hostage to fortune to open a textbook with a close reading of a poem which instructs its reader to judge its quality on how many copies it sells. By that measure, most academic volumes – even textbooks, which the publishers hope will sell in much larger numbers than most scholarly monographs do – would be a good deal 'worse' than any airport paperback, and, by the same token, most textbooks would be rather 'better' than the scholarly work (and many of the primary texts) which they purport to elucidate and explain. But to draw attention to this anxiety about the relation between the value of an item and the market for it is to signal how Jonson's epigram, superficially so remote from our own time, might be read in some ways as ushering it in. On the one hand, the poem gestures at sights and categories long since lost to our own, twenty-first century, physical and social landscapes: to reproduced title pages stuck on walls and posts and in cleft-sticks,[2] to the 'termers'[3] and to the serving men and their Knights, about whom Jonson is so snobby and

1

contemptuous. Even his fastidious horror at the thought of his book being advertised is in some ways a marker of his distance from the print culture of today, where few authors would see the dream of a book selling without the help of the 'vile arts' of advertising as anything more than an idle fantasy.

But then again, perhaps this is exactly how Jonson sees it too: his sardonic tone may belie a sense that however much he might pretend to himself and to his readers, actual (the consumer) as well as overtly implied (the Bookseller), that he can control the circulation of this particular commodity, in fact he knows all too well that he can't. He no longer has sole interest in this commodity after all: unlike the poet in a Renaissance court, whose works might be produced in a laboriously handwritten presentation copy, and donated to a dignitary, a prince or other aristocrat, whose patronage the poet desired, Jonson has relinquished control over the fruits of his labour by ceding that control to the Bookseller on whose stall the Book now lies, who has, therefore, an interest himself in whether or not it is advertised to prospective customers. Jonson's rights in his own work – his intellectual property, as later ages, including our own, might call it – is compromised from the moment his work becomes a commodity, to be sold in a market-place like any other commodity and, in a final ironic flourish, sent to Bucklers-bury, where it may have monetary- and use-value as wrapping paper if it fails to convince the consumer that its aesthetic worth merits the pennies he might spend on it at the Bookseller's stall.[4] So, in the space of twelve lines the Book becomes a commodity, and as a commodity is then fetishized, given powers which transcend its materiality, and raise it from being a simple object almost to a supernatural being, endowed with a literal as well as a figurative voice. But even as he fetishizes it, conferring upon it an identity more akin to that of a person than a book, Jonson (or his persona) articulates also his own alienation from it, and can in the end see nothing of clear value in it whatsoever except for the raw materials of which it is made. For the Book ends up in a place where the words that ought to give it its meaning are the only thing that actually have no value – neither use nor exchange – at all.

This poem thus tropes a characteristic Jonsonian preoccupation, in which everything (even in this case, waste) is a commodity and wherein commodities take on a life of their own, themselves jostle for the attention of the consumer ('make Suit to be bought') in a world which is akin to one big market place. This is an urban space, a space of Walls and stalls and market calls, a space where knights rub shoulders with serving men, and where the poet, through the medium of his book, is brought into proximity with an audience far wider and more diverse than ever he would have experienced, let alone addressed, before. Jonson was at ease writing for the traditional aristocratic patron as well, either in poetry or in the rarefied dramatic genre of the masque but his self-conscious awareness of this new, more diverse and distinctively urban landscape and audience is apparent in his drama as well as in his poetry. *Bartholomew Fair*, for example, articulates similar concerns about audience, taste and questions of financial and literary value in its 'Induction on the Stage' wherein the actors appear in the roles of stage hands and theatrical functionaries, inviting the audience into the world of the play with a contract which, though it is parodic and self-mocking, draws everyone's attention to the fact that this work of art is also a commercial exchange, money for pleasure (or at least for the ability to lament its absence). The Scrivener reads out to the Stage-Keeper and Book-holder and of course to the audience too, the 'Articles of agreement, indented, between the spectators or hearers at the Hope on the Bankside, in the County of Surrey on the one party; And the Author of *Bartholomew Fair* in the said place and County on the other party:' in which are clearly stated the amounts of aesthetic judgement allowed to each person in the audience, according to what he has paid for his ticket. 'It is further agreed', the Scrivener proclaims:

> That every person here have his or their free-will of censure, to like or dislike at their own charge, the author having now departed with his right. It shall be lawful for any man to judge his six penn'orth, his twelve penn'orth, so to his eighteen pence, two shillings, half a crown, to the value of his place. Provided always his place get not above his wit. And if he pay for half a dozen, he may censure for all them too, so that he will undertake that they shall be silent. He shall put in for censures here as they do for lots at the lottery. Marry, if he drop but sixpence at the door and will censure a crown's worth, it is thought there is no conscience, or justice in that. (Jonson 1997, induction, 72–82)

As we saw in our reading of the epigram 'To My Book-seller', Jonson's sense that he can control the adjudication and marketing of his intellectual property gives way in the end to the suspicion that actually, he probably cannot. Here too in *Bartholomew Fair*, the ostensible belief that a contract between author and audience will effectively delimit the right of the consumer to pass judgement on the work goes hand in hand with a tacit acknowledgement that, 'the author having now departed with his right', Jonson has in reality little control any more over the reception of his play, since the right to value an item – and here, even the right to articulate that valuation – is no longer (if ever it was) depend-ent on the class of the person making the judgement, or on how much he has paid to see the work he judges. '*Inprimis*', the Scrivener had begun:

> It is covenanted and agreed by and between the parties above said, [that] . . . the said spectators, and hearers, . . . do for themselves severally covenant and agree to remain in the places their money or friends have put them in, with patience, for the space of two hours and an half, and somewhat more. (Jonson, 1997, induction 62–66)

But this, of course, is exactly what *cannot* be covenanted and agreed. People can no longer be depended upon to 'remain in [their] places . . . with patience', and the humour derives in part from the ludicrousness of the claim that a covenant or contract could force them to do so.

Both of these cases arguably illustrate a tension that pervades Jonson's drama and his poetry quite systematically, at least that which is urban in its setting. A resistance to the necessity of mixing with the uncouth and the riff-raff and of being, in some senses, their servant or hireling, since it is from their pennies and not from the aristocratic patron's largesse that he now earns a large part of his keep, is mixed with a sense (of which Jonson sometimes appears to be quite conscious) of the extraordinary energies of this new commercial urban world in which much of Jonson's works are so intrinsically rooted. Like the other city comedies of the late sixteenth and early seventeenth centuries (but arguably more so), Jonson's drama is full of movement and vitality, populated by characters who burst into and out of and across the stage, expressing the energies and busyness (business) not merely of the new urban spaces of the early modern period, but also of the new urban relations between people which evolved to fit them. This, I'd claim, is one of the ways in which the early modern period looks forward to our own time, leaving behind the quiet certainties of the medieval world which predated it to embrace instead the dangerous pleasures of a world driven by the energies of burgeoning exchange and discovery, and of new inventions and realms of knowledge that were not dreamt of in earlier philosophies (see Waswo 2007).

This, in any case and at the risk of repetition, is how I would read these passages. But it is not the only way of understanding them, nor the only context in which to place them. I've offered you a brief reading here which celebrates the period's break with what predated it and gestures towards its connections with our own time and concerns, which I've tried to identify in the two passages that I discuss. But in the last essay in this volume, you will find an account which critiques those presumptions, and argues that they are liable to generate erroneous readings of the texts that we study. For Thomas Healy, whose 'Returning to the Renaissance' concludes our volume, contemporary criticism of the literature of the period, unlike that of the 1980s and 1990s, is more likely to seek to rediscover the 'era's own categories for understanding literary, social and political developments' than it is to try (as I've done here in this introduction) to '[discover in it] convenient parallels with current models for understanding the present'. He points out quite rightly that Medievalists have contested the representation of the Middle Ages as homogeneous, stable and unfractured (as opposed to an Early Modern Period held to be fraught with conflict and contradiction), and he concludes by hailing the advent of an 'innovatory' criticism which is ready and willing to see the literature of the Renaissance as 'dissimilar to the present, anchored in histories and ways of understanding history that are profoundly different to the epistemologies used to engage with the current environment'.

So, in short, at the beginning and the end of this volume you will find critics advocating, implicitly or explicitly, very different approaches to the literature of the Renaissance. That is itself not unrepresentative of the discipline: English literary criticism is a dynamic enterprise, which shifts and changes with new ideas and challenges and which seeks, as does this handbook here, to accommodate and explore various modes of understanding the texts that we read, rather than advocating only one. That tradition of debate over very funda-mental aspects of what literature can and should 'mean' to us, can be seen even in the terms we use to describe the subject of this book. As Healy points out, it is the deep differences between various approaches to the past and to its connec-tions with its own past, and with our present, which underlie the difficulty even of naming the period we are examining. Both 'The Renaissance' and 'The Early Modern Period' have been used to describe it in recent and not so recent years, the second superseding the first in the latter part of the twentieth century and now, arguably, giving way again to the original term, as the name of this volume might imply. Such choices – 'Renaissance' or 'Early Modern' – are not innocent; they reveal the attitudes that the critics who adopt them may hold about the relation of past and present, about the character of the period they are writing about, and about the enterprise of literary criticism itself.

Which approaches you find most interesting and productive is, in the end, something that every student of the subject must eventually decide for him or her self, but we hope that this handbook will allow you better to understand the works, both primary and secondary, that you read in the course of your studies, and to situate them in the intellectual, theoretical and historical contexts which surround them, from which they emerge and which they themselves often influence and inflect. Every reading of every text necessarily draws upon an array of different discourses and bodies of knowledge; here, for instance, already, in a brief examination of a very short poem and a very small extract, I have invoked a number of different terms and concepts and utilized elements of at least two theoretical approaches. I have spoken about authors, personas, poetry, drama, the masque, and city comedy, mentioned the court and the city, patronage and the book trade, class and the market place, notions of intellectual property and print culture, and I have gestured towards all of those things in the context of a reading that has borrowed its technique from New Criticism (close reading) and its concepts (class, alienation, commodity, commodity fetishism) from Marxism.

And that's within a mere couple of thousand words or so. The discourse of English literary criticism can sometimes seem dense and even occasionally impenetrable: English engages with many different intellectual traditions, and this, together with the abundant richness of the literature which is its main concern, can make it seem daunting to the student encountering it for the first time at a relatively advanced level. But its hospitality to different ideas is one of the things that make it so exciting, and about all of the categories and theories I have mentioned here, as well as many others, you will be able to learn more in the pages that follow. Brief descriptions of many key terms, from 'allegory' to 'tragicomedy', can be found in Chapter 5, 'Key Critical Concepts and Topics' by Nate Eastman. And more discursive explanations of the historical and cultural contexts that surround the literary products of the Renaissance form the basis of the first two chapters in the volume. Chapter 1, by William J. Kerwin, examines aspects of the Historical Context of English Renaissance Literature. He discusses larger, more comprehensive, aspects of the period as well as the Kings and Queens and the battles – dynastic as well as political – which frame and define our period. He explains, first of all, how conceptions of the human body itself were quite different in the Renaissance to how they are now, and details the vulnerability of the Renaissance individual to disease in an age where the causes of disease were poorly understood and the cures for them often unknown. He details some of the profound intellectual developments of the time: the return to classical learning and artistic conceptions of the perfect body which can be observed in the work of Italian artists such as Leonardo and Michelangelo and which was influential on new approaches to language and schooling in England, and on humanists such as Thomas More. He shows how means of mechanical reproduction – printing – meant that works could be printed in copies greater than ever before, and he sketches out some of the consequences of this explosion of information. He describes the conflicts of the period: the religious turmoil which engulfed Europe in the fifteenth and sixteenth centuries, for instance, in which so many lost their lives; the gender conflicts and the changes in traditional institutions such as marriage; the social tensions consequent on the rise of a new mercantile class whose interests contested those of the hegemonic aristocracy, who still held power in the period. That emergent class is itself connected to the rise of the city, which I have touched upon already in this introduction; Kerwin suggests also that these new socio-economic developments are reflected in the rise of certain literary genres, such as satire, and city comedies such as *Volpone*. Circumscribing all of these more local developments were, of course, the geographical and astronomical discoveries of the period, which Kerwin also covers in Chapter 1.

Chapter 2, by Karen Britland and Lucy Munro, offers an overview of the major Literary and Cultural Contexts of the period. They expand on some of the information provided by Kerwin, offering more material on (for example) the rise of print and its effects in England. They elaborate on the different modes of publication open to writers in the early modern period (print publication and manuscript circulation), offering more information in which (for example) to situate the kind of debates that Jonson is rehearsing in the two passages with which I opened this introduction. But with the burgeoning of printed matter, they point out, came also a growing need to control what was printed, and a later section of this chapter details the concurrent growth in mechanisms of censorship and control. They show how debates about gender overlap with those about writing and publication, and they offer some examples of women who entered this new public sphere by translating classical works or producing works of their own. Also historically neglected in this respect have been the more humble people, but they too, as Britland and Munro explain, have sometimes left their own tales to tell. Most important of all, however, were the playwrights, not just Shakespeare and Jonson, but Kyd, Marlowe, Middleton and Webster, to name just a few. As Britland and Munro explain, these men hailed from various different backgrounds, and around their work grew up for the first time an entertainment industry, composed of many competing theatre companies and theatres, with which the playwrights themselves had differing commercial relationships. The venues at which plays were performed were also very diverse: not just the theatres, the touring companies' community dramas, and the educational establishments, but also, importantly, the Tudor and Stuart courts, which were in many ways quite different from each other. Britland and Munro offer details of the particular writers – mainly but not exclusively poets – who made their careers in the Court, such as Wyatt, Spenser and Jonson.

Outside the Court, the period was marked by intense pamphleteering, as the opportunities for interventions in debates increased with the advent of print. These debates were sometimes social (over gender, for example), sometimes cultural (the attacks on the theatres and its immoral effects) and sometimes linguistic (debates over English itself, and its usage). Britland and Munro also offer here an overview of the genres adopted by Renaissance writers: poetry and drama most obviously, but prose too, in various forms: the early novellas and romances which for some prefigure the rise of the novel, the pamphlets and the broadsides, and the travel writing, which detailed the adventures of the explorers seeking out new trade routes, and new lands to conquer and subdue. Concurrent with this, many argue, was the development of a new attitude to England itself; many see this period as the one in which, for the first time, England began to be conceived as a nation, a topic which is covered in further detail in Chapters 4 and 6.

Chapter 3 leaves behind the context, and instead takes a closer look at eight literary texts from the period, dating from the early sixteenth to the early seventeenth centuries, and representing a range of genres: epic and lyric poetry, translation, satire, fiction and tragedy. Hugh Adlington, who contributes this chapter, utilizes in it a range of approaches to analyze the material he chooses. Like Healy later on in the volume, Adlington emphasizes certain differences between Renaissance notions and beliefs and modern ones, most notably in their respective ideas of originality, but also in conceptions of 'authorial sincerity, moral purpose, psychological realism [and] verbal concision'. The encounter with Renaissance understandings of such matters, he argues, will encourage us to revise our own, sometimes deep-seated comprehensions of these things. He begins with More's *Utopia* (specifically, the use of gold in that text) and Thomas Wyatt's 'They Flee from Me', which he reads to show how what may seem trivial, or incidental, can in fact be dense with meaning (the focus of the first reading is rhetorical, the second editorial). In his third reading, Adlington examines an extract from Spenser's epic poem *The Faerie Queene*, explaining what an allegory is, and showing how Spenser is both adopting and adapting the models of allegory which he has inherited, to produce something new and different to what has gone before. He also shows us how allegory 'provokes us to reflect on the act of reading itself' and to become an active rather than simply passive reader. In the following section, Adlington turns to *Doctor Faustus*, another text which exists in two very different versions, in order further to illustrate how our reading experience is affected by the form in which we encounter the text.

Adlington then addresses a female author, Mary (Sidney) Herbert, who he uses to raise questions about what we mean by authorial voice. Via a consideration of Mary Herbert's translation of a Biblical psalm, he challenges us to revise our expectations about 'the connections between an author's identity and her work'. From this, traditional form (Biblical translation) he moves to a very new kind of writing, situating Thomas Nashe's prose fiction, *The Unfortunate Traveller* in the context of a question about genre: when was the first English novel? His penultimate reading contextualizes an extract from *King Lear* in some recent feminist readings of the play; and finally, he turns to one of John Donne's Holy Sonnets, 'Show me deare Christ', which he argues is 'characteristic of certain broader traits in Renaissance English Literature' in its 'fascination with the intricacies of the relationship between words and things', its 'coupling of thought and feeling' and its invitation to its readers to devise their own answers to the questions raised.

In Chapter 4, we move from case studies in reading primary texts to case studies in reading critical ones. Here, Christopher R. Orchard examines six books of important criticism of Renaissance literature, contextualizing them in the theoretical framework from which each derives. He begins with the theory – and arguably the individual volume – which has most dominated Early Modern criticism over the last twenty-five years: New Historicism, embodied in Stephen Greenblatt's *Renaissance Self-Fashioning*, which inaugurated that critical approach. Others before Greenblatt had posited that the early modern period saw the advent of a sense of self that was new and different; Orchard explains, however, the way in which Greenblatt adopts the theoretical parameters established by Michel Foucault (most of all, his analysis of power) to track the operations of the 'self-fashioning' he identifies. Orchard's second text is Jonathan Dollimore's *Radical Tragedy*. Where Greenblatt's approach was informed by Foucault, Dollimore's main theoretical influence is Marx. 'What is important about Dollimore's work', Orchard argues, 'is not only the materialist concepts he utilizes but also the critique he offers of a tradition that has lead us to read this period in the traditionalist way that we did before [Dollimore wrote]'. From Foucault, through Cultural Materialism, to Feminism: the third book that Orchard considers is Lisa Jardine's *Still Harping on Daughters*. Feminism, he maintains, has with New Historicism had the most sustained influence on Renaissance studies during the last quarter of a century. Jardine sought to show how 'femaleness' operated in the categorization of experience, and to argue that the increased attention paid to women in the drama reflected a widespread patriarchal anxiety about social changes taking place in the Renaissance.

Feminist theory, and interest in women in literature gave way in the 1990s to a more general interest in gender, and Bruce R. Smith's *Homosexual Desire in Shakespeare's England* was an early intervention in a field that was subsequently to grow in popularity. Queer theory takes as its point of departure an interrogation of what late twentieth century culture held as axiomatic: that 'hetero-' and 'homo-' sexuality were eternal categories as applicable to other historical periods as they were to our own. Orchard explains how Smith questions the attribution of such twentieth-century concepts to the Early Modern period, and details how Smith claims that certain 'myths' of homosexual desire – male bonding, for example, or myths of class – speak to relations such as male power structures, education, private life, etc. The last two volumes Orchard examines concern England's place in the world. Andrew Hadfield's *Literature, Politics and National Identity* intervenes in the debate about the degree to which we see in this period the emergence of a sense of the nation *qua* nation, with boundaries and identities that constituted the 'imagined community' (to adopt Benedict Anderson's term (Anderson 2006)) which was England (or, more latterly, Britain). And Ania Loomba's *Shakespeare, Race and Colonialism* also examines the sense that Europeans had of themselves and of others in a world which offered new experiences of difference, in this case, racial. Like Smith, Orchard points out, Loomba raises questions about whether categories we have taken to be unproblematic (such as 'race') are as 'natural' as they had hitherto seemed, and details in the course of her volume the way in which racial categories hardened and became inflexible even as recognition of hybridity increased. After each of his examinations of these critical volumes, Orchard briefly details their influence on other criticism of the Renaissance since their publication.

Orchard's approach is to engage systematically with individual volumes and thereby to throw light on the theoretical positions each adopts. Tita French Baumlin's Critical Responses and Approaches to British Renaissance Literature, by contrast, which constitutes Chapter 6, offers a much broader explanatory context, elaborating on the various theoretical stances adopted by critics of early modern literature, so that individual works can then be situated in the theoretical landscape from which they emerge and to which they contribute. Beginning with the Swiss historian Jacob Burckhardt, whose writings on Italian renaissance art remain fundamental to our understanding of the period as a 're-birth', or 'renewal', she continues through a brief history of the literary criticism of the twentieth and early twenty-first centuries: New Criticism, Early Historicist Criticism, Structuralism, Rhetorical Criticism, Psychoanalytic Criticism both Freudian and Lacanian, Reader-Response Criticism, Deconstruction, Feminisms, Marxism, New Historicism, Postcolonialism, and Gender Studies. In each section she explicates some of the main characteristics or tenets of the theories she covers, and then draws the reader's attention to significant interventions in the field, so that those interested in a particular approach to literature may be guided in the extension of their reading beyond this volume.

Our penultimate chapter (Chapter 7), by Joshua B. Fisher, covers 'Recent Developments in the Early Modern Literary Canon' from 1968–2008. As Fisher explains, this has been a rich period for the reassessment of what we ought to read and value in the writings of the period, and this process continues to this day, as scholars seek to reclaim voices and genres which have been marginalized and overlooked. Whilst once we studied almost exclusively the drama, poetry and some prose of 'great writers' now those works might sit in syllabi alongside the private diary of a woman writer, and plays such as Brome's *The Antipodes* might be taught alongside *The Tempest*, not as a background or a supplement to their more canonical counterparts, but as equally valuable in their own right for their ability to tell us something about the world from which they emerged. In this wide-ranging and challenging chapter, you will find not only a commentary on the shifts and changes in the canon over the decades, but also an explanation of the reasons why such changes occurred. Fisher traces this history back to the medieval period, and allows us access to the voices of contemporary commentators on the canon in the Renaissance, as well as to more modern critics of it, showing as he does so that anxieties about the tainting of great literature by an influx of 'low' writing are hardly confined to the present day. Approximately half of Fisher's essay is devoted to explaining this history, and detailing the twentieth-century interventions in the debates about the canon that polarized university English departments, especially those in the States, in the late 1980s and the 1990s. The remainder of his chapter focuses on four categories that characterize the ways in which the canon of early modern literature has shifted in recent years to accommodate the unfamiliar or excluded: women writers; outsiders and 'others'; cheap print and ephemera; and documentary and source materials.

At the end of his chapter, Fisher asks if we should worry that this new hospitality to what was previously neglected has debased clear conceptions of aesthetic value and thereby diminished our understanding of what previous ages, more appropriately, acknowledged as 'great literature'; or whether, on the contrary, we should applaud the opportunities we have today to read more widely than we did before, and in less familiar texts. This polarity between the strange and the familiar also underlies Thomas Healy's essay, 'Mapping the Current Critical Landscape: Returning to the Renaissance' (Chapter 8), which assesses the state of criticism of the period as it is today. Healy opens with a discussion of Renaissance notions of originality, which he uses to introduce the debate in Renaissance studies over whether the period breaks with its past and looks forward to our own time, or remains distant, a 'less familiar culture'. As I noted earlier, Healy's approach contests the method I adopted in my own brief introductory reading of Jonson. Where I stressed continuities between the Renaissance and our own time, and emphasized its break with the Middle Ages, Healy would insist on its connection to the Medieval, and its otherness to us. Where the criticism of the 1980s and early 90s saw, for example, the 'origin of modern subjectivity', twenty-first-century scholars find instead not the liberated, self-fashioning people celebrated by those earlier academics, but a culture fearful of the dangerous temptations of treacherous Satanic urgings.

For Healy, then, this past is a foreign country, which we must recognize as such in order properly to understand it. His encounter with it is, then, different in nature to mine. But whether we see the Renaissance as an 'other' place, or as the origin of concepts which still inform us today – the early glimmer of our modernity – it is certain that its literature will remain for many years to come an enduring source of fascination, challenge, and delight and that some, at least, of the questions that it asks itself of its own world have yet to be answered by ours.

Renaissance Timeline: 1485 to 1639

Rebecca Steinberger

Year	Literary	Historical	Cultural
1485		Henry VII defeats Richard III, ending the War of the Roses and establishing the Tudor dynasty in England Accession of Henry VII, the first Tudor monarch	
1488		Bartolomeu Dias rounds the Cape of Good Hope	
1492		Columbus discovers the New World; Conquest of Granada by Ferdinand of Aragon and Isabella of Castile Spain pushes Moors out of Europe after 800 years and expels Jews	Martin Behaim constructs at Nuremberg the first terrestrial globe
1494			Aldine Press founded at Venice by Aldus Manutius
1495		Syphilis starts spreading through Europe	Leonardo da Vinci starts painting *The Last Supper* in Milan
1496		Marriage between Margaret of Austria and the Infante John of Castile	
1497		Marriage between the Archduke Philip the Fair and Joanna of Castile John Cabot sails to Newfoundland Vasco da Gama sails around the Cape of Good Hope and to India	Leonardo completes *The Last Supper*
1498		Vasco da Gama reaches India	
1500		Birth of the future Holy Roman Emperor Charles V	
1502			The first watch made in Nuremberg, Germany

Year	Literary	Historical	Cultural
1503		James IV of Scotland marries Margaret Tudor	Leonardo paints *The Mona Lisa*
1505			Picket watch first created ≈ 1505. Could be as early as 1504
1506		Death of the Archduke Philip the Fair in Spain	Leonardo returns to Milan and begins compiling the Codex Leicester Death of the painter Andrea Mantegna
1508			Michelangelo begins painting the ceiling of Sistine Chapel
1509		Henry VIII becomes King of England (r. 1509–1547); marries Catherine of Aragon Europe launches African slave trade with the New World	
1510			Death of the painter Sandro Botticelli of Florence
1513	Niccolò Machiavelli completes *The Prince* (not published until 1532)		
1515	Roger Ascham, later to be tutor to Queen Elizabeth, born	Francis I, King of France, crowned (reigned until 1547)	Copernicus writes that the earth circles the sun
1516	Publication at Basel of Erasmus' Latin translation of the New Testament		*Richard III* published between 1513 and 1518
1517	Publication at Wittenberg of Luther's Theses More's *History of Richard III* published	Martin Luther nails his theses to church door, launching the Protestant Reformation Henry Howard, Earl of Surrey born	Coffee introduced in Europe
1518		Thomas More becomes a member of the King's Council	
1519		Cortés conquers Mexico Magellan launches first round-the-world voyage	Leonardo dies in Amboise

Year	Literary	Historical	Cultural
1520		The Emperor Charles V crowned at Aachen Suleiman the Magnificent (also known as Suleiman the Lawgiver) succeeds his father Selim as Sultan of the Ottoman Empire	Death of the painter Raffaello de Santi (Raphael)
1521		Thomas More knighted by Henry VIII, and becomes Under-Treasurer of England	Cortés conquers the Aztecs
1522	Publication at Wittenberg of Luthers' German translation of the New Testament	Knights of St John abandon Rhodes to the Turks	
1523	More's *Responsio ad Lutherum* published	Thomas More becomes Speaker of the House of Commons	
1524		Francis I invades Italy	
1525	Tyndale's translation of the Bible published in Cologne		
1526	Publication at Worms of William Tyndales' English translation of the New Testament		
1527		Sack of Rome by the troops of the Holy Roman Empire	
1528			Death of the artist Albrecht Dürer
1529		Thomas More becomes Lord Chancellor Fall of Cardinal Wolsey Siege of Vienna by the Turks	
1531	Elyot publishes his *The Book Named the Governor*		
1532		More resigns as Lord Chancellor	

Year	Literary	Historical	Cultural
1533		Henry VIII divorces Catherine; marries Anne Boleyn Elizabeth, later Queen, born The Buggery Act 1533: the first anti-sodomy enactment in England	
1534	Elyot's *The Castle of Health*	Henry VIII pronounces himself Supreme Head of the Church of England	Ignatius Loyola founds the Society of Jesus (Jesuits)
1535	Publication at Zürich of Coverdale's Bible, the first printed Bible in English	Thomas More convicted of treason and beheaded	
1536	Publication of Paracelsus' *Great Book of Surgery* Calvin's *Institutes of the Christian Religion*	Anne Boleyn executed Henry VIII marries Jane Seymour	
1537		Jane Seymour dies	
1538	Elyot's Latin-English Dictionary		
1539	The Great Bible printed	Final suppression of monasteries in England (began much earlier)	
1540		Henry VIII marries Anne of Cleves in January, divorces her in July Marries Kathryn Howard	
1541			Michelangelo completes the fresco *The Last Judgement* in the Sistine Chapel
1542		The Witchcraft Act 1542 punished 'invoking or conjuring an evil spirit' with death The Inquisition established at Rome Kathryn Howard executed Sir Thomas Wyatt imprisoned	

Year	Literary	Historical	Cultural
1543	Publication of Andreas Vesalius' *On the Structure of the Human Body* Publication of Nicolaus Copernicus' *Revolutions of the Celestial Orbits*	Henry VIII marries Katherine Parr	Copernicus introduces heliocentric world system
1546		Death of Martin Luther	
1547		Death of Henry VIII Surrey executed on charges of treason Edward VI becomes King at age 9	
1552	Edmund Spenser born in London		
1553		Mary Tudor becomes Queen of England Edward VI dies	
1554	Philip Sidney born at Penshurst		
1555		Charles V abdicates as Holy Roman Emperor	
1557	Tottel's *Miscellany* printed More's collected English *Works* published Surrey's translation of Virgil's *Aeneid* published (posthumous)		
1558		Elizabeth becomes Queen of England: rise of Protestantism	
1560	The Geneva Bible printed		
1561	Francis Bacon born		
1564	William Shakespeare born in Stratford-upon-Avon Christopher Marlowe born in Canterbury		
1567	Arthur Golding's translation of Ovid's *Metamorphoses* printed		

Year	Literary	Historical	Cultural
1568	The Bishop's Bible translation published Ascham dies		Term Renaissance used in context in Vasari's *Lives of the Most Excellent Painters, Sculptors and Architects*
1569	Spenser goes to Pembroke Hall (now Pembroke College), Cambridge		
1570	Ascham's *The Schoolmaster* published posthumously		
1571	Philip Sidney leaves Christ's College without a degree in order to travel		
1572		St Bartholomew's Day Massacre occurs in Paris, resulting in the deaths of many Huguenots	
1576	Spenser graduates (MA) from Cambridge		The Theatre, the first successful public theatre, built by James Burbage in Shoreditch
1577			The Curtain, an amphitheatre, built in Shoreditch
1579	North's translation of Plutarch's *Parallel Lives* Spenser marries Machabyas Childe Spenser's *The Shepheardes Calendar* published		
1580	Sidney's *The Old Arcadia* published Marlowe goes to Corpus Christi College (Cambridge)		
1582	The Douay-Rheims Version of the Bible published Shakespeare marries Anne Hathaway		
1584			Marlowe graduates (BA)
1586		Sir Philip Sidney dies	
1587	Marlowe publishes *Tamburlaine*		The Rose built in Bankside Marlowe graduates (MA)

Year	Literary	Historical	Cultural
1588		Defeat of the Spanish Armada Thomas Hobbes born	
1589		Spenser visits London with Ralegh, and is awarded pension by Elizabeth I for the first three books of his *Faerie Queene*	
1590	Spenser publishes *Muiopotmos, Mother Hubberds Tale, Daphnaida*		
1591	Sidney's *Astrophel and Stella* published in three unauthorized editions	Robert Herrick born	
1592	Spenser's translation *Axiochus* published	Greene, famous for his coney catching pamphlets, dies	First mention of Shakespeare in London appears in Robert Greene's final pamphlet referring to him as an 'upstart Crow'
1593	Marlowe writes *Doctor Faustus* (published 1604) and works on *Hero and Leander*	Marlowe was stabbed to death on 30 May, ten days after his arrest for heresy George Herbert born on 3 April	
1594	Marlowe publishes *Edward II*	Spenser marries Elizabeth Boyle	
1595	Spenser's *Epithalamion* published		The Swan built in Paris Gardens
1596	Spenser writes *A View of the Present State of Ireland* Spenser's *The Faerie Queene* published in one volume		
1597	Bacon's first *Essays or Counsels, Civil and Moral* published James VI of Scotland publishes *Daemonologie*		
1599	Spenser's death in London		The Globe built in Southwark; timbers from The Theatre are used in its construction

Year	Literary	Historical	Cultural
1603	Jonson writes *Sejanus* Francis Bacon knighted	Elizabeth I dies in March James VI of Scotland becomes James I of England	
1604			Carel van Mander's *Painter's Manual*
1605	Bacon's *The Advancement of Learning* published	The Gunpowder Plot, which aimed to blow up Parliament, thwarted on the 5th November	
1606	Jonson writes *Volpone*		
1607		Flight of the Earls in Ireland	
1608	John Milton born		
1609	Jonson writes *Epicoene*		
1610	Jonson writes *The Alchemist*		
1611	King James Authorized Version of the Bible published		
1612		Richard Crashaw born in London	
1613			The Globe theatre burns; Shakespeare retires
1614	John Donne writes *Essays in Divinity* Jonson writes *Bartholomew Fair*		
1616	Folio edition of Jonson's *Works* published; Shakespeare dies Cervantes dies		
1618	Bacon becomes Baron Verulam		
1620	Bacon's *Novum Organum* published		
1621	Andrew Marvell born Henry Vaughan born Donne becomes Dean of St Paul's Bacon becomes Viscount St Albans		

Year	Literary	Historical	Cultural
1623	Shakespeare's *First Folio* published by Henry Condell Herrick ordained Donne writes *Devotions Upon Emergent Occasions*		
1625	Bacon's complete *Essays* published		
1626	George Sandys' translation of Ovid's *Metamorphoses* Francis Bacon dies Francis Bacon's *Sylva Sylvarum* and *The New Atlantis* are published		Herrick attains living of Dean Prior in Devonshire
1629	Milton graduates (MA) from Christ College, Cambridge		
1630	Herbert becomes rector at Bemerton		
1631	Milton writes *L'Allegro* and *Il Penseroso* Donne dies Jonson dies		
1632	Milton graduates (MA)		
1633	George Herbert's *The Temple* published posthumously	George Herbert dies	
1634			Milton's masque *Comus* performed
1635	Crashaw becomes a fellow of Peterhouse		
1637	Milton writes *Lycidas*		
1639	Crashaw takes orders	'Bishop's War'	

Part I
The Renaissance Period

1

The Historical Context of English Renaissance Literature: From Conflict to Creativity

William J. Kerwin

The English Renaissance produced what is perhaps the greatest literature in English history: the range and quality of its poetry, and most especially of its drama, surpass that produced in any other period. The extraordinary richness of the literature produced in the Renaissance might lead one to ask why some epochs nurture artistic creation so much more powerfully than others. What aspect or aspects of an historical moment enable the production of great writing? What is the relation between ideas and the history which surrounds them? There have been a number of different answers to these questions. Some have denied that history plays any significant part at all, insisting that great minds alone suffice to produce great literature. Others have claimed that art needs peace, and that the stability afforded by the end of the Wars of the Roses (which begins our period, with the accession of Henry VII) afforded the authors the time and space to write their plays and their poetry (and in some cases, even, their prose). Both of these views privilege the author (and the text) over 'history' (or context), but the mid- twentieth century saw a challenge to that view of the relation between text, author and context. Many instead suggested that in some sense it was history rather than writers that 'authored' the literature: the influential French philosopher-historian Michel Foucault, for example, referred to the 'author function', a perhaps tongue-in-cheek phrase which implies that authors are little more than an amanuensis of history.

While very few people are ready to take Foucault's claim of 'the death of the author' literally, critics of the past thirty years have paid increasing attention to the extent to which history helps produce literature, framing the aesthetic within other parts of culture. Here, in this introduction to Renaissance history, I will assume, as do the majority of contemporary critics, that history and litera-ture are deeply interlinked, and that neither has an agreed upon single meaning: history, like the literature which emerges from it, has always been multivalent, and open to interpretation. More specifically, I want in this essay to defend the claim that the best starting point for understanding where this particular trove of great literature came from is the idea of conflict. The production of literature does not demand peace; in fact, rather than flowing from a moment of cultural unity, the poems and plays that mark Renaissance literature emerged from a series of crucibles, historical moments of social and intellectual division.

In the following pages, then, I will draw on the work of recent scholars to emphasize ways in which the new challenges in the period spurred authors to imagine the world in new ways. In the concluding chapter of this volume, Thomas Healy discusses the fluid and shifting usage of the terms 'Renaissance' and 'Early Modern' to define our period (see Chapter 8). That double-vision reflects not only the Janus-like nature of that earlier time, when medieval struc-tures of living and thinking came under pressure, but also the differences of our own time, because historians and literary critics have always interpreted the period's history in conflicting ways. In a number of interrelated spheres, old ways were reconsidered and new ways were painfully brought into being. For the rest of this essay, I will explore the ways conflict marked the time and the literature. The seven sections that follow are all inter-related; for example, the 'intellectual breaks' the period makes with the medieval past are inseparable from the Reformation and the new ways of being promoted by the Reformation. It is one of the pleasures of working with this period to consider and feel that sense of multiple changes. Indeed, the Irish poet W. B. Yeats has defined Renais-sance literature in terms of its 'emotion of multitude' (1921, 215) and the Russian philosopher Mikhail Bakhtin (1968) associates this particular historical epoch as a time of 'carnival' explicitly because of the 'polyphony' of its social scene. But we will consider seven voices of conflict one at a time.

Health Crises and Body Conflicts: Plague and Pox

A good place to start our survey of the history of the Renaissance is with human health. While you might think that the body is something outside of history – something that doesn't change – what we do to bodies and how we imagine them certainly does change, and what happened to conceptions of the body in the Renaissance is a rich way to get at its overall history, perhaps more revealing than starting with kings and queens, battles and parliamentary strategies. Writers could draw upon an ancient way of understanding the body, a system that went well beyond matters of disease and medical treatment by providing a rich grammar and vocabulary for articulating and creating passion, and giving form to both individual and group identity. At the same time, crises in public health raised issues of social hierarchy, exposing cracks in inherited systems of order and belief, both medical and non-medical. By looking at the history of medicine, both in its theoretical language and its disease patterns, we can get closer to the frameworks authors had for imagining their personal struggles.

Traditional medicine was a combination of folk and learned traditions, and the most common way of imagining how one's body worked was humoral. That is, Renaissance medicine drew on the language and system of the bodily fluids – the humours – outlined by classical writers like Galen in the second century AD and augmented by learned physicians for almost two millennia. The idea that outside agents (such as germs or microbes,) were the causes of disease was not common yet; rather, people regarded health as a matter of balance or imbalance, and rigorously treated their bodies to achieve balance. Humoralism saw bodies and emotions as created by a balance of fluids different levels of which produced four 'temperaments' or personality types: the sanguine, the phlegmatic, the choleric and the melancholy. Both personality and health were influenced by changes in one's humours, which were in turn influenced by outside forces such as air, climate, food, the motions of the stars and planets, rest and even passions. The overall effect was a distinctly pre-Cartesian sense of identity, one in which body and mind were not separated, as in Descartes' philosophy, but were much more intimately inter-linked, agents in each other's creation. Thus literature was not imagined as a cerebral experience but as something that worked within the entire body: as George Puttenham wrote in *The Arte of English Poesie* (1589, 98), poetic language 'carieth his opinion this way and that, whether soever the heart by impression of the eare shalbe most affectionately bent and directed'. Writers created countless scenes of such inside-the-body drama, in which words actually changed bodies, and recently critics such as Katharine Craik (2007) and Gail Kern Paster (2004) have encouraged readers to understand the languages of affect and passion as discourses with medical as well as literary resonances. People in this time regularly saw conflicts happening inside their bodies, and they wrote about those wars of affect over and over again.

Two culture-changing diseases helped shape the history of the Renaissance and complicated the internal dramas imagined in a humoral culture. One was the bubonic plague, the 'black death' that had arrived in Europe in 1348 and recurred in England regularly until 1666. The mortality of these onsets is breath-taking: plague killed about a third of the English population in that first appearance, and similarly high rates in the scores of epidemics of the disease over the next three centuries. English men and women, and particularly Londoners, lived with repeated visitations of death on a massive scale. The second revolutionary disease, and one that did not play a role in the medieval era, was what we now call syphilis, but what was known in the Renaissance as the pox. It also had more colourful names, which carried nationalistic tones: 'the French disease' or 'the Neapolitan bone-ache'. Medical historians continue to argue over the origin of syphilis. Some say that it was a mutation of an earlier, less virulent, disease, others hold that it was brought from the Americas to Europe by returning sailors and soldiers. Whatever its origin, what is certainly the case is that it spread like wildfire throughout Europe, where the population had no resistance to it, and traditional medicine offered neither answers nor a cure. By the beginning of the fifteenth century, death from the pox was seizing the imagination of the public, much as death from HIV-AIDS did in the 1980s. The plays of Shakespeare and his contemporaries are filled with images connecting sex and desire, in which sex was a hidden carrier of death, and connected also to certain recognizable symptoms: loss of hair (the so-called 'French crowns' of many plays), collapsing facial bone structure (such as the nose and the teeth), madness, wasting and eventually death. It was the disease of disfigurement: as influential London surgeon William Clowes wrote, 'it raigneth over the face of the whole earth' (1596, 147). The era's concern with controlling women's use of 'face painting', or cosmetics, may be connected with this health fear.

The failure of traditional humoral medicine to account for or cure these new diseases may have been a factor in a gradual disillusionment with those traditional forms, and hence with the rise of a new kind of approach to the body and its health. For in this period, the persistence of traditional humoral medicine accompanies the rise of the surgeons, whose methods, such as the practice of dissection, or 'anatomy', became more widespread and more publicized, and ushered in a new sense of the body itself. The Italian surgeon Vesalius performed elaborate anatomies and, just as importantly, published drawings of what he saw, allowing people to see inside the human body in new ways. The systematic perspectives he provided of humans were part of a culture-wide reconsideration of interior spaces, beginning with the actual body but extending to the imagination and conceptions of what it means to be human. Critics such as Jonathan Sawday (1995) Katherine Eisaman Maus (1995) have argued that the Renaissance is marked by a new sense of inwardness, a privacy which cannot be fully shared, which holds the most precious meanings, and which people worked hard to protect. So when Hamlet speaks of having 'that within which passes show', (1.2.85) he may be articulating a broader, culture-wide preoccupation with how what is inside of us, body and soul, relates to the outside world, as well as the degree to which such physical and intellectual interiority can be understood, or comprehended, by the world outside of it (a reflection which we might usefully use to think about the larger representation of the isolated, the tragic hero in the period).

Intellectual Conflicts: Humanism and Modern Media

New conceptions of the body, then, may be intertwined in quite significant ways with new conceptions of selfhood, subjectivity or individuality (to use just three of the terms used by critics to define this apparent change in the conception of the person). (see Burkhardt 1878, Greenblatt 1980, Belsey 1985). This new sense of individuality was also fostered by developments in intellectual history. The history of ideas and thinkers, as opposed to political or social history, has characteristically seen the Renaissance as an heroic age, a time represented by ambitious intellects such as Shakespeare's Hamlet or Christopher Marlowe's Doctor Faustus. The rediscovery or 'rebirth' ('re-naissance') of knowledge about Greek and Latin artistic production gives the age its traditional name, as scholars and artists in Italy, and later across Europe, were reshaped by their experiences with classical life, and moved aggressively to reshape their native traditions. In Italy this provoked a revolution in the visual arts, so that the views of a classical thinker like Pythagoras, with his maxim that 'man is the measure of all things', can be seen to be echoed in the celebration of human beauty visible in the paintings of Fra Angelico, Botticelli, Leonardo da Vinci and Michelangelo. In England, classical learning inspired a new approach to language: a revised school curriculum based on Latin education was developed, and a number of grammar schools founded (especially during the short reign of King Edward VI), many of which still exist today. More generally, the age saw the birth of a reading culture that often invoked the values of the classical world. This movement was as much about making language heroic – and beautiful – as it was about particular texts or authors; art historian E. H. Gombrich wryly claims that the Renaissance came 'not so much from the discovery of Man as in the discovery of diphthongs' (Fraser 1967).

This new approach to learning that characterized the intellectual movement was known as humanism. This is a term that has meant very different things across the centuries. Renaissance humanism was something quite different from the secular humanism of the twenty-first century, being originated by very pious Christian men. What defined it were certain emphases, especially a specific approach to language, to beauty, to civic life and to the potential of the individual. These values are beautifully exemplified by the Italian writer Giovanni Pico della Mirandola in his essay 'An Oration on the Dignity of Man', (Cassirer, Kristeller and Randall 1948) as well as in the writings of continental humanists such as Petrarch, (Cassirer, Kristeller and Randall 1948) Castiglione, Machiavelli, Erasmus and Montaigne (Atchity, 1996). In England, William Lily and John Colet brought humanist values into the educational and religious life of the country's elite, bringing the spirit of linguistic purity and grace into matters of religion and civic life. That spirit is found in the life of Thomas More, author and statesman, bold politician in the court of Henry VIII, and writer of *Utopia*, wherein is exemplified one of humanism's central tenets: that humanity should use its special gifts to organize the world, and transform it into a better, fairer, place.

The advent of humanism also went hand in hand with a new age of scientific learning although, as Nicola Abbagnano has pointed out, the relationship between the two modes of thinking has been the subject of disagreement among historians of thought (1973). The brilliant Galileo, for example, was a humanist whose studies in astronomy, in particular his assertion that the earth orbited the sun, rather than the reverse, placed the new scientific learning squarely in opposition to traditional church authority (other humanists, it should be noted had a rather less fraught relationship with Catholicism; More, indeed, was canonized by Pope Pius XI in 1935). Galileo's case is an example of how a movement that started without any intention of revolution moved eventually in that direction. His worldview was based on observation, not on the teachings of the past; and like the anatomical work of Vesalius was another example of a new and more inductive approach to learning, part of the broad process that created the scientific method. In England, the most accomplished and influential player in this movement was Francis Bacon. Like Thomas More, Bacon was a 'Renaissance man' in that phrase's sense of versatility: he was a man of letters, a statesman and a proponent of scientific thinking. His essays and his lengthier works, such as *The Advancement of Learning*, helped establish the more modern way of producing knowledge, though an inductive method, part of what Bacon himself called 'the inquiry of truth' (Atchity 1996, 302). One can see the ironic narrative of the history of humanism: a movement begun conservatively let loose, genii-like, a host of new ways of seeing and living, because humanism's approach to language had fundamental conflicts with medieval sources of authority. At the level of language itself, humanist scholars found medieval Latin, or 'scholastic Latin', murky and second-rate. The willingness to put trust and even 'faith' in non-Christian writers such as Socrates and Cicero, a move that hardly seems shocking now, actually redrew the boundaries of authority in radical and irreversible ways. And the sense of rigour and inductive thinking opened the door for the secular and scientific changes of the coming ages.

But intellectual history has its own material history: it both derives from and helps to change the technical and economic infrastructure. Most importantly, all these Renaissance developments were propelled by the new medium of the printed book (see the introduction to this volume for a brief close reading of some of the effects of this transformation). William Caxton brought the technology of moveable type to England in 1476, twenty-one years after Johannes Gutenberg published his bible in Germany. The speed of change was remarkable: by 1500, about twenty million individual books had been printed in Europe, and the ensuing flood of pamphlets, broadsides and books changed the world. It would be a mistake, however, to assume that print immediately became the sole medium for literary production. Many poets continued to write in manuscript – John Donne, for just one example, avoided book publication for his poetry – and the culture of manuscripts, dominant for millennia, continued to flourish even as book culture grew (see Marotti 1995). The Renaissance was a period of overlapping technologies, much as our own era has become a hybrid period of print and electronic media; indeed, in this respect the two ages bear comparison with each other, both being worlds transformed by new technologies of information and communication: print in the Renaissance, the internet in our own time.

Religion and Conflict: The Reformation

If surgery and the vogue for anatomies both literal and figurative helped change the common imagination, and if the widespread dissemination of printed books and new literary practices encouraged solitary reading, an even broader effect came from another shift encouraging inward reflection: the great conflict over Christian religious life known as the Reformation. Begun not as a movement of revolution but, as its name indicates, Reform, Martin Luther's crusade in Germany to purify the Catholic Church was one of a number of challenges to Catholic practice, which extended well back into the middle ages. Certain practices in the Catholic Church, such as the selling of indulgences and the misdeeds of some of the clergy, came to symbolize a broad level of corruption in established religion. The most iconic moment in Luther's movement was his public posting of complaints and demands in response to those problems in the form of the famous ninety-five theses in Wittenberg in 1517. But Luther was only one of a group of reformers: Ulrich Zwingli and John Calvin in Switzerland, Philip Melanchthon in Germany and John Knox in Scotland all dedicated their lives to building new forms for Christian faith. Even countries in Western Europe which did not eventually become dominated by the new religions engaged in often violent counter-Reformation movements. In France, the St Bartholomew's Day massacre of 1572 saw the death of between 30,000 to 100,000 Protestants (known as Huguenots), while in Spain the Inquisition established courts that violently persecuted those accused of heresy. And violence spread between countries, as religious wars marred much of Europe, most notably the Thirty Years War (1618–48) in what is now Germany. No country in Western Europe was untouched by the Reformation.

How far reaching were the effects of this movement? Luther and his fellow Protestants' demands involved extended debates about doctrine, and sparked reforms including a different conception of the ritual of the Eucharist, a reduction of the number of sacraments from seven to two (communion and baptism), and an elimination of numerous other Catholic practices, including the widespread traditions of iconography, worship of saints, trust in the authority of the Pope and belief in Purgatory. But the changes went well beyond theological disputes and specific religious forms, because the new practices challenged traditions of mind and of community. For example, Protestant emphasis on private reading of the bible and other religious texts that had been translated into the vernacular, made possible by the spread of the printed book, encouraged a reading culture quite different to that which had existed before, while the invention of the printing press allowed more people than ever before to own a Bible in their home. It is arguable that a 'Protestant poetics' ultimately helped nurture a different kind of identity, a belief in a radical separateness given vivid form by Andrew Marvell in his poem 'On a Drop of Dew'. Marvell connects a dewdrop and a soul, each containing 'The greater heaven in an heaven less' (Marvell 1972, 103). Could authors such as George Herbert, John Donne and John Milton have been what they were without these changes in cultural practice and the new emphasis on inwardness that went along with them?

Politics and religion became inseparable across Europe, as the region that was previously unified in Catholicism became bitterly and violently split. In England, Henry VIII, who had previously gloried in the title 'Defender of the Faith' when that faith was Roman Catholic, demanded the creation of a Church of England, a Protestant national church of which the monarch would be the supreme head. Henry's motivations were in part personal – he wanted a legal divorce from Katherine of Aragon, which the Pope was refusing to give, so that he could marry Anne Boleyn. But he was encouraged in his radical reformation by reformers with much 'purer' agendas of change. These more zealous Protestants were the predecessors of strong-willed and demanding men and women who eventually earned the derisive nickname 'Puritan', the type of Protestantism most radical in its political and spiritual rigour. Henry's new Church of England, although it had broken from its Roman Catholic forerunner, remained close to it in many ways, maintaining many of the rituals and rhythms of 'high church' life, including a centralized church government with an archbishop in control. In contrast, some Protestant groups, such as Presbyterians, wanted a democratically governed church run by elders or 'presbyters', and others wanted even more decentralized religious life, adhering to Martin Luther's ideal of 'every man his own priest'. The result in England was a spectrum of tradition and innovation, although different religious views were alternately tolerated and persecuted in the reigns of the monarchs who succeeded Henry VIII.

By the closing decade of Henry VIII's long reign, England was entering a period of dizzying change and electrifying martyrdom. Henry's most infamous victim was his Lord Chancellor, Thomas More, who refused to swear the Oath of Supremacy acknowledging Henry as the Supreme Head of the Church in England or to support the 1534 Act of Succession (later superseded by other Acts of Succession), which legitimized Elizabeth and bastardized Mary; these refusals cost him his life. Subsequent to Henry's death, the throne went to his only son, Edward VI, who continued on the path of Reformation, but as a young prince, never able to rule independently – he reigned from the age of nine until his death at fifteen – he was not able to ensure a Protestant succession. His older half-sister Mary I took the throne, and her attempts to reassert Catholicism as

England's only legal religion earned her the nickname 'Bloody Mary'. Her public burnings of leading Protestants, most famously the Oxford clerics Thomas Cranmer, Nicholas Ridley and Hugh Latimer, and the flight of many English men and women to Protestant refuges on the continent, created an atmosphere of distrust and fear that lingered for decades. The second most popular book in England after the Bible was John Foxe's *Acts and Monuments of these Later and Perillous Days, Touching Matters of the Church*, known most commonly simply as *Foxe's Book of Martyrs*. This volume, re-issued in larger and larger editions repeatedly in the decades after Mary's reign, recounts in gory and passionate detail the death of the faithful Protestant martyrs.

When Elizabeth I took the throne in 1558, England held its collective breath as it waited to see what religious path she would take. Elizabeth took the '*via media*' or middle path, creating the 'Elizabethan compromise' that tolerated Catholicism while consolidating Anglicanism, and that came down hard only on those who tried to return to the bloody path of the preceding decades. Some tension continued: Pope Pius V excommunicated Elizabeth in 1570, expressed in a papal bull that encouraged Catholics to depose her. Several did in fact attempt assassinations, and this provoked increased state suppression of Catholic orders such as the Jesuits. Widespread fear of foreign and Catholic intervention continued throughout Elizabeth's reign, affecting debates about Elizabeth's potential marriages and increasing difficulties with Catholic Spain, fears justified by the attempt to invade England by sea in 1588. The armada's famous defeat ended that threat, but hostility to Catholics, especially Catholics on the continent, continued long into the future, and is frequently recognizable in the drama of the period in the figure of the evil Cardinal or the corrupt continental locations of Italy and Spain.

These political conflicts are one important face of the Reformation, but just as important were the personal changes: new ways of thinking that, among other things, provided a new context for literature. A Lutheran emphasis on every Christian's inner experience helped foster patterns of inwardness and individual responsibility that, some would claim, define the period, and remain characteristic of the modern Western world.

Gender Conflict: Women in Their Places

As print and a new religious culture encouraged more and more questioning of received ideas, conceptions of gender also began to shift and change. The historian Joan Kelly-Gadol famously entitled a 1977 essay 'Did Women Have a Renaissance?' and thirty years of scholarship has worked to give nuanced, if conflicting, answers to that question (see Chapters 2, 6 and 7). The period whose very name suggests liberation had a very mixed record for women, as the new gender roles created offered restrictions as often as they offered opportunity. One central aspect of the history of women in the Renaissance was the changing nature of the household, which reflected both economic shifts and the

Reformation. A new economy increasingly divided the home and the work place, and tasks that had previously been the purview of women, from brewing to administering medical care, became more and more often exclusively male. In cities, a new middle-class home often featured a husband who worked outside the household, leaving the home to become more of a female domain. Many English plays, especially 'city comedies', like Thomas Middleton and Thomas Dekker's *The Roaring Girl* and Ben Jonson's *Bartholomew Fair*, explore the tensions in London between control of and freedom for women. The nature of marriage may also have been changing: some have suggested that reformation theology encouraged a different sort of marriage to that which had gone before, where affection and mutual respect came to replace the marriages of convenience that some historians (most notably Stone 1989) argued to be more characteristic of the alliances of an earlier age. But claims that this suggests a new kind of equality – 'the companionate marriage' – perhaps need to be tempered by household manuals from the period, suggestions of a clear hierarchy which generally endorse obedience to one's husband. Although the anonymous author of the pamphlet *Haec-Vir, or the Womanish-Man* defends women and argues that 'Custom is an idiot' (Jordan, Carroll, Damrosch 2006, 1531), Robert Snawsel has a female character in his dialogue *A Looking Glass for Married Folks* tell an independent woman 'You are married now unto your husband, what manner of man soever he be; you have no liberty to change him for another, or cast him off' (Dolan 1996, 189). As Kathleen McLuskie has explored, London theatres often staged women pressing for liberty, but often the result was tragedy (1999).

Literacy in the period, a difficult concept to measure or even define, was clearly lower for women than men: by many estimates, women read and wrote at about a third of the numbers that men did. The importance of women as writers has been reconceived in the past thirty years, and Virginia Woolf's elegy about the difficulty of an imaginary 'Shakespeare's sister' to even stay alive in the period's male-dominated literary world has met considerable evidence of a different picture, one in which numerous women wrote, published and played the literary patron (Woolf 2005, and see Chapter 2). One of the most significant achievements in literary history in recent decades has been the effort to recover the voices of actual women writers and patrons from the period. Perhaps the single most extraordinary aspect of women's life in the period was the presence of a woman as ruler. Elizabeth I not only ruled but ruled independently, and provoked a full spectrum of passions among her subjects and among men in Europe. The new monarch immediately accepted and eventually cultivated an iconic stature, and her role as the 'Virgin Queen', replacing the half-sister who tried to re-establish the Catholic Church with all of its Marian associations, speaks to the shifting psychic roles that a female public figure could play as well as to the importance of the Reformation in shaping those roles. Elizabeth encouraged her courtiers to court her, and literary output in her reign, including the fashion for Petrarchan sonnets and Edmund Spenser's epic poetry, reflects that language of romantic worship (see Chapters 2 and 3). But the increasingly prominent role of women also generated a good deal of misogynistic backlash: John Knox took aim at other powerful aristocratic women, including Mary Tudor and Mary of Guise and Catherine de Medici, in his pamphlet *The First Blast of the Trumpet Against the Monstrous Regiment of Women* in 1558, and in the 1620s, pamphlets such as *Hic Mulier* and *Haec Vir* respectively attacked and defended these changes in gender roles.

The idea of a ruling woman as 'monstrous' corresponded with popular Protestant demonizing of the Catholic Church as the 'Whore of Babylon', as both converted political anxiety into the rawest misogyny, and in fact, women who stepped outside of prescribed roles were disciplined in a variety of ways. The witchcraft craze that swept Europe was less virulent in England than in many other countries, but it still targeted large numbers, most of whom were women. Plays such as Shakespeare's *Macbeth* and Middleton, Ford, and Rowley's *The Wise-woman of Hogsdon* dramatize the social and gender processes that go into converting a woman with disturbing ideas into a demonic force. A similar process can be found in the various forms of 'shrew-taming' with long-established roots in English culture, as the tamings, silencings and beatings meted out to women who talked too much for some people's tastes echoed the more fatal punishments inflicted on alleged witches. The theme of silencing women is a central one in Renaissance literature, and the extent to which plays and poems countenance as opposed to question those practices remains a central critical question.

Economic Conflict: Building a New Market World

The revolutions brought about by religious and technical changes were part of a new world. The Reformation also coincided with, and (according to thinkers like the sociologist Max Weber in his *The Protestant Ethic and the Spirit of Capitalism* [1904]), helped create a remarkable transformation of economic life. Weber's argument is that it was a new religious spirit that helped produce modern economic life, one in which individuals use markets and thrift to create new roles for themselves. This is one way of accounting for the co-incidence of religious reform and the rise of capitalism; another, more Marxist view would argue instead that is was the rise of a mercantile class (which was eventually to become the bourgeoisie) which produced the reformation, as a new class sought out new ideologies to articulate its interests (See Chapter 6). Whether the Reformation spurred economic growth, or whether new economic roles spurred the Reformation, what is undeniable is that the era was marked by an individualist spirit in both religious and economic life, and a new kind of economic life was beginning. Renaissance playwrights often staged such new entrepreneurs, usually with satiric glee; Epicure Mammon, a character in Ben Jonson's *The Alchemist*, awaits his new wealth with particular zeal:

> This is the day wherein, to all my friends,
> I will pronounce the happy word, 'Be rich;
> This day you shall be spectatissimi'. (Fraser and Rabkin 1976, 58)

While it did not have the complete rebirth imagined by the greedy Mammon, from roughly 1485 to 1660 England transformed itself, growing from an economic backwater to one of the leading centres of European and even world trade. In this time span the country's economy took on a variety of new forms, and London was transformed from a city of approximately 50,000 to a thriving metropolis of close to 350,000. Trade grew in particular directions, as England slowly shifted from being an importer of almost all finished goods, and a great exporter of raw materials (most significantly wool,) to a leader in trade. A major consequence of this transformation was a shift in population from rural to urban locations. Migration to the towns (especially to London) accelerated during the reign of Henry VIII, when aristocratic landowners began to appropriate land which had previously been available to the peasantry, who had used it to graze their animals on. This process, known as enclosure, converted previously common lands into the private lands of wealthier landlords, who used their now privatized fields for raising sheep. With no grazing rights left the newly impoverished peasantry was forced to migrate, either to the towns in search of employment, or into vagrancy (and in fact the perception of a rise of vagabonds exercised many during the period).

This was one of the causes of London's emergence as a new type of city. Not only were the population figures astounding, an explosion unprecedented in European history, but the London that emerged seemed to foster a new way of being a city dweller: urbanization created urbanism. Specialization and trade were a part of that milieu, but the most signal trait was malleability, as social life took on a protean quality, wherein it could make sense to claim, as Jacques does in Shakespeare's *As You Like It*, that 'all the world's a stage, and all the men and women merely players' (2.7.138–139). In the new city, some have claimed, there was a new freedom to play roles, to develop a different relation to money and social place, so that being a gentleman could be a matter of self-assertion and not just a matter of birth. The critic Stephen Greenblatt, the leading figure of the movement in Renaissance studies known as the 'new historicism', coined the phrase 'self-fashioning' to describe this drive at personal reinvention; certainly, the idea was a familiar one to writers in the period, as we can see in Edmund Spenser's stated intention in his introductory letter to his epic poem *The Faerie Queene* to 'to fashion a gentleman or noble person in virtuous and gentle discipline' (Spenser 1989, 15). Others have suggested that this sense of protean, shifting roles is intimately connected with the rise to hegemony of drama in the period; in 1576 the first public theatre in England was built, called simply 'the Theatre', an early part of a boom in London play-going, where the intensity of the role-playing out in the streets and markets may have found artistic transformation onto a literal rather than figurative stage (see Chapter 2).

London life brought together many types of people in many disparate places, including markets, criminal worlds, theatres, workshops, bookshops, immigrant enclaves, brothels, middle-class households, schools, churches, law courts and courts; that sense of movement and of mixed social milieu is immediately apparent in works such as Jonson's *Epigrams* or *The Alchemist* or Middleton and Dekker's *The Roaring Girl*. New city spaces created spots of conversation and contest, and out of them emerged new kinds of literature. Satire, for instance, took on new life in the areas surrounding the Inns of Court, which transformed an older genre in the matrix of a new urban world, led by the fierce 1590s satirist John Marston. Marston took on the pose of rough poetic beast, insulting his audience in introductory passages such as this one:

> Quake guzzle dogs, that live on putred slime,
> Skud from the lashes of my yerking rime. (Marston 1961, 102)

Beneath this pose of hostility, Marston and his peers brought literature into the contests of street and civic life in a new way. At the court, older modes of poetry combined European lyric modes with domestic political concerns, as can be seen in the epigrams and sonnets of John Heywood, Philip Sidney, Walter Ralegh and John Harington. The places of vice, including prostitution, gambling and blood sports, were often in the same sections of the city as the theatres, giving actors a very low social status. In Stuart London, new places to meet and gather, especially new tavern clubs or societies, and new work and reading habits, promoted a rise of a new kind of political literature, made visible in a vibrant libel culture. Merchant life helped inspire the comedies of writers such as Ben Jonson and Thomas Middleton, and the crime and bustle of the poorer parts of London inspired the wild satire of writers like Thomas Dekker, Isabella Whitney and Thomas Nashe. All these numerous locales and literatures overlapped and blended, making English Renaissance literature a chorus of radically different voices.

Outward Conflict: Looking Outside England

If we turn our gaze away from London and England, we will see that in foreign relations, as well as in matters of religious, economic and gender conflicts, England experienced conflict that shook people's senses of what their centre was. Galileo's charting of new worlds in the sky had very definite earthly parallels in the discoveries and geographical wanderings of explorers, settlers and traders around the world, as well as in the more rigorous control of the further reaches of what is now called the 'British Isles'.

Nothing demonstrates that the English Renaissance had a forward-looking vision (in addition to its reimagining of the classical past) as much as its part in exploring the western hemisphere and the newly accessible coasts of Africa and Asia. English ships set sail for ports both east and west, or as John Donne described it, 'both th' Indias of spice and mine' (Donne 1996, 80). Donne's image captures figuratively what his contemporaries embodied literally in their travels: the mixture of adventure and profit that motivated exploration. Sailors and their financiers sought out Asian spices and American gold, as well as rum, sugar and human beings, while some travellers intended to settle and build a better world, motivated by changing currents in England's religious climate. John Cabot, under the sponsorship of Henry VII, sailed to eastern Canada in 1497, establishing the claim for British control of that region, where in the 1570s Martin Frobisher furthered England's contacts, and in 1583 Humphrey Gilbert claimed Newfoundland as England's first colony in the hemisphere. The next year his brother-in-law, Walter Ralegh, founded the first English colony in what was then called Virginia, and in 1595 he explored Guiana – both of his ventures proved disastrously ill-planned. The year 1607 saw the founding of the first successful English settlement in the Americas, in what is now the United States, by John Smith in the colony of Virginia, at Jamestown, and in 1620 the Pilgrims arrived at Plymouth, Massachusetts. What was the effect of this medley of desires, of greed mixed with idealism, on the literature of the period? Texts as varied as John Donne's lyrics, Shakespeare's *The Tempest* and Francis Bacon's *The New Atlantis* provide some answers to that question.

English explorers began building a far-flung network of trade around the world that would gradually grow into empire. In 1555 the Muscovy Company was founded and for the rest of the century its leaders explored trade routes to Russia. In 1562 John Hawkins and Francis Drake initiated slave trade with America, joining in the broader Atlantic slave trade begun by Portuguese and Spanish empires. From 1577–80, Drake made a voyage around the world, part of a group of navigators opening up new possibilities for commerce, and in 1600 Elizabeth gave a charter to the East India Company, beginning the colonization of India and creating the corporation that ruled that land until the Indian Rebellion of 1857. The later-sixteenth century saw increasing trade to Europe, as well as increasing aid to Protestant communities on the continent and increased arrival of Protestant (or 'dissenting') 'strangers' into England. More radical Protestant factions at home encouraged Elizabeth to aid their co-religionists abroad, and the Anglo-Spanish war, which lasted intermittently from 1585–1604, saw a series of battles at sea and on land, especially in the Netherlands and at Cadiz in Spain. More and more of the foreign world began to move towards England as well: Edward VI had granted a charter granting certain rights of worship to Protestant immigrants, and the Dutch had been steadily moving to the island ever since. Despite repeated outbursts of anti-immigrant riots, England and particularly London continued to see the arrival of immigrants. English economic life, and the English imagination, was increasingly pushed to join Europe and the broader world.

In the islands of the archipelago – the lands including Ireland, Scotland, Wales and England – England increased its power, making major steps in dominating its Celtic neighbours. In Ireland, the sixteenth century saw the first of the 'plantations', or organized settlements of Protestants in lands seized from Catholic Irish. A series of wars in Ireland during Elizabeth's reign strained both her finances and her political control, but English plantations continued, culminating in the defeat of Hugh O'Neil and the departure of the Catholic nobles from the north in 1607, the 'Flight of the Earls'. Wales and Scotland grew a more stable part of the larger island's political union, though Scotland remained a threat, invading England in both the 1630s and 1640s, and the formalizing of an Act of Union remained unaccomplished until 1707. The tensions among these groups are captured in numerous literary texts, such as Shakespeare's *Henry V*. At home and abroad, encounters with different cultures were remaking the country and its literature.

Political Conflict: From Feudal Kingdom to Modern State

The English Renaissance is usually framed by the dates 1485 and 1660, noting two watershed political moments. The first marks the creation of the Tudor dynasty at Henry Richmond's defeat of Richard III at the battle of Bosworth Field, and the second Charles II's return to England at the Restoration of the monarchy and the end of the experiments called the Commonwealth and the Protectorate. We concentrate in this volume on the Tudor period, for another volume in the series devotes itself to the Seventeenth Century. But throughout the whole period, much of the literature produced takes as its focus the question of proper forms of government. Was the king God's designated authority, and therefore unquestionable? Did he have a divine right to rule, or did the people have a right to assert their displeasure if that rule was unjust? Plays including Marlowe's *Edward II* and many of Shakespeare's histories and tragedies – *Richard II*, for instance, or *King Lear* – are arranged around those questions. And literary critics have quite different opinions about what these playwrights believe are the proper answers. What is beyond dispute is that as the monarchy consolidated power, a new sense of England as a nation permeated the county and its imaginative literature, which often addressed the struggles of the monarchs of the Tudor line – Henry VII, Henry VIII, Edward VI, Mary I and Elizabeth I – who first built power in a central court, and then fought to maintain that power amidst the storms of Reformation politics. The great administrative accomplishment of the Tudors steadily drained power from feudal centres of authority, especially in the reign of Henry VII, when the monarchy greatly improved methods of taxation which ensured a reliable stream of financing for the national government. Henry expanded the powers of a King's Council as a counterweight to nobility, and used a special tribunal called the Star Chamber to control any nobles who stepped out of line. Similarly, an increased use of the Justice of the Peace system, on a national level, provided a network for national bureaucracy. Henry supervised building up the navy, as part of his long-term efforts to improve trade. These administrative reforms were continued in the reign of Henry VIII, that spectacular figure of personal and national appetite.

Henry may survive most luminously in popular imagination because of his six marriages, but it was his role within the rise of Protestantism in England that most changed his country's understanding of itself. The Reformation's assault on the powers and landholdings of the Catholic Church weakened the largest institution in the country, and much of that power was transferred either to an aristocracy loyal to the crown or to the crown itself. And Elizabeth in her forty-five year reign steadied the ship of state and consolidated the advances of her father and grandfather. As Richard Helgerson asserts in *Forms of Nationhood: The Elizabethan Writing of England* (1984), writers participated in a widespread attempt to imagine England as a nation for the first time.

In contrast, the Stuart monarchy which followed the Tudor dynasty in the seventeenth century presided over the dissolution of royal power, culminating in the overthrow of Charles I. The Stuarts' inflexible defense of 'the divine right of kings' galvanized the opposition from the parliamentary forces which was eventually to prove their downfall, as country split into Royalists and Parliamentarians, each with their own military forces. That conflict had both religious and economic dimensions. Parliamentary leaders found allies in Puritan radicals, as Puritan insistence on individual responsibility, and its resistance to Episcopal (let alone Papal) authority, had a corollary in resistance to monarchy; nowhere is this as clear as in the writings of that politician and poet John Milton, who wrote numerous fiery tracts defending radical liberty. The King's forces, supported mostly by the older economic interests of the aristocracy, could not hold out against the forces of new economic and religious classes, lead by Thomas Fairfax, Oliver Cromwell and the New Model Army. After purging the Parliament of its less radical members, the remaining 'rump' parliament tried Charles for treason, and he was executed on 30 January 1649. From 1649 to 1660 England had no monarch, being ruled by a republican government called a Commonwealth, and then by Oliver Cromwell, as 'Lord Protector'. After Cromwell's death a desire for national unity led to the return of Charles' son from exile, where he became Charles II, King of England, but where he never attempted to obtain the absolute authority his father and grand-father claimed as their right. How much was this conflict a matter of religious difference? How much a class war? How much a battle of personalities that could have been avoided with different decisions at key moments? How much a clash of ideas? Historians and literary critics, including David Loades (1999), Raymond Williams (2001) and Christopher Hill (1997), provide their varying opinions. There is no consensus on the meanings of the English Civil War (see Chapter 8). That conflict among professional historians is a fitting mirror for the conflicting energies driving the authors discussed in this volume, and the extremely diverse interpretations of those authors that readers have proposed in the intervening centuries. Just as earlier writers such as Wyatt, Marlowe, Shakespeare and Jonson engaged with political theory, the seventeenth-century writers such as Katherine Philips, John Milton and Andrew Marvell continued to draw on the political debates and divisions of the country to help create their literature. The conflicts had changed since the beginning of the period – the permanent diminishment of royal authority was a radical new thing – but what had not changed was that literature took its form in large part from the array of struggles of the country as whole. It was out of the radical oppositions shaping the history of the culture that individual authors derived the energy for their art.

2 Literary and Cultural Contexts: Major Figures, Institutions, Topics, Events, Movements

Karen Britland and Lucy Munro

Changes and developments in culture and literature during the sixteenth and early seventeenth centuries were often influenced by social, political and institutional pressures. As we will explore in further detail below, debates over issues such as the status and nature of women, the perceived moral failings of the theatre, the position of England within the British Isles, Europe and the wider world, all left their mark on the literary texts that were written, circulated and read. More broadly, literary production was also affected by circumstances within the nation, encompassing issues as disparate as changes in population levels and the development of print culture. To take the first of these examples, the percentage of people living in urban rather than rural areas increased during this period; this is particularly evident in the growth of London, which almost doubled its population between 1600 and 1640 and became one of the largest cities in Europe. It had around 250,000 inhabitants in 1600 and, by 1640, the population seems to have been as high as 400,000 (see Chapter 1). Other important cities in this period included Bristol, Newcastle, Norwich and York, but Norwich, the largest of these, had a population of only 20,000 in 1640. Insofar as print culture was concerned, the first book in English was printed in Bruges in 1475 by William Caxton, who in 1476 set up England's first printing press in London (see Chapter 1). The printers' guild, the Stationers' Company, gained a monopoly which confined printing for the main part to London, although the universities of Oxford and Cambridge had special permission to print books. As a result, literary culture in London developed in ways different from those in the country at large, and distinctively metropolitan cultural 'scenes' began to emerge, such as that surrounding London's playhouses.

Writing in Manuscript and Print

There were two different, though often overlapping, forms of publication in the sixteenth and seventeenth centuries. Writers might write for print publication, selling their manuscript to a publisher who would then keep the profits from this first and any further editions. Alternatively, they might circulate their work in manuscript, giving copies to friends or patrons, or hiring scribes to make copies. Shakespeare's sonnets seem to have circulated in this way before their appearance in print in 1609; in 1598 Francis Meres cited as an example of Shakespeare's work 'his sugred Sonnets among his priuate friends' (*Palladis Tamia* [London, 1598], fols. 281v–2r). Some authors, such as John Donne and Philip Sidney, were little published during their own lifetimes but found a productive posthumous afterlife in print. Manuscript might also offer advantages over print publication, especially for writers dabbling in affairs of state: print publication was subject to censorship, while manuscript circulation – of satire and libels, for instance – was much harder for the authorities to control.

Manuscript publication was not necessarily as elite or private as might be thought: some poems – such as those by Donne (see Chapter 4) – are found in huge numbers of manuscripts, and in many different versions, as readers copied them out and made their own alterations. There has been much debate about the relationships between forms of publication and the social status of authors. Although famous poets like Edmund Spenser did publish their work, the majority of poets writing at or for the court preferred to eschew the popular press and present their friends and patrons with manuscript copies of their poems. Even the future Queen Elizabeth I was involved in manuscript production: she is known to have written prayers and poems in several languages, and sometimes to have presented them as gifts to members of her family.

To circulate one's writing in manuscript, or to print it, was to make a statement about the worth of that writing. This could prove especially problematic for women. Conduct manuals that circumscribed women's roles in society, and religious exhortations like St Paul's injunction in 1 Timothy 2.11 to 'Let the woman learn in silence with all subjection', may have implied that for a woman to write (let alone to publish) contravened her prescribed social role. What she thought and what she said, so the argument goes, was the property of her husband. Publicly to publish her writing was tantamount to publishing herself: in other words, it rendered her open to accusations of wantonness and unchastity. However, it is becoming increasingly obvious that women did write and even publish throughout the Tudor and Stuart periods. For example, around 1553 Jane, Lady Lumley, translated Euripides' play *Iphigenia* out of Greek into English, while Mary Sidney, Countess of Pembroke, translated Robert Garnier's *Marc Antoine* out of French. Although they did not often receive the same kind of sustained formal, humanist educations as their brothers, who could attend the universities of Oxford and Cambridge, young noblewomen, particularly from the end of Henry VIII's reign, were sometimes educated at home by the same tutors who attended their male relatives.

It was not only aristocratic women who read and wrote. Recent scholars working on women's writing have begun to revisit and to uncover texts by authors of a lower social status than the privileged nobility (Daybell 2006; Snook 2007). Literacy rates were not so high among people of a lower social status, especially among women, although the exact levels of literacy in England have been much debated by social historians. Nonetheless, many non-elite people, including women, could read and write, and many who could not write could read. Non-elite people thus form an important audience for various forms of writing, and also feature as writers themselves. For example, Isabella Whitney, who published two volumes of her poems in the 1570s, came from a relatively humble gentry background and worked in domestic service in London. The attention now being paid to less-conventional forms of writing such as family accounts, religious writings and letters has also provided evidence of the diversity of women's experiences in the period. While such writing does not necessarily fall into conventional literary categories, it does shed light on writers' material and spiritual experiences as well as their social and familial interactions. For example, letters between Maria Thynne and Thomas, her husband, during the early 1600s demonstrate both the couple's mutual affection and Maria's involvement in her husband's business affairs: she was left in charge of his property while he was away from home, and participated in decisions about household and estate appointments (Wall 1983). Texts such as these provide a wealth of information about people's lives and in particular help to shed light on the ways in which women were constructed in more formal literary texts.

Writing for the Theatre

The most important arena for writers in this period was the theatre and playwrights came from a variety of backgrounds. Some were amateurs, many of them courtiers or educators, such as Thomas Norton and Thomas Sackville, who wrote *Gorboduc* for performance at the Inner Temple in 1562, or Richard Edwards, master of the choristers at the Chapel Royal. The majority of those who wrote for the commercial stage were from middling backgrounds: Thomas Kyd, for instance, was the son of a scrivener, Robert Greene the son of a saddler or an innkeeper, Christopher Marlowe the son of a shoemaker, Thomas Nashe the son of a clergyman and William Shakespeare the son of a glover. They were the bright, ambitious products of the humanist project of the Elizabethan grammar schools (see Chapter 1) and (in some cases) universities, many of them lured from the provinces to London (Greene from Norwich, Marlowe from Canterbury, Shakespeare from Stratford-upon-Avon). Even dramatists from more elevated social backgrounds, such as John Fletcher, the son of a bishop, and Francis Beaumont, the son of a judge, were impoverished younger sons forced to make their own way in the world. Some dramatists, such as Shakespeare, Ben Jonson, William Rowley and the older Robert Wilson, a prominent playwright of the 1580s and 1590s, seem to have worked as actors as well playwrights; Jonson was probably nothing more than a hired hand, but Shakespeare, Rowley and Wilson are known to have been shareholders in the companies for which they wrote and performed.

Playwrights' relationships with the companies who performed their plays varied considerably. Sharer-playwrights probably had a greater degree of control over their writing than the majority of writers, who would either be commissioned on a play-by-play basis or might have a long-standing informal or formal engagement with a particular company. Rowland Broughton was contracted in the early 1570s to write an improbable eighteen plays in the space of a year, while in the 1630s Brome agreed 'for the terme of three years [. . .] with his best Art and Industrye [to] write everye yeare three plays' for the company at Salisbury Court (Haaker 1968, 297). Neither dramatist was able to fulfil his contract; each was sued by the company involved. The account book or *Diary* of Philip Henslowe, who owned theatres and pay-rolled companies in the 1590s and 1600s, suggests that the actors might specify particular genres or subject-matter to writers; many entries in the diary have spaces where titles were to be interlined, the plays are instead described as a 'tragedy', 'comedy' or even, in one case, 'a Pastorall ending in a Tragedye' (Foakes and Rickert 1961, 266).

Many dramatists collaborated on plays, either in pairs or in larger groups. For instance, payments in Henslowe's *Diary* demonstrate that a lost play called *Caesar's Fall* (1602) was written by Thomas Dekker, Michael Drayton, Thomas Middleton, Anthony Munday and John Webster. Middleton collaborated regularly with Dekker on other plays, and with William Rowley on *A Fair Quarrel* (c. 1616) and *The Changeling* (1622); Webster is better known for solo plays such as *The White Devil* (1612) and *The Duchess of Malfi* (1614), but also collaborated with Dekker on *Westward Ho* and *Northward Ho*, written around 1605–06. Even Ben Jonson, who published his *Works* in 1616 and who liked to present himself as a fiercely independent writer, was a frequent collaborator; he worked as part of a team for Henslowe in the 1590s, and was still collaborating in 1605, when he wrote *Eastward Ho* with George Chapman and John Marston. His tragedy *Sejanus* (1603) was originally written with another dramatist, but Jonson rewrote his collaborator's contributions when he published the play. Shakespeare also seems to have collaborated periodically throughout his career. Early plays such as *1 Henry VI* and *Titus Andronicus* are thought to include the work of Thomas Nashe and George Peele respectively, and Shakespeare may have been one of the dramatists who contributed to *Sir Thomas More*, a play which survives in manuscript. In 1607–08 he wrote two plays collaboratively, *Pericles* with George Wilkins and *Timon of Athens* with Thomas Middleton, and at the end of his career in 1612–13 he wrote three plays with John Fletcher: *Henry VIII or All is True*, *The Two Noble Kinsmen* and the lost *Cardenio*. Fletcher also famously collaborated with Francis Beaumont, with whom he wrote plays including *The Maid's Tragedy*, *A King and No King* and *Philaster*, but he also wrote widely with other dramatists, notably Philip Massinger, and wrote some plays alone.

Theatrical Traditions
The business of playing changed significantly between the early sixteenth and mid-seventeenth centuries. At the beginning of the period, there were three major traditions of theatrical performance. The first was amateur performance within communities, expressed in forms as disparate as cycles of liturgical mystery plays and civic pageants. The second was professional performance by troupes of players, many of them patronized by members of the nobility, who toured locally or nationally and who also performed at court. The third was performance within educational establishments such as universities, grammar and choir schools; the students performed plays as part of their education and before invited audiences, and some groups were summoned to perform at court. In the course of the sixteenth century, professional performers gradually eclipsed the amateurs and the children, but the process was by no means coherent or continuous.

Venues for Performance
A number of venues were available for theatrical performance throughout the period: noble households; the royal court; town halls and churches; inns and taverns; schools, universities and the Inns of Court (where legal education was centred). The late sixteenth century saw an innovation in English playing with the development of permanent playing spaces, some purpose-built and others converted from inn-yards or other existing buildings. The earliest of these appears to have been the Red Lion (1567), a playhouse built by John Brayne in the grounds of a farmhouse in Whitechapel, to the east of the City of London. Brayne and his son-in-law James Burbage later built the Theatre (1576), an open-air amphitheatre in Shoreditch, to the north of the City. The Theatre appears to have been a success with audiences, and it was followed by other amphitheatres, most of them clustered in areas to the north and south of the City:

the Curtain (1577); the Rose (1592); the Swan (1595), the Globe (1599) and the Fortune (1600). Inn-yard conversions included the Boar's Head (1598) and The Red Bull (*c.* 1604), which was still in use after the Restoration. These playhouses were substantial, open-air structures, the largest of which could admit up to 3,000 spectators. According to the available evidence, their audiences appear to have been a cross-section of London society, both male and female: the nobility in the most expensive seats; respectable gentry and citizens; apprentices and students; and thieves and prostitutes who visited the playhouses for profit and recreation. The lasting value of the amphitheatres is demonstrated by the fact that at least two – the Globe and the Fortune – were speedily rebuilt when they were the victims of fire. Sometimes there were attempts to combine the theatre with other forms of popular entertainment. A project to build a combined theatre and bear-baiting house, the Hope (1614), was apparently not a success; the players quickly departed, though the venue was still being used for baiting and fencing shows in the 1630s. The precise reasons for the venture's failure are not known, but they probably include problems of noise, odour and (from the actors' point of view) unwanted proximity with dangerous animals.

The open-air amphitheatres were not the only venue for professional or semi-professional performance. In 1576, Richard Farrant, master of the choristers at the Chapel Royal, converted rooms in an old monastery building to form a permanent playhouse, the First Blackfriars theatre. This theatre was used by Farrant's charges, known as the Children of the Chapel, a company of choir-school pupils who mounted semi-professional performances and performed regularly at court. The adult companies quickly took note of the potential of indoor playhouses. In 1596 James Burbage bought up buildings in the Blackfriars precinct which he converted into a new theatre, the Second Blackfriars. Later indoor theatres included the Cockpit or Phoenix (1616) and the Salisbury Court (1629). The indoor theatres were much smaller than the outdoor amphitheatres – the Second Blackfriars, which was the largest, may have admitted around 600–1000 spectators, while the theatre at St Paul's Cathedral may have admitted as few as 50. As a result of their smaller size, they seem to have charged higher prices for admission: while the cheapest admission at the Theatre in the 1590s was 1 *d.*, rising to 6 *d.* for the Lord's room above the stage, the Blackfriars' minimum price was 6 *d.*, rising to 2 *s.* 6 *d.* for a box alongside the stage. A higher entrance price meant that the spectators were probably wealthier on average than those in the amphitheatres, but this did not mean that only the nobility and gentry were present: affluent citizens and law students also seem to have attended in numbers.

Theatre Companies

Two kinds of professional and semi-professional theatre companies were active in the course of the sixteenth and seventeenth centuries: adult companies in which all female roles were played by boys or youths, and companies composed entirely of children. The adult companies began the period as travelling players, criss-crossing the country on long-established touring routes which included major towns and cities such as London, Norwich and Bristol, the royal court, and the households of the nobility and gentry. They did not stop touring on the emergence of the purpose-built theatres. Indeed, the most important company of the 1580s, the Queen's Men, was primarily a touring organization, and companies were still touring in the 1630s and 1640s. By this time, many actors had become well-known celebrities. Famous performers of the late sixteenth and early seventeenth centuries included Richard Burbage of the Chamberlain's Men (later the King's Men) – who performed many of Shakespeare's most famous roles, including Hamlet, Othello and King Lear – and Edward Alleyn of the Admiral's Men (later Prince Henry's Men), the original performer of roles including Hieronimo in Thomas Kyd's *The Spanish Tragedy* and the title roles in Christopher Marlowe's *Doctor Faustus* (see Chapter 3) and *The Jew of Malta*. Comedians, including Richard Tarlton, William Kemp, Robert Armin, John Shank and Andrew Keyne, were also well known and loved by audiences. Acting was not at that time a profession open to women: all women's parts were played by boy actors aged between around fourteen and twenty-one years of age, some of whom went on to have successful adult careers.

The composition of the children's companies varied between troupes. In 1599–1600 the boy actors in the Chapel Children and the Children of Paul's seem to have been aged between around nine and fourteen years of age, but there is evidence for the involvement of older actors at other times and in other companies. In the 1570s, 1580s and in the early 1600s, the children were prominent in the court calendar, performing innovative plays by the likes of Lyly, Peele, Marlowe, Jonson, Chapman, Beaumont and Fletcher. These groups performed some of the most experimental and politically aware drama of the period, and seem to have posed a sustained challenge to the adult companies, as comments in Shakespeare's *Hamlet* about the 'little eyases' who have forced an adult company to go on tour suggest.

The advent of the purpose-built theatres seems to have influenced the performance styles of the companies – the settled theatres offering more potential for special effects, for instance – and the range of plays performed by individual companies. When a company was primarily a touring organization, the number of plays needed was comparatively small; when they used a purpose-built theatre, a rotating repertory was needed in order to attract audiences day after day. In June 1596, for instance, the Lord Admiral's Men performed sixteen different plays: their repertory included tragedies (Marlowe's *Doctor Faustus* and *The Jew of Malta*, and a lost play about the siege of Troy), history plays (the anonymous play *The Famous Victories of Henry V* and *Longshank* [probably George Peele's *Edward I*]), plays with exotic settings (the lost *Tamar Cham*), plays about English life (the lost plays *The Siege of London* and *The Wise Man of Westchester*) and comedies (the lost play *Crack Me This Nut*). The companies maintained this repertory system throughout the period, but some plays began to be played in longer runs, such as Thomas Middleton's *A Game at Chess*, a scandalous political satire which was performed by the King's Men for nine days in a row in 1624.

Kinds of Writing

Drama

Renaissance English drama had its roots in a variety of vernacular and Latin traditions (see Chapter 8). These traditions were comprised of a range of sub-genres: religious plays including the cycles of liturgical mystery plays performed in many English cities, which survived until well into the sixteenth century despite their official suppression during the Reformation, and morality plays such as *Mankind* (*c.* 1465) and *Everyman* (*c.* 1509–19); secular interludes such as Henry Medwall's *Fulgens and Lucrece* (*c.* 1497) and John Heywood's *The Four Ps* (*c.* 1520–30); and classical plays by authors such as Terence, Plautus and Seneca, some of which were performed in grammar schools (see Chapter 1). In the mid-sixteenth century, plays began to intermingle these sources, resulting in plays such as the comedies *Ralph Roister Doister* (*c.* 1552) and *Gammer Gurton's Needle* (1566), Richard Edward's tragicomic *Damon and Pithias*, and the first English blank-verse tragedy *Gorboduc* (1562) by Thomas Norton and Thomas Sackville. These modes would be developed in various ways in the years that followed.

One of the most influential comic writers was John Lyly. In plays such as *Campaspe* and *Sappho and Phao* he combined classical settings with topical allusion to court and country, while in *Gallathea* he explored the mutability of gender and set a fashion for narratives in which girls chose or were forced to disguise themselves as boys. The next generation of playwrights, including Robert Greene and Shakespeare, were quick to seize on the possibilities of his work in their own romantic comedies. For instance, Rosalind's male disguise in *As You Like It* echoes those of Lyly's Gallathea and Phyllida; like them, she is forced by circumstances outside her control to take on the disguise, but while Gallathea and Phyllida feel constrained by their disguises, Rosalind's gives her greater room to manoeuvre and enables her to renegotiate her position as the object of romantic attention.

In contrast with romantic comedy, and often reacting against it, were more satiric forms of comedy. These included a brief craze for 'humours' plays (such as George Chapman's *An Humorous Day's Mirth* (1597) and Ben Jonson's *Every Man in his Humour* (1598)) and a more sustained tradition of 'city comedy' which encompassed plays such as Thomas Dekker's *The Shoemaker's Holiday* (1599), Jonson's *Volpone* (1605) and *The Alchemist* (1610), John Marston's *The Dutch Courtesan* (1605), and Thomas Middleton's *A Trick to Catch the Old One* (*c.* 1605) and *A Chaste Maid in Cheapside* (1613). In the early Jacobean period, a more formal fusion of tragedy and comedy emerged which was strongly influenced by Italian tragicomedy. Although early experiments such as John

Fletcher's *The Faithful Shepherdess* (c. 1607) were unsuccessful, popular plays such as Beaumont and Fletcher's *Philaster* (c. 1609–10) and *A King and No King* (c. 1610) and Shakespeare's *The Tempest* and *The Winter's Tale* (c. 1610–12) led to tragicomedy becoming one of the dominant dramatic modes of the late Jacobean and Caroline periods.

Renaissance tragedies encompassed revenge plays such as Thomas Kyd's *The Spanish Tragedy* (c. 1589), Shakespeare's *Hamlet* (c. 1600–01), Marston's *Antonio's Revenge* (c. 1600–01) and Middleton's *The Revenger's Tragedy* (1606); romantic tragedies such as Shakespeare's *Romeo and Juliet* (c. 1595); domestic tragedies such as *Arden of Faversham* (c. 1591) and Thomas Heywood's *A Woman Killed With Kindness* (c. 1603); and political tragedies such as Chapman's *Bussy D'Ambois* (c. 1604) or Shakespeare's *King Lear* (c. 1605) and *Macbeth* (c. 1606). *The Spanish Tragedy* and Marlowe's *Doctor Faustus* (c. 1588) were especially popular: they were still being performed, and influencing new generations of playwrights, forty years after their debuts. There were also traditions of more classicized tragedy. These included not only 'closet' plays intended primarily as reading material (such as Fulke Greville's *Mustapha* (1596) and *Alaham* (1600) and Elizabeth Cary's *Tragedy of Mariam* (1613), the first original English play written by a woman), but also plays written for the commercial stage such as Marlowe and Nashe's *Dido Queen of Carthage* (c. 1587), and Jonson's *Sejanus* (1603) and *Catiline* (1611).

History plays, which could be comic, tragic or tragicomic in form, were one of the most popular modes of the 1590s, encompassing such disparate plays as Greene's *James IV* (c. 1590), Marlowe's *Edward II* (c. 1592) and Shakespeare's first and second tetralogies. Later developments included a line of so-called 'elect nation' plays dealing with Reformation history and featuring Henry VIII and Elizabeth I as characters; these include Heywood's two-part play *If You Know Not Me You Know Nobody* (c. 1604–05), Samuel Rowley's *When You See Me You Know Me* (c. 1605), and Dekker's *The Whore of Babylon* (1606).

Poetry

Poetry was published in a bewildering variety of forms. Some genres were popular throughout the period. The most prized of literary genres, the epic, was represented prominently by Spenser's *Faerie Queene* (1590, 1596), a sweeping chivalric allegory examining England's religious and political history and destiny (see Chapter 3). Similarly important was religious poetry. The best-known religious poets of the period include John Donne (see Chapter 3) and George Herbert, while the genre also provided a means of expression for poets who were otherwise marginalized: Roman Catholic 'recusant' poets such as Chidiock Tichborne and Robert Southwell, and female poets including Mary Sidney and Aemilia Lanyer.

Many poetic genres had political associations. In the early sixteenth century Thomas Wyatt and Henry Howard, Earl of Surrey, pioneered the formal satire in England, and John Skelton attacked the excesses of Cardinal Wolsey in *Speak,*

Parrot (*c.* 1521) and *Colin Clout* (*c.* 1521). Skelton's deliberately rough style had a shaping influence on the style of later satirists, such as John Marston and John Donne. This style was not without critics. Ben Jonson wrote that such poets 'erre not by chance, but knowingly, and willingly' and compared them with people who dress in a deliberately outrageous way: 'they are like men that affect a fashion by themselves, have some singularity in a Ruffe, Cloake, or Hat-band; or their beards, specially cut to provoke beholders, and set a marke upon themselves' (Jonson 1640, 98). Wyatt's poems depicted court intrigue in sharp detail, and his depiction of Henrician tyranny is reflected in the work of Sir Walter Ralegh and other courtier-poets in the 1580s and 1590s. Pastoral writing also often took on a satiric cast, developing the interrogative style of Vergil's *Eclogues*. Prominent examples include Spenser's *Shepheardes Calendar* and *Colin Clout's Come Home Again* (printed 1595), which were imitated by a generation of 'Spenserian' poets. Not all political poetry was overtly satiric. Publications such as *The Mirror for Magistrates* (suppressed on its first publication in 1553, published in 1559 and expanded in successive editions) featured the first-person confessions of prominent historical figures such as Richard II, Owen Glendower and Jack Cade.

Some genres, such as the sonnet sequence, were popular for relatively brief periods of time (see below). For example, an outburst of Ovidian erotic narratives occurred in the 1590s and early 1600s, which included Lodge's *Scillae's Metamorphosis* (1589), Marlowe's *Hero and Leander* (*c.* 1593, printed 1598) and Shakespeare's *Venus and Adonis* (1593). More explicit erotic writing can be found in Donne's elegies and Nashe's wittily obscene *A Choice of Valentines* (written *c.* 1593–97), both of which circulated in manuscript.

Prose

The most important form of prose fiction was the romance,[1] a forerunner of the novel, albeit generally without the novel's unified narrative or focus on psychologically complex or consistent character (see pp 78–81). Instead, romances might be huge, sprawling narratives featuring outlandish settings, exaggerated emotions and casts of thousands; they often cross time-periods, continents and even worlds. Perhaps surprisingly, romance was a genre which carried a relatively large amount of political and social comment beneath its surface. Important examples include William Baldwin's *Beware the Cat* (*c.* 1554, printed 1570), which is sometimes termed the first English novel, John Lyly's witty and stylized *Euphues: The Triumph of Wit* (1578), which influenced English prose for generations, and numerous pastoral tales including Sir Philip Sidney's *The Countess of Pembroke's Arcadia* (written *c.* 1581 and *c.* 1583–84, first printed 1590), Robert Greene's *Pandosto* (1588) and *Menaphon* (1589) and Thomas Lodge's *Rosalyne* (1590). Other forms of prose fiction included utopian narratives such as Thomas More's *Utopia* (1516) (see pp 64–67), originally published in Latin, celebrations of citizen endeavour such as Thomas Deloney's highly popular narratives *Jack of Newberry* (1596) and *The Gentle Craft* (1597), and accounts of the rather less praiseworthy activities of rogues and criminals, such as Greene's 'cony-catching' pamphlets of the early 1590s. Particularly striking is the idiosyncratic, linguistically exuberant and virtually uncategorizable work of Thomas Nashe, which includes *Pierce Penniless his Supplication to the Devil* (1592), *The Unfortunate Traveller, or the Life of Jack Wilton* (1594) and *Nashe's Lenten Stuff* (1598), a text dedicated to (mocking) praise of the herring.

The most important non-fictional prose genre of the period was probably the sermon, of which huge numbers were printed and consumed. Notable examples include the works of John Fisher, Hugh Latimer and Henry Smith in the sixteenth century, and those of Lancelot Andrewes and John Donne in the seventeenth century. Other religious material was also consumed avidly, including William Tyndale's exchange of pamphlets with Thomas More in 1529–32, the *Examinations* of Anne Askew (1546–47), and John Foxe's Protestant hagiography, *Acts and Monuments of the English Martyrs* (1559, 1563), which was ordered to be displayed in churches. Other important religious and political prose works of the sixteenth century include Tyndale's *The Obedience of a Christian Man* (1529); John Knox's *First Blast of the Trumpet against the Monstrous Regiment of Women*, which was aimed at Mary I but offensive also to her successor, Elizabeth I (see Kerwin, this volume, Chapter 1); and Richard Hooker's *Of the Laws of Ecclesiastical Polity* (1593, 1597).

Biographical and autobiographical writing also developed during the early modern period. The earliest examples of life-writing are diaries and spiritual biographies, such as William Roper's *The Life of Thomas More* and Grace Mildmay's autobiography in the mid-sixteenth century, and the diaries of Margaret Hoby (1599–1605) and Anne Clifford (1616–19) in the late sixteenth and early seventeenth centuries.

Writing at Tudor and Stuart Courts

If the public playhouses constituted one location that fostered new writing, then the royal courts provided another. Indeed, it might be argued that literary success at court far outweighed that which could be obtained in the public theatre. Patronage from the reigning monarch, or an influential member of the nobility, could bring benefits to a poet that ranged from presents of food or money to more lasting gifts of positions in a noble's household or in institutions such as the church. Ben Jonson's famous poem to the Countess of Bedford, beginning 'Madam, I told you late that I repented', exemplifies the kind of gift exchange inherent in the first type of award: Jonson describes how he received a gift of venison from the countess, and presents her his gratitude in a poem which praises her generosity in return, publicizing her virtues in a manner which shows the poet/patron relationship to be fruitful and reciprocal.

Poets associated with the courts fall into roughly two categories: members of the nobility whose families' positions led to their attendance on the monarch (for example, Wyatt, Surrey, Sidney); and educated members of the lesser nobility and gentry who attempted to gain patronage and preferment through their services (literary or otherwise) to the monarch or prominent members of the nobility (such as Shakespeare, Jonson, Daniel). Success as a court poet depended less on one's ability to publish one's work in printed books, and more on its circulation in manuscript among a specific group or coterie.

Tudor Courts

The two most renowned court poets of the early Tudor period are probably Sir Thomas Wyatt and the Earl of Surrey, who are credited with bringing the sonnet tradition to England from Italy. Wyatt, a courtier and diplomat during the reign of Henry VIII, translated the work of the Italian Petrarch (1304–74) into English, producing famous poems such as 'Whoso list to hunt' (based on Petrarch's sonnet 190, 'Una candida cerva'), reputed by some to be about Wyatt's feelings for Henry VIII's paramour, Anne Boleyn, Wyatt also produced poems of his own, most famously the poignant lyric 'They Flee from Me' (see Adlington, this volume, pp 67–70).

The sonnet tradition flourished during Elizabeth's reign, its most famous practitioner being Sir Philip Sidney, whose *Astrophil and Stella* (written *c.* 1582, printed 1591) has become one of the most well-known of all Elizabethan sonnet sequences. Notable later examples include Samuel Daniel's *Delia* (1592) and Michael Drayton's *Idea's Mirror* (1593). Sidney's niece, Lady Mary Wroth, consciously followed in her uncle's footsteps when she wrote a sonnet sequence, 'Pamphilia to Amphilanthus', which was published in 1621 at the end of her long prose romance *Urania*. (The *Urania* itself was influenced by her uncle's prose tale *The Countess of Pembroke's Arcadia*.)

Nowadays, the most famous collection of Elizabethan sonnets is undoubtedly William Shakespeare's. His poems, probably written over a period of several years, were finally published in 1609. They draw on the Elizabethan sonnet tradition inaugurated by Wyatt and Surrey, but play with its conventions in several ways. For example, in sonnet 130, which begins 'My mistress eyes are nothing like the sun', Shakespeare consciously subverts the sonnet conventions that praised a beloved's beauty in overly extravagant terms.

The idea of Elizabeth I as a virgin queen took on an iconic importance in court poetry during this period that cannot be underestimated, and directly informed the work of poets such as Edmund Spenser and Sir Walter Ralegh. The first three books of Spenser's *The Faerie Queene* were dedicated and presented to Elizabeth in 1590, and, as Spenser noted in a letter to Ralegh, many of the characters shadowed the queen's virtues within the grand allegorical scheme of that epic poem (see Chapter 3). Ralegh himself expressed his devotion to Elizabeth in verse, most famously in his poem, 'The Ocean to Cynthia', which arguably uses the language of love to promote the poet's political interests. Elizabeth was not, however, a passive recipient of such poems: on at least one occasion, she appears to have written poetry back. Around 1587, Ralegh, concerned at the rise of a new court favourite, wrote verses to express his dismay at being displaced from the queen's affections. Elizabeth's poem in return begins with the lines, 'Ah, silly Pug, wert thou so sore afraid? / Mourn not, my Wat, nor be thou so dismayed', and concludes with the admonishment: 'Revive again and live without all dread, / The less afraid, the better thou shalt speed' (Elizabeth I 2000, 308–9). The queen's participation in this discourse shows how integral poetic writing was to the court and its politics.

Stuart Courts

After Elizabeth's death in 1603, James VI of Scotland's accession to the English throne changed the tenor of the English court. Where the final years of Elizabeth's reign were characterized by anxieties about the succession, James brought with him two ready-made heirs, his sons James and Charles. He was an educated king and cognizant of his role as the head of the Protestant church in England. Like Elizabeth, he too was a writer, and, as king of Scotland, had already printed some of his works, notably a paraphrase on the book of *Revelation* and a pamphlet about kingship entitled *Basilikon Doron* that laid out for his son Henry his understanding of the rights and duties of a monarch.

Ben Jonson, who shared James' passion for classical learning, soon became the most renowned court writer of the Jacobean reign and was employed to write courtly entertainments, not only by the king, but by Queen Anna and the royal favourite, the Duke of Buckingham. Under Jonson's influence, the old Elizabethan tilts and pageants changed into elaborate court masques which were performed to a much more exclusive audience than the older entertainments. These entertainments praised James as a Solomon or Jupiter and lauded the way he managed to maintain the nation's peace in a time of European conflict.

Many among the English, though, wanted England to intervene in the religious wars of the Continent and saw in Prince Henry someone who could take up Sir Philip Sidney's mantle as the saviour of international Protestantism. Jonson's *The Masque of Oberon*, performed by the Prince in 1611, carefully balanced Henry's desires for military involvement in Europe with his father's policies of non-engagement. Henry's costume for this entertainment was martial, and loosely based upon Roman precedents, emphasizing his military ambitions and his desires for rational, masculine order. The promises of the masque, however, eventually came to nothing: Henry died suddenly in 1612, and hopes for active English intervention on behalf of the Protestant cause in Europe faded with him.

James I's own death in 1625 occurred at almost the same time when Prince Charles, his only surviving son, married the French princess Henrietta Maria. For the first time in many decades, England had a young couple on the throne and the 1630s saw the flourishing of dramatic activity at court, with Henrietta Maria sponsoring productions in which, following the French traditions within which she had been brought up, she danced, sang and even acted. Ben Jonson soon fell out of favour, and was replaced by writers preferred by the Queen such as William Davenant and Walter Montagu. It has often been argued that the Caroline court was inward-looking, and overly concerned with glamour and theatrical entertainments to the detriment of the government of the country (Ashton 1978, 30–31). However, this may be an overly simplified view of the situation: Charles, after all, managed to maintain the neutrality of his country for nearly fifteen years, no mean feat, perhaps, in a Europe riven by religious wars.

The opinions of those who wished to enter into the European conflict and those who advocated the maintenance of peace at home never ceased to be aired in poems and plays of the period. For example, a poem by Aurelian Townshend on the death of Gustavus Adolphus, the Protestant king of Sweden, which called for English intervention in the conflict, was countered by another from his friend Thomas Carew which asserted the benefits of England's avocation of domestic peace. Ultimately, though, the religious wars could not be held at bay. Throughout the 1630s, divisions over the form that religious worship should take in the country, combined with unpopular taxes and other centralized ways of raising money (such as the selling of monopolies), meant that political positions became polarized. Eventually, after an invasion from the north by discontented Scotsmen and two unsuccessful Parliaments, the King raised his standard near Nottingham in what was to be seen as the beginning of the English civil wars, or (interpreted from a differently inflected theoretical perspective) the English Revolution (see Chapter 8).

Writing and Political/Cultural Debate

Literary and theatrical activities were immersed in political and cultural debates throughout the sixteenth and seventeenth centuries. Some of these debates focused on the status of literary or theatrical activities themselves. For instance, pamphleteers attacked the theatre from the early days of the purpose-built theatres in the 1570s through to the 1630s. Although the contexts of the debate shifted, the basis of their attacks remained surprisingly consistent: according to writers such as Philip Stubbes, Stephen Gosson and William Prynne, theatres drew uncontrollable crowds, they spread disease, they encouraged lewd and criminal behaviour, they broke biblical authority by having boys play the female roles, and their actors broke social conventions by pretending to have higher status than they actually had (Stubbes 1583; Gosson 1579; Prynne 1633). Their arguments were countered by others, including some professional dramatists such as Thomas Lodge and Thomas Heywood.

Other writers examined the status of literature, and of English literature; the most famous piece of literary criticism of the period is probably Philip Sidney's *Apology for Poetry* (written *c.* 1581, published 1595), a defence of literary writing against the rival claims of history and philosophy in which Sidney famously declares that the poet's imagination 'in making things either better than Nature bringeth forth, or, quite anew, forms such as never were in Nature . . . Her world is brazen, the poets only deliver a golden' (Sidney 2002, 85). A more practical approach is taken in *The Art of English Poesy* (1589), usually thought to have been written by George Puttenham, which outlines rhetorical and stylistic effects available to the writer.

Debates about the language itself were also prominent. The 'inkhorn' debate of the late sixteenth century focused on the introduction of words borrowed or adapted from other languages into English. Some writers thought that English needed to be amplified with new words if it was to stand alongside Latin as a legitimate literary language; others preferred what they saw as the purity of existing English words (see Healy, this volume, Chapter 8). The Elizabethan humanist Sir John Cheke commented in 1561, 'I am of this opinion that our own tung should be written cleane and pure, unmixt and unmangeled with borowing of other tunges'.[2] The inkhorn debate also entered the theatre. In Shakespeare's *Love's Labour's Lost* (*c.* 1594), for instance, Don Armado is a one-man Elizabethan language debate, his speech mixing up new and old words; the King describes him as 'A man in all the world's new fashion planted, / That hath a mint of phrases in his brain' (1.1.161–2). The debate features in an even more concrete fashion in Ben Jonson's play *The Poetaster* (1601), in which a thinly veiled caricature of John Marston – a rival playwright who had a penchant for neologisms – is made to vomit up the indigestibly complicated words he has been using. Some of the Latinate words introduced into English during the Renaissance have endured, such as 'agile', 'education', 'ostracize' and 'system'; others, such as 'exolete' (obsolete, insipid) and 'fatigate' (to fatigue) have disappeared.

Other debates focused on social, political and religious issues. For instance, debates about the nature and status of women flared up at intervals during the sixteenth and seventeenth centuries. In one prominent example, Joseph Swetnam's *The Arraignment of Lewd, Idle, Froward and Unconstant Women* (1615) saw a number of responses. Some, such as Rachel Speght's *A Muzzle for Melastomus* (1617), were written by women, others were published under female pseudonyms: Esther Sowernam (a riposte to 'Swetnam', which could be pronounced 'sweetnam') and Constantia Munda (the Latin for 'moral constancy'). A play, *Swetnam the Woman-Hater, Arraigned by Women*, entered the debate in 1617–18, when it was performed at the Red Bull playhouse. A couple of years later, a new debate stirred around the fashion for women to wear supposedly masculine clothing; King James was said to have instructed the clergy to 'inveigh vehemently and bitterly in theyre sermons against the insolencie of our women' (Chamberlain 1939, 286–7), and the pamphlet response included *Hic Mulier; Or, The Man-woman* and *Haec Vir; or, The Womanish Man*, dialogues featuring debates between a masculine woman and an effeminate man (see this volume, Chapters 1, 6 and 7).

Drama was a prominent political genre throughout the period. Works such as Skelton's *Magnificence* (*c.* 1519, which criticized Cardinal Thomas Wolsey, chief advisor to Henry VIII and Henry's young courtiers) and Bale's anti-Catholic history *King Johan* (1538, an important precursor of the Elizabethan history play), had a political and polemical edge which was maintained in many later plays. For instance, Nicholas Udall's *Respublica*, performed at court in front of Mary I by a group of boy players in 1553, was an anti-Protestant moral interlude, while Thomas Norton and Thomas Sackville's *Gorboduc*, performed at the Inner Temple in 1562, is as notable for its attempt to intervene in political affairs by advising Elizabeth I about her possible marriage and succession as for its being the first English blank-verse tragedy. After Elizabeth's death and the accession of James I, political drama included a lost play about the assassination of the Earl of Gowrie (1604), Samuel Daniel's *Philotas* (1604, which was thought to comment on the fall of the Earl of Essex), George Chapman's *Conspiracy and Tragedy of Charles Duke of Byron* (1608, which focused on recent French history) and Thomas Middleton's hugely popular *A Game at Chess* (1624, a political allegory about Anglo-Spanish relations).

Writing and Nation

Popular perceptions of the Tudor period are perhaps most often articulated around Henry VIII's development of England's navy and the 1588 defeat of the Spanish Armada. The period certainly saw a great colonial expansion, with England competing with other European nations for a stake in the New World and establishing colonies in Virginia, Providence and Maryland. Shakespeare's *The Tempest* is often invoked in the context of the new world: it is thought that one of the main sources of the play is a description of the shipwreck in Bermuda of a group of colonists travelling to Virginia. Pamphlets about the colonists' experiences were published in London in 1610, a fact that helps to date the composition of Shakespeare's play. More recently, the play has been linked to modern discourses about colonialism, with much good work being done on, for example, Caliban's position as a subjugated native (Greenblatt 1990; Vaughan and Vaughan 1993).

The opening up of trade routes led to the importation, not only of goods, but of new words to describe them. The excitement of discovery can be felt in the literature of the period which overflows with description and an enjoyment of variety. Take, for example, the opening of Ben Jonson's *Volpone* in which Volpone, the play's chief character, expatiates at length upon his hoard of gold, employing a mythological and quasi-religious vocabulary to express his excitement about his riches; that 'dumb god, that giv'st all men tongues' (*Volpone*, 1.1.22). Volpone's excitement in his goods and the wealth of words he has to describe them is seductive. However, this excitement in the copiousness of goods and words also generated anxieties about cultural invasion. The inkhorn debate (discussed above) was one such manifestation of this anxiety as words imported into English from European languages were regarded suspiciously and were thought by some to have the potential to weaken the sinews of the English language.

The joy in new things and places was also expressed in travel writing; a genre that became very popular during the period. Probably the most famous piece of this kind of writing is Thomas Coryat's *Crudities* (1608) which described a journey the author took through Europe to Germany, France and Italy. Similarly, George Sandys, a younger son of the Archbishop of York, who was involved with the management of the colonialist Virginia Company, wrote and published about his experiences in the Ottoman Empire in a work entitled *A Relation of a Journey* (1615). He also translated Ovid's *Metamorphoses* on his voyage out to Virginia, completing it while he was there, and, on his return to London in 1626, presenting a copy of the work to King Charles. With its emphasis on strange places and fantastical transformations, Ovid's *Metamorphoses* was a very appropriate text for someone involved in colonial exploration.

The development of England as a maritime nation was accompanied by a desire to establish England as a literary and cultural force within Europe. Writers such as Edmund Spenser sought to establish England's cultural credentials by producing major works in the vernacular, rather than in the more traditional Latin. Spenser's *The Faerie Queene* not only tries to create a canon of English literature by harking back to writers such as Chaucer; it also establishes Elizabeth as the rightful heir of Brutus, and England as a new Troy, the direct inheritor of a literary tradition that is seen to have moved from Greece to Rome to England. In effect, it positions England as the heart of a new empire, a worthy successor to the empires of Greece and Rome.

James I's accession to the English throne in 1603 saw the beginning of a controversial literary and political movement that sought to unite England, Scotland, Ireland and Wales under the name of Britain. William Shakespeare's *King Lear* has been associated with this project: Lear's reign was imagined to have seen the fragmentation of the United Kingdom of Britain, while James' reign was seen as a reuniting of the kingdoms. Court entertainments, such as Jonson's *Irish Masque* (1612) promoted the idea of a united kingdom, although the realities of rule were very different and were complicated by differences in religious belief (Nicholls 1999; Lee, Jr 1990; Bradshaw et al 1993). King Charles' attempts to follow his father's lead and promote uniformity, particularly in religion, in his kingdoms was especially controversial. In 1637, his attempts to enforce *The Book of Common Prayer* in Scotland led to huge Scottish discontent. A Scottish army crossed the border into England in 1639, in an act that was later to be seen as one of the defining events in the outbreak of the English civil wars.

Writing and Censorship

Another intersection between literature and the political arena can be seen in the operation of censorship in the sixteenth and early seventeenth centuries. Scholars have taken differing views of the impact and influence of censorship: some have argued that the various systems of censorship had negligible effects on writers, while others have suggested that much writing of the period is marked by self-censorship and by the implicit presence of the censor. Apparatus existed for the censorship of works in print and in the commercial theatre, and we will look briefly at each in turn. Both aimed to control the discussion of political issues and events; they were especially concerned to suppress public criticism of the monarch and prominent politicians.

Print

There were two main forms of print censorship in the sixteenth and seventeenth centuries: pre-publication censorship aimed to control what was published, while post-publication censorship suppressed any dissident works that made it into print. Although press censorship was in operation for most of the sixteenth and seventeenth centuries, it did not always function in the same way and was generally less monolithic and more contingent than was recognized by earlier scholars. The monarch, religious authorities and parliament all took part in the regulation of the press, and at various times their interests might not coincide. As a number of critics have noted, the book trade was not merely the object of censorship; its organizing body, the Stationers' Company, was a partner of the state and religious authorities in controlling what was published (Johns 1998).

In the sixteenth century, successive rulers of England sought to promote the book trade by offering publishers certain forms of commercial protection, but they also sought to control it through parliament, orders by the Privy Council and the law courts. In 1557, Mary I granted the Stationers' Company a patent giving them not only an effective monopoly on printing but also the responsibility of regulating the printing trade; this patent was renewed by Elizabeth I when she came to the throne in 1558. In 1586, the legal court of Star Chamber issued decrees which regulated printing further and formalized an already existent system of pre-print censorship: it stipulated that the Archbishop of Canterbury and the Bishop of London should inspect all texts before publication, and that the Archbishop could approve or refuse the establishment of new printing presses. But having a rule was one thing, implementing it another. The issue of further acts to control printing in 1623 and 1637 suggests that printers and publishers were ignoring government instructions, and a good number of books were never licensed.

The authorities were concerned to control inflammatory religious writing Protestant propaganda under Mary, and Catholic and extreme Protestant polemic under Elizabeth and her successors. Other censorship aimed to control texts which questioned the ruler's authority, dignity or probity. For instance, in 1581 parliament issued a statute stating that the death penalty could be imposed on people who were found guilty of any involvement in the publication of a text 'containing any false, seditious, and slanderous matter to the defamation of the Queenes Majesty . . . or the incouraging, stirring or moving of any insurrection or rebellion' (Clegg 2001, 33). As we noted above, another concern was to constrict printing to particular locations; although printing presses were allowed in Oxford and Cambridge, it was generally felt that printing was safer in London, 'in the eye of gou*ernment*' (Mendle 1995, 310).

Only a very small percentage of texts were subjected to post-publication censorship. A prominent example is a scandal of the late 1580s, during which unlicensed and daringly satirical tracts criticizing the bishops and church hierarchy were issued from a secret printing press under the name of Martin Marprelate. The printer was never caught, but some of his alleged supporters were tried and fined, although the fines were later waived when the Archbishop of Canterbury intervened. In 1611, the High Commission was issued a patent which enabled it to 'inquire and search for . . . all heretical, schismatical and seditious books, libels and writings' (Clegg 2001, 52) and all those involved in their publication. The High Commission took action not only against religious writings but also against more secular political publications, such as the news-books on foreign affairs issued during the early years of the Thirty Years' War in the 1620s. In 1620, James I issued a warning to all his subjects to 'take heede, how they intermeddle by Penne, or Speech, with causes of State and secrets of Empire, either at home, or abroad' (Clegg 2001, 58). As this suggests, some works might be suppressed because their publication was badly timed. For instance, John Haywood's *The First Part of the Life and Reign of King Henry the IV* was burned at the Bishop of London's house in 1599 and provoked a ban on the printing of histories; this may have been because it was dedicated to the ill-fated Earl of Essex and treated the deposition of Richard II at length, both things which would have disturbed nervy politicians in the last years of Elizabeth's reign. Indeed, it is probably no coincidence that 1599 also saw measures taken against satirical and erotic poetry, including works by Christopher Marlowe, John Marston and Joseph Hall, the future Bishop of Exeter and Norwich.

Theatre

Theatrical censorship was administered by the Master of the Revels, who was appointed by the crown. Although Ben Jonson came close to gaining the office in the 1620s, the Master was usually a courtier; holders included Sir Edmund Tilney (1579–1610), Sir George Buc (1610–22), Sir John Astley (1622–23) and Sir Henry Herbert (1623–42). For a brief period early in the reign of James I, Samuel Daniel was given the position of licenser to a specific company, the Children of the Queen's Revels, but this was both short-lived and unusual; censorship was generally concentrated in the hands of the Master of the Revels. In addition to censoring plays, the Master of the Revels was responsible for all performances at court; censorship was thus part of a delicately balanced set of commercial and patronage relations. Manuscripts were supposed to be submit-ted to the Master of the Revels before a play was performed, and the companies were to pay a fee for the privilege of having their play licensed.

Dramatists and companies often trod a fine line: they wanted their plays to have exciting topical relevance, but also had to be careful not to make too pointed a reference to contemporary personalities and events. The surviving manuscript of Fletcher and Massinger's *Sir John Van Olden Barnavelt*, performed by the King's Men in 1619, contains annotations by Buc criticizing its presentation of living politicians; 'I like not this' he writes, 'neith^r do I think y^t the pr{ince} was thus disgracefully vsed' (British Library, MS Add. 18653, fol. 5v). Some plays that slipped through censorship might be suppressed after one or more performances, such as the lost tragedy about the treasonous scheme of the Earl of Gowrie to assassinate James I when he was King of Scotland; the letter-writer John Chamberlain commented, 'whether the matter or manner be not well handled, or that yt be thought unfit that princes should be played on the Stage in theyre life time, I hear that some great Councellors are much displeased with yt, and so is thought shalbe forbidden' (Sawyer 1725, 2: 41). A few years earlier, a collaboration between Thomas Nashe and Ben Jonson called *The Isle of Dogs* caused a political scandal and was denounced by the Privy Council as 'lewd . . . seditious and sclanderous' (Charles Nicholl, *ODNB*, s.v. 'Nashe, Thomas'). In 1606, the 'Act of Abuses' forbade actors to 'jestingly or prophanely speake or use the holy name of God or of Christ Jesus or of the Holy Ghoste or of the Trinitie, which are not to be spoken but with feare and reverence' (Chambers 1923, 2: 238).

Part II
How to Read Renaissance Texts

Case Studies in Reading 1: Key Primary Literary Texts

Hugh Adlington

Chapter Overview

Introduction

The beginning, and end, of any study of Renaissance literature is the literature itself, but how should modern readers approach it? What does one need to know about life, language and literary conventions in Britain in the sixteenth and seventeenth centuries to get the most from the extraordinary writing of the period? The following micro-studies of extracts from Renaissance literature seek to explore these questions via demonstrations of close reading. The eight primary texts selected extend in chronological terms from the early sixteenth century to the early seventeenth, and cover literary genres from epic and lyric poetry, and biblical translation, to prose satire, fiction and dramatic tragedy. Close readings of these texts are informed by a number of relevant critical and interpretative methods, with particular methods selected for use with particular texts. These methods may be classified broadly as formal/rhetorical (including analysis of conventions of metre, genre, allegory and translation); historicist/ ideological (including cultural materialist and feminist readings); and biblio-graphical (drawing on recent editorial theory). The aim throughout will be to demonstrate how best to engage with the primary material. At the same time, the chapter also seeks to identify distinctive characteristics of British Renaissance literature: its imitation and transformation of classical and contin-ental European literary forms; its striking emphasis on rhetorical performance; its vibrant experimentalism and love of paradox and contradiction; and its modes of textual transmission (via manuscript and print).

According to the Platonic concept of anamnesis (from the Greek ἀνάμνησις, meaning recollection or reminiscence), to learn, or to read, is simply to recall what we already know. Such is the experience of reading Renaissance literature (see Introduction and Chapter 8). What the following close readings hope to do, therefore, is to restage this initial shock of recognition, while going on implicitly to ask in what ways, and to what extent, our lives, language and literature are similar to or differ from those of our literary forebears of half a millennium ago. One difference in particular will become apparent in the following pages: namely, the disparity between Renaissance and modern notions of originality. Unlike the nineteenth-century Romantic fascination with tracing the imagina-tive qualities of literary works back to their origins in the thoughts and feelings of authorial subjects, or the modernist injunction to 'make it new', Renaissance writing is characterized by its focus on effects rather than origins, and its conse-quent reworking of older texts (see Healy, Chapter 8, this volume). Shakespeare is paradigmatic in this respect; the majority of his plots were appropriated from other, often classical, sources. Similarly, More, Wyatt, Marlowe, Spenser, Mary Herbert, Nashe and Donne: all consciously build upon, adapt and transform their literary models and sources. Post-Romantic notions of 'originality', there-fore, prized so highly in other epochs, come to seem, if not anachronous, then at least in need of redefinition in early modern literature. As with originality, so it is with other cherished literary virtues: authorial sincerity, moral purpose, psy-chological realism, verbal concision. Our willingness to reconsider, redefine and revise our initial assumptions and attitudes to these and numerous other aspects of Renaissance literature will be crucial to the following eight case studies.

Chamber Pots of Gold: Rhetorical Conventions in More's *Utopia* (1516)

What lies at the root of crime and social discord? Is it simply the amorality, cruelty or greed of individual men or women? Or might society itself – its customs, laws and beliefs – be as much to blame for driving some to illegality? In addressing these questions, Thomas More's (1478–1535) political essay, *Utopia*, written in Latin and first published in Louvain in 1516, paints a picture of the all-too evident failings of early sixteenth-century Christian Europe: the war-mongering of kings, the parasitical idleness of noblemen, the cruel punishment of petty thievery, the degradation of the clergy. The voice of this withering critique is Raphael Hythloday, a fictional sun-burned mariner recently returned to Antwerp from a voyage to the New World. In the first of *Utopia*'s two books, More lends plausibility to his creation by staging discussions between Hythloday and fictional versions of himself, 'More', and of another 'real' person – Peter Giles, city official and citizen of Antwerp. Hythloday tells the sceptical 'More' that the only way to eradicate social injustice (and especially capital punishment for trivial offences) is to replace private ownership of property with a communism of goods. But why, counters 'More', should a man work if he cannot reap the rewards of his own labour? Dispense with the laws of property and the result will be anarchy. In response to More's doubts, Hythloday proceeds to give a first-hand account of the successful workings of a communist society in the New World island commonwealth of Utopia (see Chapter 1).

In Utopia private property is anathema. Utopian clothes, houses and cities are identical. Private life is virtually non-existent. Meals are communal, conversation is public, idleness and sloth is deplored. The contrast between the ultra-rational society described by Hythloday, and the degenerate Christian Europe of More's day could hardly be greater. This antithesis reaches its peak in the following extract, when Hythloday turns to the subject of gold and silver, and the value placed upon them by Utopians.

> For whereas they [the Utopians] eat and drink in earthen and glass vessels which, indeed, be curiously and properly made and yet be of very small value, of gold and silver they make commonly chamber-pots and other vessels that serve for most vile uses not only in their common halls but in every man's private house. Furthermore, of the same metals they make great chains, fetters, and gyves wherein they tie their bondmen. Finally whosoever for any offence be infamed, by their ears hang rings of gold, upon their fingers they wear rings of gold, and about their necks chains of gold, and, in conclusion, their heads be tied about with gold. Thus by all means possible they procure to have gold and silver among them in reproach and infamy. And these metals, which other nations do as grievously and sorrowfully forgo, as in a manner their own lives, if they should altogether at once be taken from the Utopians, no man there would think that he had lost the worth of one farthing. (Bruce 1999, 71)

Chamber pots of gold and silver? This, as Christine Rees has observed, is 'the Midas touch in reverse' (16), in which the Utopians seek to transmute gold into non-material assets; in this case, human virtue. Classical precedents of disdain for gold and silver abound, with Plato's Republic and Lycurgus' Sparta being among the best known; in the early sixteenth century Vespucci notes the native

Americans' indifference to gold and gems. Yet how seriously in *Utopia* are we meant to take this? We might, for example, smile at the incongruity of the image of the golden chamber pot, but still assent to the anti-materialism it proposes. In which case, we will be inclined to think that Thomas More the author, rather than the character 'More', is in favour of Hythloday's political views. On the other hand, we might laugh out loud at the image, as an idea taken to the point of absurdity. In which case we are liable to think, as some critics have, that More means us to take Hythloday's account of Utopia's communism with a generous pinch of salt, if not to reject it out of hand. How, then, are we to decide between these two possible ways of reading the passage (and the work as whole)?

To answer this question it is worth looking again at the uses to which precious metals are put in Utopia. Golden pissoirs may seize our attention, and the wearing of gold rings and necklaces as badges of dishonour may strike us as novel, but should an ideal commonwealth have any place for 'chains, fetters, and gyves wherein they tie their bondmen'? *The Oxford English Dictionary* (*OED*) tells us that 'gyves' are shackles; 'bondmen' are slaves. Aside from the technical incongruity of using a soft metal like gold for chains and fetters, doesn't the fact that Hythloday condones slavery in Utopia undermine both his and the Utopians' moral legitimacy? At first glance it would seem so, lending further weight to the view that More intends to satirize the political model of Utopia, rather than endorse it. A moment's reflection, however, makes this view seem less tenable. In Utopia slavery is used to punish criminals who would be put to death in sixteenth-century England. Can we really think, then, that More condemns mercy of this kind?

Further clues might be considered. The proper names used by More play on Greek words. 'Utopia' means 'no place', 'Hythloday' means 'expert in non-sense'. Surely such denotations indicate More's rejection of the communist enterprise? Perhaps, but it seems equally likely that such names are simply a playful way of distinguishing fictional places and persons (Utopia, Hythloday) from real ones (England, More, Peter Giles). Critics who read *Utopia* as predominantly ironic in tone also point to 'More's' apparent disclaimer at the book's conclusion: 'I can not agree and consent to all things that he [Hythloday] said' (Bruce 1999, 123). Such disclaimers, however, were a common ingredient of Renaissance dialogues, intended to protect the author should the work cause offence to the powerful. They serve a function similar to that of the legal provisos placed at the beginning (or end) of modern novels and films: 'Any resemblance to actual events, locations, or persons, living or dead, is entirely coincidental.' What at first sight appears to be a clue to the 'true' meaning of the text, turns out to be a rhetorical commonplace of its time and genre.

In many ways, it is far easier to find parallels rather than opposition between Hythloday's Utopia and More's known views. Utopia is an almost exemplary concentration of many of More's most cherished values: asceticism, discipline, community, piety, learning. Does this mean that More intended Utopia to stand as a viable model of a future commonwealth? Not necessarily. Listen to the way the character of 'More' concludes *Utopia*: 'so must I needs confess and grant that many things be in the Utopian weal-public which in our cities I may rather wish for than hope after' (Bruce 1999, 123). The practical, political distinction between 'wishing' and 'hoping' is crucial. The latter hints at a potentially realizable social programme, whereas the former, 'More's' view, suggests only a distant dream.

In his later years, following the inception of the Protestant Reformation in 1517 and its break with older forms of authority, Thomas More retreated even further from the potentially radical implications of *Utopia*. He declared that he would rather burn *Utopia* than see it translated into English, afraid that a work conceived of as an intellectual game or speculation might be adopted and put to practical use by what he saw as the forces of heresy and disorder. Though not translated into English until 1551, sixteen years after More's death, the literary and political reverberations of More's fictional commonwealth, whether he intended them to be so or not, were far-reaching. The name 'Utopia' passed into general usage, and has been used to describe a host of later fictional worlds, inspired directly or indirectly by More's work, including Francis Bacon's *New Atlantis* (1626), James Harrington's *The Commonwealth of Oceana* (1656), and William Morris' *News from Nowhere* (1890).

We might conclude, then, that the Utopian's golden chamber pot acquires a fresh literary and political interpretation with each new turn of political history itself. What appears at first sight to be a fanciful, ambiguous, even absurd scene or skit, can in fact tell us much about changing times, tastes and attitudes. Sensitivity to the interpretative potential of even the most apparently trivial aspects of the text is thus a first step in learning how to read the literature of Renaissance Britain. The following section aims to build on this first step, show-ing the kinds of inference that may be drawn from apparently minor textual variations.

Thomas Wyatt's Lyric Poems: Metrical 'new fangleness'? Textual Variation (Editorial)

In the sixteenth century, one of the most important developments in Renaissance English literature was the evolution of the lyric poem, shaped in particular by English translation and adaptation of Italian verse (notably Petrarch). Foremost among such translators was Thomas Wyatt (1503–42), courtier and diplomat in the reign of Henry VIII. Wyatt's poems circulated in manuscript among aristo-cratic readers during his lifetime, the most important extant manuscript being Egerton 2711, now held in the British Library (see Chapter 2). Fifteen years after Wyatt's death, Richard Tottel included ninety-seven poems attributed to Wyatt in a collection of poetry by Henry Howard, earl of Surrey. In his desire to satisfy contemporary tastes, Tottel frequently emended the manuscript versions of his authors, removing archaisms and smoothing out rhythm and accent. The follow-ing brief explication will explore how these emendations of diction and metre affect tone and meaning, using Wyatt's 'They Flee from Me' as a case study. The text of Wyatt's poem, taken from MS Egerton 2711, is presented in its original layout and punctuation, but in modernized spelling for ease of comprehension.

> They flee from me that sometime did me seek
> with naked foot stalking in my chamber
> I have seen them gentle tame and meek
> that now are wild and do not remember
> that sometime they put themself in danger
> to take bread at my hand & now they range
> busily seeking with a continual change
> Thanked be fortune it hath been otherwise
> twenty times better but once in special
> in thin array after a pleasant guise
> when her loose gown from her shoulders did fall
> and she me caught in her arms long & small
> therewithall sweetly did me kiss
> and softly said dear heart how like you this
> It was no dream I lay broad waking.
> but all is turned through my gentleness
> into a strange fashion of forsaking
> and I have leave to go of her goodness
> and she also to use new fangleness
> but since that I so kindly am served
> I would fain know what she hath deserved (Harrier 1975, 131–2)

Before examining emendations made by Tottel in print, what can we say about Wyatt's poem in manuscript? Formal observations first. The poem is written in three rhyming stanzas of seven lines each (ababbcc). This is rhyme royal, a form often used by Chaucer, but employed less frequently by later, Elizabethan poets such as Spenser and Shakespeare. The poem's metre appears, generally, to be iambic pentameter, though there are frequent deviations from this pattern. Such deviations often occur at pivotal points in the poem's unfolding. 'It was no dream I lay broad waking' comprises only nine syllables instead of ten, the last of which is a feminine, or unstressed, syllable. The caesura or pause in the middle of the line is especially drawn out, providing the metrical equivalent of pinching oneself to distinguish waking from dreaming.

The poem's ostensible subject or setting, however, is harder to pin down. In the first stanza, the 'They' of 'They flee from me' appears to refer to some kind of animal ('gentle tame and meek / that now are wild'), which has taken bread from the speaker's hand. 'They' possibly refers to deer or birds (pigeons or birds of prey). The latter is suggested by the reference to 'naked foot', a term used in falconry to denote birds sufficiently tamed not to need tethering. The speaker's evocation of the recollected scene is vivid but dream-like, giving insufficient specific information to say for sure who or what took 'bread at my hand'. In the second stanza, an equally vivid and sinuous image recalls the seduction of the male speaker – 'her loose gown from her shoulders did fall / and she me caught in her arms long & small' (*OED*: 'small' = slender) – but once again Wyatt leaves the pronoun 'she' tantalisingly unqualified and unidentified. All we can be sure of is that the hunter has become the hunted, the tables turning on the erstwhile powerful male lover.

In the third stanza the role reversal is complete. The speaker's mistress gives him 'leave to go' and permits him to 'use new fangleness'; that is, to pursue other loves. To his dismay, however, she extends the same latitude to herself in this 'strange fashion of forsaking'. What has led to this unwelcome turn of events? The speaker identifies his own moral behaviour, his former 'gentleness', or courtesy in love, as the culprit through which 'all is turned'. When his own liberality is matched by the 'goodness' of his mistress, the irony is a bitter one. The speaker no longer seeks a multitude of lovers – his 'heart' (a play on 'hart', or deer) has been won by his mistress. This brings the speaker in the final couplet to his bemused, anguished inquiry: 'but since that I so kindly am served / I would fain know what she hath deserved'. Must the defeated lover accept his lot, measuring his mistress' actions by the standard of his own earlier promiscuous actions? Or, having been wronged by a faithless woman, is the speaker justified in his implied wish for retribution?

Now, let us turn to another version of the poem (presented, once again, in original layout and punctuation, but with modernized spelling).

'The Lover Showeth How He is Forsaken of Such as He Sometime Enjoyed'

They flee from me, that sometime did me seek
With naked foot stalking within my chamber.
Once have I seen them gentle, tame, and meek,
That now are wild, and do not once remember
That sometime they have put them selves in danger,
To take bread at my hand, and now they range,
Busily seeking in continual change.
    Thanked be fortune, it hath been otherwise
Twenty times better: but once especial,
In thin array, after a pleasant guise,
When her loose gown did from her shoulders fall,
And she me caught in her arms long and small,
And therewithal, so sweetly did me kiss,
And softly said: dear hart how like you this?
    It was no dream: for I lay broad awaking.
But all is turned now through my gentleness,
Into a bitter fashion of forsaking:
And I have leave to go of her goodness,
And she also to use newfangleness.
But, since that I unkindly so am served:
How like you this, what hath she now deserved? (Howard 1557, fol. 22ᵛ)

Richard Tottel's 1557 printed version of Wyatt's poem shows that tastes and expectations concerning metrical regularity were changing fast in the early sixteenth century. Tottel frequently adds a syllable to a line (as in lines 2, 3, 4, 5, 16) to smooth out Wyatt's rough, expressive rhythm. In line 17, 'strange fashion of forsaking' in the Egerton manuscript is replaced by Tottel with 'bitter fashion of forsaking'. With the exchange of single word, Tottel skews the speaker's tone of contemplative, if pained inquiry into one that is harsh and accusatory. But perhaps the most important change is saved until last. Here, in the poem's closing couplet, Tottel replaces 'kindly' with 'unkindly', and transforms the pensive mood of the manuscript's last wish, 'I would fain know what she hath deserved', into a far more belligerent request for third-party moral adjudication: 'How like you this, what hath she now deserved?' Abstract nouns such as 'kindly' are shorn of their ambiguity in Tottel's version, thereby lending weight to the moral case against the speaker's mistress.

What have we learned, then, from this cursory comparison of the manuscript and print versions of Wyatt's poem? One crucial insight relates to the apparent correlation between changing tastes in both poetic form and in morality. In Tottel's version of the poem, printed just fifteen years after Wyatt's death, both metrical irregularity and ethical anomalies are smoothed away. If nothing else, Tottel's editorial policy reflects the powerful influence of contemporary fashions, or 'new fangleness', on both literary taste and social mores. By studying a poem's textual transmission therefore, we learn not only about the poem's internal workings, but also remind ourselves of an insight gleaned from our reading of More's *Utopia*. That is, that British Renaissance literary history is far from being a monolithic, static entity, but rather it constantly ranges, 'busily seeking with a continual change'.

Edmund Spenser, *The Faerie Queene* (1590–96): Dark Conceits: Theories of Allegory

What is the nature of Spenser's allegorical method in his epic poem, *The Faerie Queene*, published in six books between 1590 and 1596? The first and best place to look for an answer is in the text of the poem itself. The stanza below is from Book 2, Canto 9 – a canto in which Spenser constructs his own extended comparison of architecture and anatomy in the allegorical sequence of the castle of Alma (a.k.a. the house of Temperance). Alma (translated as 'the soule of man' by John Florio in 1598) welcomes her guests Prince Arthur and Sir Guyon, the Knight of Temperance, and leads them through the castle, stanza by stanza (in Italian, 'stanza' means 'room'). Each separate part of the castle corresponds to a part of the human body. Thus we pass from twin gates (upper and lower jaws) to the porch (chin), to the portcullis (nose) and into the barbican (mouth), guarded by warders (teeth).

> Thence she them brought into a stately Hall,
>   Wherein were many tables fayre dispred,
>   And ready dight with drapets festiuall,
>   Against the viaundes should be ministred.
>   At th'upper end there sate, yclad in red
>   Downe to the ground, a comely personage,
>   That in his hand a white rod menaged,
>   He Steward was, hight *Diet*; rype of age,
> And in demeanure sober, and in counsell sage. (Spenser 2007, 240)

The hall, in this stanza, appears to equate to the throat in the castle-body. Tables are set out ('fayre dispred'), covered with cloths ('ready dight with drapets festiuall'), and await the arrival of food ('Against the viaundes should be ministred'). The castle's chief officer, the Steward, responsible for the overall smooth running of the castle-body, represents the back of the throat and is thus 'yclad in red'; his white rod stands for the uvula, here the symbol of royal power (Spenser 2007, 240). The identification of the Steward with the virtue of temperance, curbing the gluttonous demands of appetite, is underscored by alliteration: a series of words beginning with 'd' ('dispred ... dight ... drapets') culminates in '*Diet*'. The moral sobriety of the Steward is also emphasized by the Spenserian stanza's rhyme scheme (ababbcbcc), in which the triple 'c' rhyme comprises 'personage ... age ... sage'. Moreover, the parallel clauses of the longer last line (hexameter instead of the usual pentameter), brings the depiction of the Steward as the personification of temperance to a plangent conclusion: 'And in demeanure sober, and in counsel sage'.

Spenser's metaphorical parallel between virtue enshrined in the well-regulated human body, and the great house besieged by adversaries, has a long literary pedigree. From the Bible we derive the image of the human body as a vessel of clay, under siege by the devil (2 Corinthians 4.7–12). The allegorical conflict of vices and virtues can be found in Prudentius' *Psychomachia* (late fourth or early fifth century), and thereafter in works as diverse as the *Roman de la Rose* (c. 1230–75), *Everyman* (c. 1509–19), and in Ariosto's *Orlando Furioso* (1532). Spenser's poetic achievement in Canto 9 is to elaborate on these earlier allegorical models by including both a visit to the castle of Alma and its siege by the seven deadly sins and five vices (Canto 11). As a consequence, the *Fairie Queene* demonstrates not only the resistance of Sir Guyon (as the Knight of Temperance) to the twin temptations of sensual sloth (Acrasia's Bower) and avaricious pursuit of wealth (Mammon's Cave), it also prompts the reader to recognize his or her own part in the construction of the poem's meaning. This process of self-recognition occurs, in part, because as Rosemond Tuve reminds us, the subject of each book in *Faerie Queene* is *sought* virtue (Temperance, in Book 2), not simply biography or psychological analysis or exploration of archetypes (1966, 91). The reader of Spenser's allegory, therefore, is highly active in a way commensurate with the subject of each book – reading and interpreting in the arduous search for virtue.

Recent historically inflected commentary has drawn attention to a number of political aspects of Spenser's use of allegory: to evade political censorship (Kelsey 2003, and see Chapters 2 and 3); the influence of colonialism on Spenser's fashioning of an English national epic in *Faerie Queene* (McCabe 2002, and see Chapter 4); and to connections between the virtues depicted in the poem's six books and Elizabeth I's political character. But perhaps the most far-reaching development in modern criticism has been to show how allegory is engaged by the reader, in contrast to the tendency of traditional critics to locate its doubleness of sense inside the text (Teskey 1990, 16). Thus, rather than think of Spenser's 'darke conceit' as something hidden and textual, requiring us to excavate its meaning, we do better to conceive of the 'continued Allegory' as a principle or rule of interpretation. Iconic narrative details, such as the body-castle of the house of Alma, suggest a deeper framework of meaning. Other aspects of the poem are then seen by the reader through the lens of this frame-work. Aesthetic and thematic patterns seem to emerge the further one reads: the *idea* of the 'darke conceit' has thus shaped our experience of drawing nearer to truth as the poem proceeds.

Far from offering a clear-cut correlation between outward appearance and inner essence, therefore, Spenser's extraordinary allegory provokes us to reflect on the act of reading itself, to revel in the range of possible correlations between the terms of comparison, and to oscillate between the local significance of the allegorical part (here, the 'stately Hall' or throat in the House or Body of Temperance) and the general yet illusory, and ever out-of-reach truth of the poetic whole. Building on this sense of the activeness of the reader of allegory, the next section draws attention to the way in which our reading experience is also shaped by the form in which the text comes to us, and its possible vari-ations. We turn now from Sir Guyon, the embodiment of Temperance, to one of the most intemperate figures in all literature, Doctor Faustus.

Christopher Marlowe, *Doctor Faustus* (1604/16): One Minute to Midnight: Textual Variation (Censorial)

There are few authors in Renaissance English literature more colourful than Christopher Marlowe (1564–93). Scholar, poet and playwright, Marlowe was also reputed to be an atheist, homosexual and spy, murdered at the age of twenty-nine in a fight in Deptford. Such a sensational life is matched only by the controversial subject matter and rhetorical daring of Marlowe's four hugely popular, major dramatic works: *Tamburlaine* (1587–88), *The Jew of Malta* (1590), *Edward the Second* (1592) and *Doctor Faustus*. But how closely do the play texts that we read correspond with what Marlowe actually wrote? And how far might the emendations, distortions and deletions that accrue in the text's jour-ney from its sixteenth-century origins to modern printed editions affect both the way we interpret the play and how we think about its authorship? Of Marlowe's works, *Doctor Faustus* most clearly demonstrates the problems inherent in the transmission of texts. The play exists in two significantly different versions, the so-called 'A-text' of 1604 and the 'B-text' of 1616. This brief essay compares the A- and B-texts of the climactic scene of *Doctor Faustus*, and aims to show how crucial differences between the two versions can lead us to see in a new light the questions of authorship, textual stability and the meaning of the play itself.

According to Henslowe's *Diary*, *Doctor Faustus* entered the repertoire on 30 September 1594, more than a year after Marlowe's death in 1593. The first printed quarto of the play, the A-text, was not published until 1604 (it was not in the actors' financial interests to release the manuscript of their play to a publisher). The following extract is taken from Act V, Scene 2 of the A-text (1604).

> FAUSTUS. Ah Faustus,
> Now hast thou but one bare hour to live,
> And then thou must be damned perpetually.
> Stand still, you ever-moving spheres of heaven,
> That time may cease and midnight never come!
> Fair nature's eye, rise, rise again, and make
> Perpetual day; or let this hour be but
> A year, a month, a week, a natural day,
> That Faustus may repent and save his soul!
> *O lente, lente currite noctis equi!*
> The stars move still; time runs; the clock will strike;
> The devil will come, and Faustus must be damned.
> O, I'll leap up to my God! Who pulls me down?
> See, see where Christ's blood streams in the firmament!
> One drop would save my soul, half a drop. Ah, my Christ!
> Ah, rend not my heart for naming of my Christ!
> Yet will I call on him. O spare me, Lucifer!
> Where is it now? 'Tis gone; and see where God
> Stretcheth out his arm and bends his ireful brows!
> Mountains and hills, come, come and fall on me,
> And hide me from the heavy wrath of God! (Marlowe 1993, 194–8)

All hope is lost. For a brief, desperate moment, Faustus glimpses salvation high above him ('See, see where Christ's blood streams in the firmament!'), only for it to vanish (' 'Tis gone'), and be replaced with the awful, pendant threat of divine retribution ('see where God / Stretcheth out his arm and bends his ireful brows!'). Faustus' speech is studded with figures of speech indicative of a mind *in extremis*. Exclamation, rhetorical questions (*epiplexis*), paratactic compression ('The stars move still; time runs; the clock will strike'), verbal repetition or *epizeuxis* ('rise, rise . . . *lente, lente* . . . See, see'): each contributes to the frenzied, staccato rhythm of Faustus' blank verse, distorting and disrupting its metrical pattern. For Faustus there is nowhere left to hide. His speech ends, thirty lines further on, with the despairing cry, 'My God, my God, look not so fierce upon me!', clearly echoing Christ's words on the cross: 'My God, my God, why hast thou forsaken me?' (Matthew 27.46).

Is Marlowe's play suggesting by this parallel that God is somehow complicit in Faustus' downfall? By turning to the B-text we may be able to shed further light on this interpretative possibility. The B-text of *Doctor Faustus* first appeared in quarto in 1616, and it contains a number of important additions, deletions and emendations to the earlier A-text. The majority of current scholarly opinion now holds that the 1604 quarto is set from an authorial manuscript composed of interleaved scenes by two dramatists, one of whom was Christopher Marlowe. The longer B-text is thought to represent a mix of authorial and theatrical provenances that included extensive revision in 1602 (by two dramatists referred to in Henslowe's *Diary*: Samuel Rowley and William Bird). Roma Gill also speculates that the play may have been modernized to compensate for the anticipated retirement from the Admiral's Men of the company's leading actor, Edward Alleyn (Marlowe 2002). But whatever the provenance of both versions of the play, what can be said about the textual differences apparent in Faustus' last scene?

The most obvious difference is the addition in the B-text of a final scene in which Faustus' scattered limbs are discovered, 'All torn asunder by the hand of death'. The effect of this scene is to underline the religious orthodoxy of the play, to demonstrate in graphic fashion the price of dealing with the Devil. Moreover, Faustus' final speech in the B-text appears to have been censored in accordance with the Act of Abuses of 1606, which threatened to exact heavy fines on any play that 'jestingly or prophanely speake or use the holy Name of God or of Christ Jesus'. The consequence of such censorship is to dull the vibrant imagery and reduce the dramatic power of Faustus' agonized outpouring. The B-text contains no extraordinary vision of Christ's blood streaming in the firmament, and all references to 'God' are replaced with 'heaven', creating a clear separation between God and Lucifer. The A-text's dynamic unfolding of divine wrath – 'and see where God / Stretcheth out his arm and bends his ireful brows!' – is muted and stilled in the B-text: 'And see a threatening arm, an angry brow'. The deletion of the word 'Stretcheth' also eliminates a potentially fascinating echo of a similar line in Marlowe's earlier play, *Tamburlaine*: 'Jove himself will stretch his hand from heaven / . . . and shield me safe from harm' (Act 1, Scene 2). What is the A-text's half-submerged allusion hinting at? That we, the audience, should draw our own conclusions about the contrast between the divinely protected Tamburlaine and the divinely-threatened Faustus? Whether such verbal echoes suggest that Faustus in the A-text is in fact more sinned against than sinner is a debatable point. In the B-text, however, it is not even a question.

One further emendation deserves consideration. Presumably to conform to the 1606 Act of Abuses, the B-text replaces 'My God, my God, look not so fierce upon me!' with 'O, mercy, heaven, look not so fierce upon me!' The scriptural echo is thus lost, and with it the Christ-Faust comparison; but even more interpretative richness is abandoned than may at first appear. This is due to the typological foreshadowing in Psalm 22.1 of Christ's words on the cross. 'My God, my God, why hast thou forsaken me?' is in fact a verbatim quotation of David's words in Psalm 22.1. Since Psalm 22 goes on to become a hymn to divine victory (vv. 22–31), it might be argued that Jesus is far from despairing on the cross; rather he quotes Psalm 22.1 to make it clear that he understands the ultimate purpose of his suffering, and to demonstrate his confidence in God's ultimate deliverance of him through resurrection of the body. What, then, of Faustus' echo of Christ's words in the A-text? Are we to infer that Faustus, 'Excelling all . . . / In heavenly matters of theology' (Marlowe 1993, 107), is in fact contrasting himself with Christ's assurance of salvation? Or, more subtle yet, that Faustus the learned theologian has misread Christ's dying words, interpreting them literally as a cry of despair? In which case, might we not see Faustus' blunted perception as a result of the noetic effect of sin, the loss of 'inner knowing' or intuition? Of course, it is difficult to say to what extent a contemporary Elizabethan or Jacobean audience would discern such interpretative possibilities in the A-text. What is abundantly clear, though, is that the B-text's removal of those possibilities makes it an utterly different play.

As we have seen, small textual differences may have large interpretative consequences. The complicated journey of play-texts via authors, actors, publishers, censors, compositors and editors to the words of a modern edition leads us to question our assumptions about the nature of an authorial text. The next section expands upon this inquiry into the nature of authorship, moving into the realms of translation and gender.

Mary (Sidney) Herbert, Countess of Pembroke: Translation, Gender and the Author's Voice

What do we mean when we speak of an 'author's voice'? Do certain aspects of authorial identity – gender, race, class or religion – leave unmistakeable traces in a writer's work, such that a distinct 'voice' is always apparent? Or is a writer's literary style shaped more by specifically literary factors (such as rhetorical and generic conventions) than by aspects of biography? To explore these questions it will be instructive to consider the work of Mary (Sidney) Herbert, Countess of Pembroke (1562–1621), sister of celebrated courtier and author, Sir Philip Sidney (1554–1586). After Sidney's death, Mary Herbert completed her brother's metrical paraphrase of the Psalter (*Book of Psalms*), adding more than one hundred verse translations of her own to the forty-three composed by her brother. Widely circulated in manuscript, and dedicated to Queen Elizabeth I, the Sidneys' collection of psalms exercised a powerful influence over the work of seventeenth-century religious lyric poets such as John Donne and George Herbert. Deeply indebted to an array of sources in English, French and Latin, including the *Book of Common Prayer*, the Geneva Bible of 1560, and the *Psaumes* of Clément Marot and Theodore Beza, Mary Herbert's verse translations nonetheless stand brilliantly apart, not least for their witty lyricism and highly inventive deployment of varied stanza forms. Clearly, Mary Herbert's poetic achievement is significant. But to what extent does it constitute a specifically 'feminine' early modern poetic voice? And given the severe cultural restrictions on female authorship in the late sixteenth century – as a woman, Mary was not permitted to contribute to any of the volumes of elegies published in honour of her brother – is it possible, or in any way desirable, to read or interpret Mary Herbert's poetry except through the critical lens of gender? (see Chapters 1, 2, 4, 6 and 7)

Consider the following example. Psalm 58 is a bitter lament at the wickedness of men (in particular, the wickedness of the judges and counsellors of Saul, who conspired against David), and a prayer for their punishment. In the Geneva Bible of 1560 and in the Bishops' Bible of 1568, Psalm 58 comprises eleven verses. These verses were transposed by John Hopkins in 1562 into eleven hymnal stanzas for the purposes of congregational song. In her own verse translation, Mary Herbert renders the psalm in one sixteen-line stanza, followed by the two eight-line stanzas shown below (spelling and punctuation have been modernized):

> Lord, crack their teeth; Lord, crush these lions' jaws,
>   So let them sink as water in the sand.
> When deadly bow their aiming fury draws,
>   Shiver the shaft ere past the shooter's hand.
> So make them melt as the dis-housed snail
>   Or as the embryo, whose vital band
> Breaks ere it holds, and formless eyes do fail
>   To see the sun, though brought to lightful land.
>
> O let their brood, a brood of springing thorns,
>   Be by untimely rooting overthrown,
> Ere bushes waxed they push with pricking horns,
>   As fruits yet green are oft by tempest blown.
> The good with gladness this revenge shall see,
>   And bathe his feet in blood of wicked one;
> While all shall say: the just rewarded be;
>   There is a God that carves to each his own. (Rathmell 1963, 133–4)

Even a casual reader is struck by the visceral quality and force of the images and sentiments in these lines. Such an uncompromising tone derives in part from the biblical prose translations of the psalm available to Mary Herbert. Yet crucial verbal substitutions and phrasal additions infuse Herbert's version with a pungency and immediacy absent from her biblical sources or earlier translations in French (Marot and Beza) or English (Hopkins, Anne Lock, Matthew Parker, Robert Crowley, George Gascoigne). For example, Herbert's version of the psalmist's supplication ('Lord, crack their teeth; Lord crush these lions' jaws') generates an audible impression of retributive violence (via alliteration and onomatopoeia) not heard in the straightforward repetition of the verb 'break' found in Hopkins and in the biblical sources. Intense imagery and insistent alliteration are also evident in the third and fourth lines of the Countess of Pembroke's first stanza above. The Countess' version picks up on Hopkins' alliterative use of 'shafts' and 'shoot', but also deploys the highly expressive 'Shiver' (*OED v¹* = to fly in pieces; to split) to rework her biblical sources to kinetic effect. In both of these examples, Herbert introduces subtle metrical variations, disrupting the iambic rhythm (unstress-stress) on which her paraphrase is based. The supplication, 'Lord, crack their teeth', emphasizes divine power through the use of a spondee (stress-stress); while nimbleness and speed are conveyed through the use of a trochee (stress-unstress) in 'Shiver'. It is such fine-grained yet highly effective rhythmic variations that distinguish the sound patterning of Herbert's version from that of the consistent ballad rhythm (iambic tetrameter and iambic trimeter) of Hopkins' simpler lyrics.

Cross-rhyme, interlocking the two quatrains in each stanza (ababacbcb), and enjambment, provide further cross-referencing of sound and sense in Herbert's version, while other patterns of rhetorical repetition function to accentuate allegorical meaning. An example of the latter is Herbert's use of *anadiplosis* (beginning a new clause or phrase with the last word of the previous clause or phrase), in the opening line of the last stanza: 'O let their brood, a brood of springing thorns / Be by untimely rooting overthrown.' By emphasizing 'brood' Herbert draws out the implicit theme of the Hebrew lyrist – that wickedness begets wickedness – reflecting Herbert's use of scholarly glosses (such as Calvin's commentary and Beza's paraphrase) which were unavailable to earlier English psalmodists. Such metaphorical suggestiveness is a function, in part, of the fact that the Sidneian versions were intended for use in private devotions. Hence, Mary Herbert was not constrained by the need to provide simple and memorable texts for use in church services (Rathmell 1963, xiii–xiv; Zim 1987, 185–202). It is this alertness to the Psalter's underlying sense that leads Donne to say of the Sidneian psalms: 'They tell us *why*, and teach us *how* to sing' (Donne 2001, 368).

To what degree, however, can we say that Mary Herbert's skilful transformation of her biblical sources enabled her to develop her authorial voice as an early modern female writer? Although it is possible to situate Mary Herbert's *Psalms* within a 'female literary tradition' (other notable sixteenth-century female translators included Anne Cooke-Bacon, Elizabeth I, Anne Locke, Joanna [Jane] Lumley, Dorcas Martin, Margaret More-Roper and Margaret Tyler), does this therefore mean that her translations are intrinsically 'feminine' (Trill 1996, 148)? Is there any particular aspect of Herbert's poetic art that can be said to be gendered? In tackling this question most critics agree that Mary Herbert's *Psalms* resist any straightforward or literal biographical reading. Indeed, locating authorial identity in psalm translations is especially difficult given that the translations of the Psalms produce a kind of 'nested voice', in which the voices of God, David and the translator each overlap one another in the voice of the narrator. Thus, as Trill suggests, a more fruitful approach to the question of authorial identity in Herbert's *Psalms* may be to examine the self-consciously poetic nature of her translations. By emphasizing the role of the speaker and the manner and form of her telling, Mary Herbert positions herself as female poet-praiser of God (151). Moreover, Mary Herbert's implied insistence throughout the *Psalms* is that a woman's experience can represent the experience of all Christian believers. Thus it seems that the gendered identity of the author cannot be discounted, even when the work itself contains no overt allusion to that gender.

A caveat is often raised at this juncture. Some critics regard Mary Herbert's *Psalms* as evidence of her desire to remain within the 'acceptable' sixteenth-century boundaries of female expression (i.e. focusing on religious subject matter and on translation, which was perceived to be a 'feminine' genre). Yet it is also true to say that the translation of psalms was central to the construction of Protestant subjectivity in the period, and thus practised by women and men alike. If nothing else, therefore, Mary Herbert's psalm translations show that while a female author may work within an established literary tradition (here, psalm paraphrase), she may also expand, enrich and even transform that tradition through her 'sweet learned labours' (Donne 2001, 369). And in so doing, Herbert's translation of metrical psalms challenges her readers, today as then, to revise their assumptions and expectations concerning the connection between an author's identity and her work.

Thomas Nashe: Polyphonic Prose Fiction; or, When Was the First Novel?

What, and when, was the first English novel? The answer to this frequently asked question depends, of course, upon how we define 'novel' (Italian, *novella*, 'new', 'news' or 'short story of something new'). Due to the powerful influence of Ian Watt's study in literary sociology, *The Rise of the Novel: Studies in Defoe, Richardson and Fielding* (1957), the first novel in English is often said to be Daniel Defoe's *Robinson Crusoe* (1719). *Crusoe* conforms, according to Watt, to 'the primary criterion' for the novel form: 'truth to individual experience' (13). Other critics reach back a further thirty years for the first English novel to Aphra Behn's *Oroonoko* (1688). Still others find the substantive origins of the novel in John Bunyan's allegorical narrative *The Pilgrim's Progress* (1678). But as even a cursory glance at the shelves of modern-day bookshops will show, the 'novel' is a particularly capacious generic category, containing an array of subgenres such as the epistolary novel, the historical novel, detective fiction, *Bildungsroman* (novel of 'education'), comic fiction and the picaresque novel. Perhaps we need to go beyond Watt's criterion, and further back in time, in our search for the first English novel.

One earlier candidate can be found in the picaresque novel subgenre (from the Spanish *pícaro*, a wily trickster): Thomas Nashe's *The Unfortunate Traveller, or The Life of Jack Wilton* (1594). *The Unfortunate Traveller* resembles modern concepts of the novel in that it is an extended fictional narrative depicting the fortunes of a central character; in this case, Jack Wilton, a page attending the court of Henry VIII at the siege of Tournay in 1513. Thomas Nashe's (1567–1601) fidelity to idiomatic English in this work – a characteristic he shares with other writers of prose fiction in the period such as John Lyly, Robert Greene and Thomas Deloney – is also in accord with a sixteenth-century notion of the novel in which the stylistic plainness of its form was held to be distinct from the more fanciful elaborations of romance. Yet the narrative structure and rhetorical character of *The Unfortunate Traveller* are far from plain. Roger Pooley describes Jack Wilton's speech as 'a supercharged colloquialism which is closer to the eloquence of inebriation than sober plainness' (Pooley 1992), and narrative elements such as abrupt time-shifts and a cacophony of voices and genres have led some commentators to link Nashe's *The Unfortunate Traveller* to the works of Modernist authors such as James Joyce and Wyndham Lewis (Jones 1983, 61). This brief essay, therefore, considers two instances of Nashe's polyphonic style in *The Unfortunate Traveller*, and asks to what extent we are justified in regarding the work as an early prose fiction forerunner of later developments in the novel form.

Nashe's headlong gallop though an assortment of sixteenth-century oral and written forms takes in jest-book anecdotes, newsbook reporting, satire, lyric verse, revenge tragedy, humanist oration and Church of England sermon. 'Like a crow that . . . follows aloof where there is carrion' (Nashe 1972, 277), Jack Wilton travels from the English camp at Tournay in 1513 to the Anabaptist uprising at Münster in Germany in 1534 in the space of one page of narrative, and jumps from first-hand account to pulpit oratory. The narrator calls for quiet in the voice of a preacher:

> Peace, peace there in the belfry: service begins . . . let me dilate a little more gravely than the nature of this history requires or will be expected of so young a practitioner in divinity: that not those that intermissively cry 'Lord, open unto us, Lord, open unto us, enter first into the Kingdom; that not the greatest professors have the greatest portion in grace; that all is not gold that glisters. When Christ said "The Kingdom of Heaven must suffer violence" he meant not the violence of long babbling prayers, nor the violence of tedious invective sermons without wit, but the violence of faith, the violence of good works, the violence of patient suffering. The ignorant snatch the Kingdom of Heaven to themselves with greediness, when we with all our learning sink to hell.' (Nashe 1972, 279–80)

The prose style of Nashe's attack on 'what it is to be Anabaptists, to be Puritans, to be villains' (286) is notable for its self-reflexiveness. The sermon opens with a mock-call for silence, 'Peace, peace there in the belfry', and acknowledges how anomalous such a narrative register must seem in a picaresque novel, especially when uttered by such a roguish character as Jack Wilton:

'let me dilate a little more gravely than the nature of this history requires or will be expected of so young a practitioner in divinity' (279). Other stylistic aspects also call attention to the sermon's own literariness. The rhetorical device of *anaphora* (the repetition of the same word or phrase at the beginning of successive clauses) imitates the scriptural style of sermon delivery: 'that not those that intermissively cry . . . that not the greatest professors . . . that all is not gold that glisters'. The sermon is structured about phrasal parallelism and antitheses of syntax, sound and sense: 'not the violence of long babbling prayers, nor the violence of tedious invective sermons without wit', are opposed to, 'the violence of faith . . . of good works . . . of patient suffering'. Similarly, Nashe alerts the reader to the particular generic style he is adopting in his later turn to pastoral interlude: 'To tell you of the rare pleasures of their gardens . . . were to write a second part of *The Gorgeous Gallery of Gallant Devices*' (an allusion to Thomas Proctor's 1578 poetic miscellany). Nashe's narration continues:

> I saw a summer banqueting house belonging to a merchant that was the marvel of the world, and could not be matched except God should make another paradise. It was built round of green marble like a theatre without; within there was a heaven and earth comprehended both under one roof. The heaven was a clear overhanging vault of crystal, wherein the sun and moon and each visible star had his true similitude, shine, situation and motion, and, by what enwrapped art I cannot conceive, these spheres in their proper orbs observed their circular wheelings and turnings, making a certain kind of soft angelical murmuring music in their often windings and going about; which music the philosophers say in the true heaven, by reason of the grossness of our senses, we are not capable of. (327)

Nashe's sudden plunge into pastoralism exemplifies Lorna Hutson's description of *The Unfortunate Traveller* as 'a parodic medium of dozens of public voices' (Hutson 1989, 4). Each passage of parodic ventriloquism is precisely observed. Here, the piling of clause upon clause in Nashe's long, loose prose paragraph imitates the 'windings and going about' of the celestial movement described. For the modern reader, used to the sentence as the primary unit of syntax and argument, Nashe's Renaissance 'period', composed of *cola* (colon-to-colon) and *commata* (comma-to-comma), can seem circuitous and baffling. But for sixteenth- and seventeenth-century readers, used to the period as the dominant method of organizing prose, Nashe obeys rhetorical decorum in exemplary fashion by adopting appropriate prose styles for each new change of scene and subject matter.

Even from this briefest of glances at Nashe's multi-vocal narrative style we can see that there are obvious parallels with the parodic, playful and allusive prose of canonical Modernist works such as Joyce's *Ulysses* (1922). There is insufficient room here to discuss whether such stylistic similarities extend to thematic or generic ones, or whether we can trace the multivoiced narratives of Renaissance and Modernist literature back to a common ancestry in ancient folk ritual and Menippean satire (as suggested by Mikhail Bakhtin, the Russian

Marxist-Formalist critic). What is clear from this micro-study, however, is that the development of literary genres such as the novel appears to be far from linear or straightforward; that literary self-consciousness is as much a characteristic of Renaissance literature as it is a feature of Modernist works; and that the beginnings of the novel in English may reach much further back than often thought.

William Shakespeare: Women on the Verge: Feminist Views of *King Lear*

In 'Before My Time', Johnny Cash sings: 'And in the dim of yesterday / I can clearly see / That flesh and blood cried out to someone / As it does in me.' But just how clearly and how far can we, as modern readers, see into the 'dim of yesterday'? Our historical distance from the prevailing mentalities of Renaissance Britain throws up perennial questions for modern critics of the literature of the period. How, for example, should we approach the depiction of gender in Renaissance literature? Should modern critics attempt to reconstruct the social and cultural attitudes of Spenser, Shakespeare, Jonson and the rest, or is this effort always bound to be coloured by unexamined aspects of our own ways of thinking? Would it not be more plausible, and honest, to 'update' Spenser, Shakespeare or Jonson by recreating the works of these authors in images that makes them fully compatible with contemporary tastes and value? In short, how much of what we say about a text comes from us, the critics, and how much from the text itself?

An example will illustrate how different approaches may inform our reading. In the following brief passage from Act V, Scene 1 of *King Lear*, Lear's eldest daughters, Goneril and Regan, are brought together with Edmund, bastard son of the Duke of Gloucester, in an uneasy alliance to fight an invading army from France. Much of the dramatic tension of the scene depends upon the fact that Edmund alone knows the precise nature of his intimate and political relations with each of the sisters.

REGAN   Now, sweet lord,
   You know the goodness I intend upon you:
   Tell me but truly, but then speak the truth,
   Do you not love my sister?
EDMUND   In honoured love.
REGAN
   But have you never found my brother's way
   To the forfended place?
EDMUND   That thought abuses you.
REGAN
   I am doubtful that you have been conjunct
   And bosomed with her, as far as we call hers.
EDMUND   No, by mine honour, madam.

REGAN
  I never shall endure her. Dear my lord,
  Be not familiar with her.
EDMUND   Fear me not –
    Enter with drum and colours ALBANY, GONERIL,
                  [*and*] soldiers.
    She and the Duke her husband.
  GONERIL [*aside*]
  I had rather lose the battle than that sister
  Should loosen him and me. (Foakes 2005, 357–8)[1]

The passage is suffused with the language of alliance – political and sexual – and associated mistrust, jealousy and fear of deception, as first Regan and then Goneril doubt the security and exclusivity of their bond with Edmund. Edmund, by contrast, betrays no such anxiety. The difference in the representation of their psychological states is evident in the rhythms of dialogue. Regan's speech keeps harping on the same theme: she seems obsessed with the fear that Edmund has committed adultery with Goneril ('But have you never found my brother's way / To the forfended place?'). Her probing questions are all variations on the same theme: 'I am doubtful [anxious] that you have been conjunct / And bosomed with her, as far as we call hers.' Close attention to Regan's words here reveals important nuances. According to the *OED*, 'conjunct' carries a double sense: joined together or united (whether in a political or carnal sense), but also joined in a subordinate capacity (as though Edmund were at Goneril's service). Similarly, 'bosomed with her' conveys the meaning of 'to receive into intimate companionship' (*OED*), but can also mean to be enclosed, hidden or confined within the bosom – another hint at clandestine activity on the part of Edmund and Goneril. Goneril too adopts the same vocabulary of political and personal alliance in her pun on 'lose' the battle and 'loosing' him and me ('loose' was a common spelling for 'lose' in the period). By contrast, Edmund's speech is notable for its reference to abstract virtue to defend his innocence ('honoured love', 'by mine honour'), and the remarkable construction, 'That thought abuses you'. In his separation of the thought from the thinker (we might say, 'that thought is unworthy of you') Edmund makes a crucial distinction. The effect of this distinction is to prompt the audience to notice how Edmund seems in control of dissimulation and lying (i.e. he is capable of separating truth from fiction), while Goneril and Regan have become prey to their passions and no longer know where the truth lies. But is this difference in representation, between the coolly malicious Edmund and the anxiety-ridden sisters consumed with jealousy, necessarily a gendered one?

By this advanced point in the play, the sisters have turned against their father, presided over the torture of Gloucester, and now compete for the affections and support of Edmund, the play's black-hearted Machiavel. Goneril and Regan appear to be cast in the mould of Cinderella's Wicked or Ugly sisters: vain, selfish, and ruthless. Feminist critics have commented widely on the dramatic representation of Goneril and Regan. Kathleen McLuskie argues that, 'the narrative, language and dramatic organisation all define the sisters' resistance to their father in terms of their gender, sexuality and position within the family' (McLuskie 1985, 98). This is in contrast to the situation in the chronicle play *King Leir*, a source for Shakespeare's work, in which the sister's wickedness is much more evidently a function of the plot. According to McLuskie, however, in Shakespeare's version the treatment of Lear meted out by Goneril and Regan reverses existing patterns of rule and is seen not simply as cruel and selfish but as a fundamental violation of human nature (98–9). The play thereby dramatizes the material conditions which lie behind power structures within the family. Ann Thompson, in turn, shows how this type of feminist criticism actively reads Shakespeare's play in the *present*; it does not attempt to accommodate Shakespeare to contemporary feminist mores, but is keenly insistent on historicising Shakespeare while urging critics to resist the ideology of femininity that Shakespeare historically represents (Thompson 1991, 126).

Another recent study, by Christina León Alfar, builds on this historicist analysis of power relations to show how the behaviour of Goneril and Regan reproduce existing forms of power. In Alfar's reading, the sisters' 'actions are not evidence of their innate "evil" but are symptomatic of the patrilineal structure of power relations in which they live' (Alfar 2003, 169). Thus, the attempt by Goneril and Regan to neutralize their father's power reflects precisely the kind of power given to them by Lear: unstable and self-interested. The torture of Gloucester is similarly of a piece with the way in which traitors are treated under Renaissance notions of rule – 'the methods by which the stability of the nation must be preserved' (183). Furthermore, desire for political survival also drives, at least partially, their involvement with Edmund. 'Both sisters . . . seize on Edmund . . . as a means to legitimize their own desire and exercise of power through an affiliation with the new, and satisfactorily ruthless, earl of Gloucester' (185). As in the culturally materialist criticism of McLuskie and Thompson before her, Alfar seeks to show how Goneril and Regan act not so much according to naturalized gender distinctions, but rather in response to other determinative causes, such as Renaissance notions of assuming and maintaining both political and personal power.

That Goneril and Regan are portrayed unsympathetically in *King Lear*, most notably in contrast to the loyalty and long-suffering of Cordelia, is not in dispute. But would Shakespeare's contemporary audience have responded differently to the representation of Goneril and Regan than we might do today? How much of our response is conditioned by our own modern preconceptions of gender and gender relations, and how much by what we find in the text (the problem of the so-called 'hermeneutic circle' (Baldick 2001, 111))? As I hope this brief review of recent feminist critical opinion of *King Lear* has demonstrated, our historical 'belatedness' presents a central and enduring challenge to our efforts at interpretation, with each new critical approach refining rather than resolving the nature of the task before us. But the likelihood that we will never achieve a final, unified 'answer' ought not to deter us from the exhilarating, if painstaking, pursuit of meaning in our reading. As our experience of reading Renaissance literature shows, interpretation and the knowledge that derives from it is accretive.

Self-Reflection and Paradox: John Donne's Holy Sonnets and the Characteristics of Renaissance Literature

As the previous case studies have shown, one of the distinguishing traits of English Renaissance literature is its self-reflexive use of language. Whether in plays, poems, prose fiction or psalm translation, the kind of writing practised by More, Wyatt, Marlowe, Mary Herbert, Nashe, Spenser and Shakespeare is writing that investigates itself; words serve not only to convey thought, but also to interrogate thought. Reasons for this preoccupation both with the effects and mechanics of language are not hard to find. The disciplines of language – included in the trivium of grammar, logic, rhetoric – lay at the heart of education in the period (see Chapters 1 and 2). The highly prized skills of debate and disputation, of arguing on both sides of a case (*in utramque partem*), relied upon mastery of rhetorical techniques, and formed the pattern for many English Renaissance literary texts (e.g. More's *Utopia*, Sidney's *Defence of Poesy*, Shakespeare's sonnets and the flowering of Elizabethan and Jacobean drama in general). And no writer in the period was more alive to the possibilities of the argumentative, or disputational literary style than John Donne (1572–1631), lyric poet, author of prose works of religious controversy, and one of the greatest writers of sermons in the English language.

In Donne's holy sonnet below, 'Show me deare Christ', secular and sacred vocabularies are mingled, and the sonnet form reconfigured, for the purposes of spiritual inquiry. The astonishingly bold fusion of erotic and devotional imagery in Donne's sonnet lends credence to Samuel Johnson's observation in his *Life of Cowley* that in such poetry 'the most heterogeneous ideas are yoked by violence together' (1781, I. 29). This concluding section, therefore, asks whether Donne's apparent poetic plea for ecumenism and religious tolerance is helped or hindered by his startling, provocative imagery, and how such language might be understood by readers, then and now.

> Show me deare Christ, thy Spouse, so bright and cleare.
>   What is it She, which on the other Shore
>   Goes richly painted? Or which rob'd and tore
> Laments and mournes in Germany and here?
> Sleepes She a thousand, then peepes vp one yeare?
>   Is She selfe truth and errs? now new, now'outwore?
>   Doth She, and did She, and shall She evermore
> On one, on Seauen, or on no hill appeare?
> Dwells She with vs, or like adventuring knights

First trauaile we to seeke and then make Love?
Betray kind husband thy Spouse to our Sights,
    And let myne amorous Soule court thy mild Dove,
Who is most trew, and pleasing to thee, then
When She is embrac'd and open to most Men. (Stringer 2005, 19)

At the heart of Donne's poem is a review of the competing claims of the various Christian Churches in the early seventeenth century (Roman Catholic, Anglican, Lutheran and Calvinist). Opening with a direct request to 'deare Christ', the speaker of the poem asks to be vouchsafed an unimpeded vision of 'thy Spouse'. This conceit, of the true Church as the bride or spouse of Christ, finds its principal scriptural source in Revelation (19.7–8, 21–22), and in the Song of Solomon (2), and runs throughout Donne's sonnet, allowing him to use metaphors of human courtship to illustrate religious affairs. A topical allusion, to she 'which rob'd and tore / Laments and mourned in Germany and here', refers almost certainly to the defeat of German Protestant forces in 1620, and allows us to place the composition of the poem at a relatively late stage in Donne's career. Donne's references to the appearance of the true Church 'On one, on Seauen, or on no hill' are generally thought to indicate, respectively, Ludgate Hill, on which stood the Anglican St Paul's Cathedral; the seven hills of Rome; and the flat plain of Geneva, centre of Calvinism.[2]

The first eight lines, or octave, of the sonnet conform to the Italian model of two quatrains with the enclosed rhyme scheme of abbaabba. As so often in Donne's poetry, however, formal conformity is leavened by rhythmic variation. An opening spondee (with stresses placed on both 'Show' and 'me') gives way to the base metrical pattern of iambic pentameter, only for the last three lines of the octave to end with anapaestic feet (unstress-unstress-stress), the effect of which is to increase the urgency and rapidity of the poem's insistent rhetorical questioning. It is just such metrical irregularity, placed in the service of logical and syntactic coherence, that prompted Coleridge's famous verse on Donne's poetry, concluding: 'Rhyme's sturdy cripple, fancy's maze and clue, / Wit's forge and fire-blast, meaning's press and screw.'

Donne's most notable formal innovation, however, comes in the sonnet's sestet. In the manner of a Shakespearean or Spenserian sonnet Donne constructs the sestet from a quatrain and concluding rhyming couplet. Unlike Shakespeare or Spenser, however, Donne's conventional rhyme-structure runs counterpoint to the sestet's syntax, in which an opening couplet is followed by a quatrain. In the couplet – 'Dwells She with vs, or like adventuring knights / First trauaile we to seeke and then make Love?' – Donne mocks the knight-errantry of medieval romance, and by implication the elaborate rituals of courtly love. He thereby draws attention by contrast to his own, altogether more worldly and frank sensibility and literary style. Donne's decision to conclude the sonnet via the carefully staged suspense of the quatrain, rather than via the neat, conclusiveness of a heroic couplet, seems entirely in keeping with the confrontational directness of this style, especially when we consider the final, shocking proposition that the poem makes: that the true Church 'is most trew, and pleasing to thee, then / When She'is embrac'd and open to most Men.'

Ernest Gilman has argued that this audacious image acts as a final admonitory twist to the poem, serving to reveal the idolatrous, and adulterous, aspect of the speaker's desire to embrace an image of the true Church (Gilman 1986, 85), 'And let myne amorous soule court thy mild Dove'. What is certainly beyond dispute is that images derived from physical love in the final quatrain imbue the abstract concept of divine love with a palpability that seems calculated to shock. In mitigation, Frank Kermode has suggested that such shock in the modern reader may arise because the metaphor, the Bride of Christ, is no longer commonplace (Kermode 1957, 39). Other critics have argued that in this final image, Donne is not being literal so much as reminding us of the radical nature of divine grace: the shocking metaphor is intended to startle us into recognition of how very different God's love is from our own (Young 1994, 172). In attempting to make sense of such apparent paradoxes, of the conjunction of sacred and profane, the reader is therefore prompted to a deeper realization of religious faith, thus suggesting that Donne's use of erotic imagery may help rather than hinder his plea for greater religious latitude.

In at least two respects, then, Donne's divine poetry is characteristic of certain broader traits in Renaissance English literature. In the poem's deliberate self-reflexiveness, calling attention to the artifice of its own making, Donne's sonnet exemplifies the period's fascination with the intricacies of the relationship between words and things. In its provocative fusion of sacred and profane imagery, the poem testifies to Renaissance literature's affinity for teasing, riddling formulations, for the mental and verbal challenges posed by apparent paradox and contradiction. And it is in this coupling of thought and feeling – witnessed in 'Show me deare Christ' in the interrogative attitude of the poem's speaker-hearer relationship – that the reader is invited to devise his or her own answers to the questions that are raised. In doing just this, in encountering Renaissance literature on its own terms, we begin to read anew, recognizing afresh the contingencies and continuities of each literary epoch, not least our own.

Case Studies in Reading 2: Key Theoretical and Critical Texts

Christopher R. Orchard

Chapter Overview

Brief Overview

Theory tends to gravitate towards categorization, and our discipline encourages recognizable taxonomies such as periodization. Similarly, as scholars and teachers, we are expected to announce our theoretical affiliations/positions and are readily identified according to our specialization. Arguably, this is how academic discourse is structured. Unsurprisingly then, while the organizational principles of this chapter are based on case studies, the reader will encounter each writer's commitment to a recognizable theoretical field/s. Therefore, this chapter has been written so that each case study is framed by its theoretical background. It should also be noted that many of these writers collectively share a conceptual language concurrent with each particular theoretical emphasis. Repeatedly the reader will encounter a mutual interest in the circularity of discourses, synchronically and diachronically, and a challenge to ahistorical readings, all testifying to the legacy of New Historicism, which I would argue has been the most pervasive theory in this field over the past twenty-five years. As John Brannigan (1998) points out, this shared discourse should not be surprising given 'the mutation of New Historicism into postcolonial, feminist and queer readings' (121). Finally, but equally important is the afterlife of the work. Given the importance of each case study to the field of Renaissance studies, references are made to the legacy of the work, emphasizing the contribution that other scholars have made in building on the approaches taken in these key critical texts.

Stephen Greenblatt, *Renaissance Self-Fashioning: From More to Shakespeare* (1980)

Edition cited: *Renaissance Self-Fashioning: From More to Shakespeare*, Chicago: University of Chicago Press, 1980.

Theoretical Foregrounding

There is little doubt that New Historicism has dominated theory in the Early Modern period in the last quarter of a century. The essays of its proponents, collected in editions such as Aram Veeser's *New Historicism* (1989) and Greenblatt and Gunn's *Redrawing the Boundaries* (1992), emphasized their interdisciplinary roots in the work of the anthropologist Clifford Geertz and proclaimed the importance of 'thick description', the detailed analysis of a single event or anecdote, in order to detect the representation of any given culture. Other features of New Historicist approaches include the following. First, a concern to historicize the dialectic between the present and the past, each being seen to reshape the other so as to establish what Montrose calls 'a dialogue between a poetics and a politics of culture' (for practitioners see Parker and Quint 1986, Marcus 1990, Corns 1992 and Brink and Gentrup 1993). Second, a preoccupation with identity and the cultural construction of the self (Greenblatt 1980). Third, the complicit inclusion of the critic's own text and personal preoccupations (Greenblatt 1988). Fourth, the adoption in its terminology of the language of Reaganomics: words such as 'exchanges', 'networks' of trades and trade-offs, competing 'representations', 'negotiation', the idea of the market and the invisible large economy being some salient examples (Bretzius 1997). This 1980s rhetoric also, and importantly, embraced the economic metaphor of circularity that was said to characterize all constructions of reality, literary and otherwise. Finally, New Historicist criticism entails a continual concern with what are often overwhelming displays of power, and with the manner in which authority is contested or acknowledged.

Self-Fashioning and Fashioning

Greenblatt's *Renaissance Self-Fashioning* is one of the best known in its field; it exemplifies the tenets of New Historicism regarded as synonymous with Greenblatt himself. Greenblatt foregrounded the idea of the subjective intervention of the critic in the work, holding that the critic cannot completely re-enter the culture of Renaissance nor leave behind his or her own contemporary situation. For Greenblatt, the Renaissance and the early 1980s were intimately interconnected: 'We . . . are situated', he claims, 'at the close of the cultural movement initiated in the Renaissance, and . . . the places in which our social and psychological world seem to be cracking apart are those structural joints visible when it was first constructed' (175). (He is, however, sometimes frustratingly vague on this point, and generally does not elaborate on precisely what it is that connects our own 'social and psychological world' with that of our Renaissance counterparts.)

The main tenet of Greenblatt's study is a concern with both selves and a sense that they can be fashioned. In other words, while the self has the power to shape itself, there exists outside the self a general power which controls identity. Greenblatt also announces that the purpose of New Historicism is to avoid limiting literature as either timeless or an autonomous product of artist but instead is 'part of a system of signs that constitutes a given culture' (4) (see, Healy, this volume, Chapter 8). The aim is to investigate 'both the social presence to the world of the literary text and the social presence of the world in the literary text' (5), to understand how 'the written word is self-consciously embedded in specific communities, life situations, structures of power' (7). Thus, he focuses on writers who best express 'the historical pressure of an unresolved and continuing conflict' (8). He sees the same patterns involved in power: expressed first in the church, then the book, then the absolutist state, a shift from celebration to rebellion to subversive submission and the creation of a literary profession. Self-fashioning thus always occurs with a partial submission to something that lies outside the self, whether this is God, a book or an institution, and that self-fashioning occurs in relation to something that is alien which is always present, pervasive and which threatens the authority that exerts power to attack it. As a consequence, the threat to the self is always part of the nature of self-fashioning and self-fashioning always paradoxically entails a degree of self loss. For Greenblatt, there are 'no moments of pure, unfettered subjectivity; indeed, the human subject itself began to seem remarkably unfree, the ideological product of the relations of power in a particular society' (256).

The first chapter of *Renaissance Self-Fashioning* deals with Sir Thomas More and the 'writings of self-fashioning and self-cancellation, the crafting of a public role and the profound desire to escape from the identity so crafted' (13). Power is a charade whose sign is the imposition of one's own fiction on the world and the inevitable participation of everyone in this fiction. This reflected a political world which for More created an increasing sense of his own alienation from his society, friends and himself. More's playful rhetorical strategies in *Utopia* enable moments where 'blind spots' of sociohistorical forces emerge to sit alongside the seemingly immobile nature of Utopia itself, and this, for Greenblatt, mirrors More's own awareness of his life as a self-reflexive one that causes self-estrangement, a sense of the 'shadow of other selves' (31). This sense of a conflict within More's identity is constituted in a social role apparent in his participation in institutions and in a text, (*Utopia*) that 'cancels such an identity by eliminating, among other things, most of the highly particularized corporate categories in which a man could locate himself and by means of which he could say, "I am *this* and not *that*" ' (42). For Greenblatt, this self-cancellation explains the difference between More's public persona and his inner self, the place of unexpressed judgements and thoughts. It is also a response, he argues, to the rise of Protestantism: More *imagines* the dismantlement of individual identity but he cannot cancel it since his Catholicism 'opposes those who dare to set themselves off from the community and to lay claim to a private truth' (62).

Greenblatt's revelation of contradictory impulses between the self and culture and within the self itself is a rhetorical strategy typical of New Historicist readings. Its presence is felt in the second chapter in which Greenblatt examines the authority of the book, specifically Tyndale's *Obedience of the Christian Man* and his translation of the *New Testament*. Greenblatt examines a Protestant discourse which figures the self as Christ, so creating, Greenblatt argues, 'a simultaneous affirmation and effacement of personal identity' (77). For Greenblatt, the printed book and Tyndale's work for the reader 'provides a way of being in the world and shapes the reader's inner life' (84); Tyndale's work, he claims, begins the transition from one mode of interiority to another: 'we may watch the fashioning of the Protestant discourse of self out of conflicting impulses: rage against authority and identification with authority, hatred of the father and ardent longing for union with the father, confidence in oneself and an anxious sense of weakness and sinfulness, justification and guilt' (85). The momentum of transition also informs the move from Catholicism to Protestantism as texts replace auricular confession as the prime means of self-fashioning while the New Testament becomes a form of power; the book offers all that the Church *qua* institution, had once arrogated to itself. The book became the personal history of the individual reader. But this is not a matter of an individual agency, freed from outside fashioning: the New Testament now functions as a spiritual version of societal power. God's work represented an inner state 'that must, nonetheless, be experienced as the irresistible operation of a force outside the self, indeed alien to the self. The man of faith is seized, destroyed and made new by God's Word. He gives up his resistance, his irony, his sense of his own shaping powers, and experiences instead the absolute certainty of a total commitment, a binding, irrevocable covenant' (111).

Such intersections between the spiritual and the secular also inform Greenblatt's reading of Sir Thomas Wyatt's controversial translation of the penitential psalms of 1530s and 1540s. Greenblatt argues that for Wyatt, both God and Henry VIII are viewed as 'irascible autocrats' (116). Wyatt's individuality as a translator is compromised by his involvement in the social game: his work responds to values of domination and submission in the system of power oriented around the absolutist state. Hence Greenblatt shows how material that can seem removed from the concerns of the Tudor state, such as Wyatt's borrowing from Aretine of the historical prologues involving King David's adultery with Bathsheba is in fact closely related to it, his translation situated firmly within the context of the world of royal power he inhabits.

The fourth chapter marks the start of the second half of the book in which Greenblatt considers Spenser, Marlowe and Shakespeare as locating 'a heightened investment of professional identity in artistic creation' (161). Remarking on Spenser's observation to Ralegh in *The Faerie Queene* (see Adlington, this volume, Chapter 3) that a gentleman can be fashioned, he focuses on the Bower of Blisse episode to remark about its contradictory impulses. He sees this episode as showing that the self created by Spenser reflects his culture's violent desire to resist a sensuousness to which it is drawn with more intensity precisely because it must be destroyed and yet simultaneously to embrace its temperate side in which sexuality, expressed as love, leads to virtuous action. So, if excess threatens, it justifies the control of an institutional power over sexuality and hence 'over the inner life of the individual' (177). As a result, self-fashioning requires both an enabling institution such as the court and a 'not-self' that threatens from without; in this manner Greenblatt associates the episode in the Bower of Blisse with European control over indigenous people in North America.

Chapter five focuses on Marlowe who Greenblatt reads through the lens of a fear of cultural effacement, the sense that in using up intellectual and economic resources nothing will be left behind. For Greenblatt, Marlovian characters embrace disciplinary paradigms: in Barabas for example, we have a character who, in responding to Christian plans, is '*bought into being* by the Christian society' (206). In Marlowe therefore, characters are continuously engaged in repeating a self-constitutive act in order to continue to be the same on the stage and hence resist the changes of time: 'identity' Greenblatt argues, 'is a theatrical invention that must be reiterated if it is to endure' (201). This sense of improvisation, 'the ability both to capitalize on the unforeseen and to transform given materials into one's own scenario' (227) is at the heart of Greenblatt's discussion of Iago in the final chapter and arguably one of *Renaissance Self-Fashioning*'s most enduring legacies to criticism. Greenblatt reads the figure of Iago not so much as a character, but as a figure for something rather greater than himself. Iago's strategy is part of a larger European calculation of insinuating itself into pre-existing cultures of indigenes and turning them to its advantage, an exercise of Western power even as it is an effacement of self. Iago imagines his own non-existence so he can live in another's and eventually displace and absorb the other. Othello himself is a text, but not necessarily of his own making: 'Iago knows that an identity that has been fashioned as a story can be unfashioned, refashioned, inscribed anew in a different narrative' (238).

Influence

New Historicism's domination of criticism of the Early Modern period has generated retrospectives and modifications as well as critiques of its operating assumptions. Its earliest practitioners now take a more moderate position about some claims than they once did: Louis Montrose, for example, still holds that primacy should still be given to the social and cultural context in which Elizabethan drama was created but now he recognizes complexities and multiple contrary perspectives that he did not acknowledge before, rejecting binary oppositions of subversion and containment model of power relations in favour of positions that are 'relationally located and circumstantially shaped' (104) (Montrose 1997). Those critics who identify themselves as disciples of the original theoretical tenets of New Historicism still affirm its vitality and insist on the historicity of texts, the textuality of history and a desire for historical truth but some wish to avoid the throwaway conflations of the past and the present that characterized the theory in its early days (Comensoli and Stevens 1998, and see Chapter 8). New scholars have extended the focus of New Historicism beyond the court and its hierarchies, focusing instead on the ordinary or taken-for-granted, believing that attention to the details of everyday life complements a further interest by second-generation new historicists in materiality such as the graffiti found in households and churches (Fumerton and Hunt 1998). And there have been critics aplenty who have attacked New Historicism for its monolithic depictions of the past together with a self-interested rejection of critical predecessors. (Bradshaw 1993). These studies suggested that texts were not inevitably embedded in ideological matrixes and because they were resistant in their very structures they could resist totalizing interpretative strategies (Strier 1997).

Jonathan Dollimore, *Radical Tragedy: Religion, Ideology and Power in the Drama of Shakespeare and his Contemporaries* (1984)

Edition cited: *Radical Tragedy: Religion, Ideology and Power in the Drama of Shakespeare and his Contemporaries*, Chicago: University of Chicago Press, 1984.

Jonathan Dollimore's *Radical Tragedy* shares New Historicism's insistence on the primacy of history in the analysis of literary texts, but the intellectual forbears underlying his approach lie in Marx, not Foucault (see Baumlin's Chapter 6 and Healy's Chapter 8, this volume). In his introduction to *Cultural Materialism: Theory and Practice* (1995), Scott Wilson, however, argues that Cultural materialism differs from traditional Marxism in that it plays down class as a signifier of difference and incorporates feminism, Queer theory and post-colonialism instead. Dollimore and Alan Sinfield defined cultural Materialism in *Political Shakespeare* (1985) as 'a combination of historical context, theoretical method, political commitment and textual analysis' (cited in Wilson vii) in the service of a particular, and overtly political, agenda: the eradication of tendencies towards values of immanence, transcendence, conservatism and tradition. As all texts are produced by history and provide knowledge at only a certain contingent moment of that history, therefore all texts are 'partial, interested, political' (Wilson 9). For Dollimore and Sinfield, cultural materialism 'registers its commitment to the transformation of a social order which exploits people on the grounds of race, gender and class' (cited in Wilson viii). In other words, as Wilson points out, from the cultural materialist perspective 'The whole point of academic life is not to search for poetic or aesthetic truth . . . but to seek to transform society for the good . . . Education should not have an ideal but a useful, material purpose' (16). As Wilson notes, 'this definition helps distinguish it from New Historicism which was less overtly partisan about its political commitment' (55).

The Materialist Dialectic

Dollimore's influences include materialist dialecticians such as Raymond Williams and dramatists such as Brecht over critics such as A. C. Bradley and T. S. Eliot; (see Baumlin, this volume, Chapter 6). He holds that drama is not 'a transhistorical symbol of human depravity, [but] a historically specific focus for a contemporary critique of power relations' (4); and maintains that drama reacted to the political and social crisis of the early modern period not by '[retreating] into aesthetic and ideological conceptions of order, integration, equilibrium' but by '[confronting] and [articulating] that crisis, indeed . . . [helping to] precipitate it' (5). The key then is to avoid teleology and stress instead the dialecticism behind historical processes. Such cognitive and materialist views of ideology were prefigured at the time, Dollimore claims, in Baconian and Hobbesian models, and exemplified by views which recognized religion as political expediency and history as contingent rather than providential. Thus Dollimore examines John Marston's plays as an investigation of the changing nature of subjectivity, possessed of the conviction that reality cannot be explained by absolutes and the universe is not providentially governed. This leads in revenge plays to a violent re-entry into society out of a state of grief: 'The Jacobean malcontent can in turn be seen as a prototype of the modern decentered subject, the bearer of a subjectivity which is not the antithesis of social progress but its subject . . .' (50).

What is important about Dollimore's work is not only the materialist concepts he utilizes but also the critique he offers of a tradition that has led us to read this period in the traditionalist way that we did before. He shows how criticism of Jacobean tragedy in the twentieth century, especially in Bradley and Eliot, betrayed an ideal of harmonic integration in which history was excluded or transcended and in which drama was expected to reflect some reality. Dollimore uses Brecht as a corrective model, seeing how dialectical materialism, rooted in a preference for estrangement, creates an awareness of characters and incidents caught up in historical contingency. He distinguishes between two kinds of mimesis in conflict: idealist (didacticism in drama with order restored) and realist (historical and contemporary) found in the theories of Bacon and Fulke Greville in which providentialist belief disintegrates and is replaced by scepticism about its retributive intents. He notes the Renaissance dramatists' obsessive concern with chaos as a marker of real social inability and change and sense of universal decay as a contradiction of an immanent God because it presupposed the primary existence of fate and fortune. Transgression is born out of this disjunction and results (for example) in Faustus transgressing limits 'which, among other things, renders God remote and inscrutable yet subjects the individual to constant surveillance and correction; which holds the individual subject terrifyingly responsible for the fallen human condition while disallowing him or her any subjective power of redemption' (115) (see Adlington, this volume, Chapter 3).

Dollimore's third section focuses on the decentering of man; for him 'the essentialist concept of "man" mystifies and obscures the real historical conditions in which the actual identity of people is rooted' (153). Instead, Dollimore offers a Marxist perspective filtered through Brecht on the one hand (human consciousness is determined by social being) and Foucault on the other (the idea that it is power that constitutes people). Both of these he ties back to Galileo and Machiavelli's concept of praxis. He insists that identity is not metaphysically derivative but connected instead with a new geographical and social mobility, so that for individuals what matters is less their function within an order than the ability to initiate and choose certain directions – what I want to be. An essential, autonomous self is not possible, and identity is either fiction or representation, not fixed. Thus in George Chapman's *Bussy D'Ambois*, man's 'essential nature goes missing as does the universe's teleological design . . . Chapman concentrates on the social realities disclosed by their absence' (183). Similarly, Dollimore rejects an essentialist reading of *King Lear* as humanist tragedy focused on redemption based on courage and integrity, arguing instead that the play is about property and power, and shows that 'Human values are not antecedent to these material realities but are, on the contrary, in-formed by them' (197).

Dollimore's reading shares some conclusions with the readings of New Historicist critics, however. Both tend to see progressive or subversive ideologies as, frequently, contained by the power structures they attempt to confront, as 'a revolutionary (emergent) insight is folded back into a dominant ideology' (201). Hence in *Coriolanus* loyalty to the state allows the idea that reputation proceeds from a man's virtue but dissent with the state represents a contradiction 'which reveals both reputation and state to be prior to and in some sense constitutive of virtus.' (218). And, like New Historicism, Dollimore's cultural materialism is concerned to emphasize connections between our own time and the period we are analysing; he seeks, he says, to 'invite a positive and explicit engagement with the historical, social and political realities of which both literature and criticism are inextricably a part' (249–50).

Influence

As Brannigan (1998) has suggested, cultural materialism has retained its theoretical shape, still emphasizing, through writers such as Felicity Nussbaum, its Marxist origins and its commitment to social engagement. Its viability as a theory has continued to be reiterated by covering issues such as cultural production, reading non-heterosexually, investigating the limits of Queer reading and detailing rape and Rights (Sinfield 2006).

Lisa Jardine, *Still Harping on Daughters: Women and Drama in the Age of Shakespeare* (1989)

Edition cited: *Still Harping on Daughters: Women and Drama in the Age of Shakespeare*, 2nd ed, New York: Columbia University Press, 1989.

With New Historicism, feminism has probably had the most sustained influence on Renaissance studies in the last quarter of a century. Typically, feminist work in this period can be characterized by two main areas: (1) the reaction by women critics, women authors and female characters to patriarchal attempts to shape gender; (2) twin concerns with domesticity and female interaction with, or intervention into, public discourse.

In her new introduction to the second edition of *Still Harping on Daughters*, Jardine acknowledges that being labelled a new historicist critic since the first edition came out in 1983, has enabled her to view the individual female subject as a cultural artefact, and place her history 'at the intersection of systems of behavior, customs, beliefs, out of which, I consider, personal identity is constructed' (ix). She recognizes, however, that new historicist tenets have not always been compatible with feminist scholarship of this period and argues that recent scholarship has sometimes failed to 'retrieve *agency* for the female subject in history' (vii). But she does appreciate the ways in which disagreements among scholars over theory and methodology (she contrasts her preference for social relations and materiality over a psychoanalytical emphasis on individual subjectivity) have aided in an engagement with real issues.

Jardine's introduction to some degree takes issue with earlier feminist studies of Shakespeare because they focused either on female characters or the sexist attitudes of male characters. What results from this approach, Jardine claims, is that either Shakespeare's female characters' qualities are held to be immutable, Shakespeare merely mirroring the variety he saw around him, or his society is represented as unmitigatingly chauvinistic, so that Shakespeare's own maleness inevitably entails a warping of his female characters. Jardine seeks instead to align cultural issues with perspectives on the treatment of women in drama, examining how the interconnections of stage representation and concerns outside the theatre might '[suggest] a way in which "femaleness" was significant in a network of possibilities for categorizing and discriminating experience' (6). However, rather than argue that the increased interest in women in drama reflects more social possibilities for them, Jardine posits that it reflects a patriarchy's anxiety about larger social changes in the period.

Jardine's first chapter concerns female roles and Elizabethan eroticism. She considers the context of biblical and patristic traditions which denounced stage transvesticism, accusing it of generating subversive homosexual desire in the male members of the audience for 'the erotically irresistible effeminate boy' (17) or hermaphrodite. She examines how Shakespeare's treatment of Rosalind differs from his source in Lodge (25) and argues that Shakespeare's heroines are 'sexually enticing *qua* transvestied boys, and that the plays encourage the audience to view them as such' (29). The second chapter focuses on drama's interconnection with social discourses about women's engagement in Protestantism, humanist education and marital relations. Jardine explores the tension between expected and acceptable social roles and independence, the latter being represented on stage as adultery and sexual promiscuity. Moral writers, she claims, inevitably saw opportunities for women as indicative of a world turned upside down, but, she suggests even liberal interpretations of possibilities for women, articulated mostly in humanist writings, expected moderation in the pursuit of these activities. Protestant reformist writings held that any depiction of women allowed to interpret scripture must be tempered by Pauline models of obedience and seriousness; and the family hierarchy, based on a Protestant model, encouraged the wife and mother to be the disciplinarian, hardly a liberal role (see Baumlin, this volume, Chapter 6). For Jardine, humanist education produced a docile, pure, modest woman, consequently warding off not only idleness, but also interest in social and political issues (56).

In her third chapter, Jardine argues that strong women in the drama do not reflect real-life emancipation of women in Renaissance society; for Jardine, such representations are reflective of a male point of view, and are morally reprehensible: strong women in the drama in the end must always be redeemed through a conversion to acceptable female virtues such as chastity, patience and chastity and any signs of female sexuality breach decorum. A similar corrective is brought to bear in the final three chapters on the figure of the scold, satirically depicted as the quick tongued woman who 'threatens to sabotage the domestic harmony which depends upon her general submissiveness' (106); the cross dresser (such as Moll in *The Roaring Girl*,) and the heroic woman, divested of any real power through her elevation to an archetypal status as the patient sufferer, who are who 'is appropriated as ... figure[s] representative of all society's nervousnesses where the relations between men and women are concerned' (161).

Influence

Jardine's scepticism about the degree of women's advances during the Renaissance has not been adopted by all of the feminist critics who have followed her. Some have argued that women could circumvent restrictions through irony or voice (Ferguson, Quilligan and Vickers 1986; Beilin 1990; Mendelson 1987);

others that women in the period showed an activist commitment to engaging in a discourse of political dissent (Smith and Appelt 2001) and flourished despite the prohibitively patriarchal ideologies which surrounded them at the time (Krontiris 1992). Others reject the notion of women as silent, suggesting that women, particularly in popular culture, acted as agents of ridicule and satire to countermeasure domestic violence (Brown 1998); still others claim that women writers participated in erotic aggression, and articulated their opposition to male unfaithfulness, in order to enable them to fight for control over their own bodies and for an important, if limited, degree of autonomy (Sondergard 2003). Much of the debate over the role of women during the Civil War period has focused on the question of whether women's writing articulated confidence or self effacement (Nevitt 2006; Seelig 2006), and on whether the closet drama practiced by Cavendish and Finch among others, was deliberately chosen to air political issues or, by contrast, necessitated by political circumstances (Straznicky 2004; Chalmers 2004).

What has fundamentally changed since Jardine published her book is the availability of resources for feminist criticism of the Renaissance period. Anthologies that include canonical writers (Haselkorn and Travitsky 1990), continental women (Wilson 1990) and non-elite women writers (Trill, Chedgzoy and Osborne 1998) have vastly extended the range of writing available to scholars. Some show how women writers were resisting patriarchal ideology (Lewalski 1993) others argue that we ought to sidestep the idea of a female writing community in favour of examining individual priorities and concerns. But collectively, they illustrate a range of writing that was unimaginable a generation ago.

Bruce R. Smith, *Homosexual Desire in Shakespeare's England: A Cultural Poetics* (1991)

Edition cited: *Homosexual Desire in Shakespeare's England: A Cultural Poetics*, Chicago: Chicago University Press, 1991.

Since the beginning of the 1990s, the engagement of Queer theory with Renaissance literature has steadily increased. One of its most pressing questions has been whether modern concepts of homosexuality can be applied to the early modern period (Sedgwick 1985; Summers 1992). Many argue that homosexual identity only came into focus in the eighteenth century with the prosecutions of those caught in Molly houses (Bray 1982). And Renaissance definitions were different to those of today: they focused exclusively on sexual acts rather than on a conception of an individual's sexual identity. For these reasons, most queer theorists today would claim that to import the term 'homosexual' uncritically into a discussion of the Renaissance would be to risk anachronism.

Smith's study is concerned with setting up the parameters for investigating Renaissance literature using queer discourse. His focus is on cultural subjectivity regarding 'deviant' sexual practice – what is one person's bestiality is another's legitimate pleasure – issues of power and definition. Using a Foucauldian analysis that holds that 'structures of power in society help define sexuality in that society' (7), Smith examines how what is being said (knowledge) and how it is being said to someone else produces power in the field of sexuality: 'Sexuality is the interpenetration of external social controls with internal experience' (9). He suggests that, unlike today, in the Renaissance sexuality was not the starting point for anyone's self-definition. Homosexual was not a term and buggery and sodomy were inexact since they could cover heterosexual acts too. In other words, such acts were part of a larger moral arena and were understood as acts on a spectrum of depravity to which all of mankind might be subject. Smith warns that the distinction between homosexual and heterosexual is a contemporary definition which misleadingly 'takes sexual desire as a point of departure for personal identity. It presupposes a sexual essence in the desiring subject' (12). For Smith power in a text is also exerted over the reader who then exerts control over the self: power is not just prohibitions but 'a matter of positive excitations: it is people, situations, and objects that a particular culture endows with erotic value. That is to say, sexuality is not simply subject to power, it manifests power' (12).

While acknowledging the existence of legal, moral and medical discourses about homosexuality, Smith's focus is on the poetic or imaginative because of the importance that symbolic discourse plays in culture. If we look at sexual activity only as an external matter, Smith argues, we miss what it means to the people doing it; that is, we miss the subjectivity it expresses. Therefore we need to look at private fantasies that reorganize reality to satisfy individuals' various wishes, fantasies which are most intimately accessible through imaginative discourse because it doesn't have to be logical and consistent and because it entails a more complicated relationship between speaker and listener. Whereas the other discourses posit the writer as the authority and the reader as passive, areas of imaginative reality create collaboration in which power is constantly being renegotiated: 'fiction making is a *performative* act in which the reader or the listener is as much a participant as the author' (17). Moreover, whereas other discourses are concerned with sexual acts alone, 'only poetic discourse can address homosexual *desire*' (17), that which can only be defined by talking about it because it is an internal feeling. So, Smith is interested not only in how structures of power shaped homosexuality but equally the kinds of imaginative vocabulary with which writers could talk about homosexual desire. His book is organized around six myths of homosexual desire that speak to social relations: male power structure, education, festival occasions, religion, social class and perhaps most importantly the private life in which Marlowe and Shakespeare create a homosexual subjectivity, which Smith identifies as a radically hitherto unmapped area of human sexuality. These are myths because they 'enact in symbolic terms what the relevant social institution fosters in actual behavior' (22). And each myth has connections with the other 'official' discourses of medical, moral and legal in which 'poetic discourse often *mediates* between the official ideal and the quotidian real' (22).

The first myth Smith looks at is male bonding, the overarching myth for all the others he discusses. Examining the changing nature of sodomy laws, he shows how charges of sodomy never focused on an interest in sexual relations between two consenting male adults. The emotional interconnections suggested by poetic discourse were important markers of sexual desire. For example, North's translation of Plutarch told male readers how to be male and emphasized bonding but also advocated keeping one's emotional distance: this produced both love and hate for the man, which Smith argues suggests the conjunction of violence and desire in Shakespeare's martial plays or, in say, Iago. So the dilemma for young men facing the necessity of marrying within a patriarchal society 'was not, am I heterosexual or am I homosexual, but where do my greater emotional loyalties lie, with other men or other women' (65). In other words, it was a question of how a woman's presence set at odds friendship between two men. While Renaissance culture saw homosexual potential it only officially sanctioned marriage; moreover, Smith claims, 'Behavior that we would label homosexual, and hence a rejection of maleness, was for them an *aspect* of maleness' (75).

The second myth focuses on place, whether the field or forest, as charged with erotic feeling and the exclusion of women. Smith sees the pastoral as homologue for all male-institutions such as the schools where masculine identity was learned. Latin was 'the tribal language of educated men' (83; translation into English was reprehensible because 'it was to divulge male secrets to women' (84)). Smith identifies Virgil's *Eclogues* as containing both the pleasing landscape with erotic potential but also the place that teaches the perspective of the harsher worlds of social and political life that prevents desires from being realized. Place may also represent the youthful dalliance for the writer and reader before they move on to higher things, in life and in a literary profession. Examples include E. K.'s preference for spiritual pederasty between Colin and Hobbinol in *The Shepheardes Calendar*, the golden age friendship between Leontes and Polixenes before the despoliation of heterosexual love intrudes on their boyhood friendship or Richard Barnfield's masturbatory poems for young men before they progress to the Inns of Court.

The third Myth focuses on festivals: all male cast of morris dancing, for example, or the transvestite role of Maid Marion in which males could flirt with other males precisely because it was a contingent and ephemeral occasion: 'The luminal festivities of Renaissance England, like fraternity hazing in our own day, exorcize homosexual desire by turning it into a game' (128). Working through the homoerotic descriptions of Marlowe's Leander, Smith settles on Beaumont's comment to his 'Salmacis and Hermaphroditus' that he hopes his reader will turn 'halfe-mayd' in reading it. But all the poems he describes, Smith argues, are not about the consummation, but the frustration of male desire for the objects that are described. It is arousal produced in the reader rather than activity apparent in the text itself which is significant here, the youthful androgyny of the subjects appealing to memories of the readers' own adolescence. Hence while there is cross – dressing aplenty in Sidney's *Arcadia*, ultimately, Sidney obeys the convention of genre and treats homosexual desire as a game: 'At the story's end we leave the sexual freedom of Arcadia and return to the strictures of Elizabethan society. It is these strictures, after all, that make romance romantic' (143). Furthermore, the conventional endings of books and plays served, for the reader and spectator, 'as ways of *separating* himself from the fantasies in which he had reveled' (154).

In the fourth myth, Smith focuses on satires as homologues to institutionalized morality. Juvenal and Horace and Martial are used to 'bait men who take sexual pleasure with other men' (161) while making the reader complicit in siding with the moralist and his targets. Smith distinguishes between romance 'which is focused on the boy as an object of desire', and satire which is 'focused on the man who is subject to that desire' (166). Renaissance satirists, he argues, based their descriptions of those who consented to these acts on the court records of prominent lawyer Sir Edward Coke whose descriptions often amounted to caricatures of haughty, overweight aristocrats with too much time in their hands. Ultimately, satire worked by suggesting that 'to give up homosexual desire was to give up one's social and even psychological identity' (185).

The fifth myth examines class: 'homosexual activity in early Modern England, like illicit sexual activity of all sorts, usually involved a person in a superior position of power exercising his social prerogative over a person in an inferior position' (193). And in this discrepancy lay the sexual energy. Smith shows how the 'boy' can figure as a social term of class and opprobrium through the Jove/Ganymede narrative and in renditions of court narratives such as the Villiers/James I relationship. Central to the discussion of sexual desire is the question of political power: in *Edward II*, for example, because social discrepancy is what attracts Edward to Gaveston, we witness 'an eroticization of class difference. [Thus] male bonding is a phenomenon that transcends class distinction' (216).

The final myth focuses on Shakespeare's sonnets and their connection with the intimacy of Horace's love lyrics which positions the reader as a 'secret sharer'. What Smith sees as unique is that the Sonnets are private, often addressed to another man and consider love *after* rather than before sexual consummation. What is important is less Shakespeare's homosexuality than that the 'poems insinuate sexual feeling in the bonds men in general made with one another in early modern England.' 'In the sonnets, Shakespeare seeks to speak about homosexual desire with the same authority that Petrarch assumes in speaking about heterosexual desire. In pursuit of that end Shakespeare invokes three different modes of discourse: Horace's language of erotic experience, the traditional language of courtly love, and the language of Christian marriage' (264). And this subjectivity is what, as Smith claims, makes Shakespeare modern to us.

Influence

Since Smith, there have been numerous studies of sodomy, its range of categories from the catamite to Ganymede, the 'masculine whore' and early Tudor sodomy discourse, its sublimity and its legal discourse. Textual sources range from Marlowe's *Edward II* and Shakespeare's *Troilus and Cressida* to the court letters of Spenser to William Bradford's narrative of a 'sodomite' colonist in the New World (Bredbeck 1991; Goldberg 1992; Halpern 2002). Sodomy has been read in terms of Freud's theories of displacement and condensation to argue that the category epitomized a sexual deviance that stood in for a whole spectrum of evil behaviour, or for an inability to talk about social conflicts such as race and gender (Dollimore 2001). Some studies that emphasize the inevitability of the success of heterosexual over homosexual relations elaborate also the sense of loss inhabiting the work of some of the authors in the period, as they come to recognize the apparent impossibility of a fulfiled homoerotic desire (Sinfield 1994; Guy-Bray 2002). Other critics have used the insights of reader response and reception theory to identify an invitation to read in a homoerotic fashion (Summers and Pebworth 1993), or have critiqued the heterosexist readings of other literary critics (Goldberg 1994).

Andrew Hadfield, *Literature, Politics and National Identity: Reformation to Renaissance* (1994)

Edition cited: *Literature, Politics and National Identity: Reformation to Renaissance*, Cambridge: Cambridge University Press, 1994.

Given the current preoccupation with devolution in the past fifteen to twenty years, including the widespread commentary on the marking of the three hundredth anniversary of the 1707 Act of Union, it should not be surprising that Renaissance studies have likewise focused on nationalism, national identity and the tensions that exist between England, Scotland, Wales and Ireland. A central debate has arisen over whether early modern England ushered in self-conscious nationalism in its role as forerunner of a transformation from an old to a new order (Greenfeld 1992), that was later copied by America, France, Germany and Russia; or whether Englishness and English national identity only developed in the nineteenth century (Kumar 2003). Writers such as Willy Maley have recently argued that Britishness is what defines the writings of Shakespeare, Ford and Spenser. (Maley 2003). Other studies consider how Britishness was constructed and then reified in Civil War and Jacobite literature. (Baker and Maley, 2002). Many studies examine how, through the subjects of law, cartography, exploration, writers were engaged in the idea of writing England (Helgerson 1994). Embodied in this nationalistic project was a desire to fashion a national poetry (see Chapter 8). Spenser's enquiry to his friend Gabriel Harvey, 'may not we . . . have the kingdom of our own language?' is reflected in reading Spenser's *Shepheardes Calendar* and Philip Sidney's *Old Arcadia* as attempts to present a specifically English literary style (Shrank 2005). Other studies define nationalism from a religious rather than political perspective. Thus the reign of Mary Tudor is seen as a watershed in detaching national identity from the personhood of the sovereign while Charles I's execution was in part prepared for by Henry VIII's break from Rome and the subsequent secularization of the state (Grabes 2001).

Hadfield's work is a decisive contribution to the discourse about nationalism/s, although his work is informed also by other theories. For Hadfield, literature was an essential medium through which writers imagined, re-imagined and renegotiated the national community they addressed, but this is not, for him, a teleological process: 'Literary history forms a discontinuous narrative even in terms of its own intra-textual process and to read it as a gradual development is absurd' (4). Hadfield takes issue with both Greenblatt and Dollimore: 'Greenblatt', he claims, 'frequently assumes that all literature functions to contain seemingly subversive utterances ... whereas Dollimore often asserts the converse case, that literature is *ipso facto* oppositional' (19). Hadfield argues instead that no one in the Tudor period was sure about how to write this kind of literature or what it was supposed to do. Should an English literary culture rival a European one? Should it imitate the classics? Should it be produced in the vernacular? The theory which he finds most useful here is Habermas' notion of the public sphere, where citizens gather to argue over matters of public interest. For Hadfield, the political and literary public spheres often overlap: 'Indeed,', he states, 'one might suggest that many sixteenth-century writers explicitly attempted to link the "imagined community" of the nation to a "public sphere," in that they used their fictions to create a critical national literature' (8). And for him, the adoption of the vernacular was pivotal because writers now had to '[renegotiate] the relationship with the political authority under which this writing would exist' (9). As a result, Sixteenth Century writing betrays diverse and sometimes contradictory impulses: 'Literature could be seen as a form of ideological cement in helping to constitute the nation; but also as a public sphere in that it provided writers with a means of separating their utterances from the political constraints of state-approved discourses. It was thus a site of knowledge saturated with ideology and simultaneously a Utopian hope of a free, interactive critical space' (10).

Hadfield starts with a chapter on John Skelton whose poems about laureateship balanced Latin and vernacular English and provided a medium through which he argued for the intervention of the poet in public affairs. His second chapter considers John Bale, whose unwavering Protestant commitment to the absolute rights of the monarch placed him in opposition to those who placed sovereignty in the people. But Hadfield also recognizes Bale as a nationalistic writer, a compiler of a 'recognizable British history of writing, a native voice, to complement the history of a distinct native church established in his other writings' (70). The third chapter focuses on *Mirror for Magistrates*. Hadfield suggests that John Lydgate's *Fall of Princes* was a precursor of *Mirror* melding unchanging moral lessons for man with 'an awareness of historic change which negates this certainty and is acutely conscious of a national development' (89). Subsequent, revised editions of *Mirror* sought to 're-work British and English material to form a chronological account of the nation's origins' (101). Most fruitful is his suggestion that even literary theory during the period had nationalism as its focus. He explores Thomas Wilson's invocation of a specifically Protestant national reader who could empathize with his experiences with Mary I and commit to use language in such as way as to preserve the hierarchical order in the state. With George Puttenham, Hadfield argues that we have the emergence of the courtier-poet 'who by rights claim the English public sphere' (131).

In a chapter on Sidney's *An Apologie for Poetry*, Hadfield argues that Sidney contributed to Puttenham's desire to identify poetry as the 'site of national knowledge' (138) by recording his shame at the current state of poetry. Without poetry, a national identity might perish. So heroic poetry links the fate of nations with individuals who lead them. Particular poets, like Surrey, are picked out by Sidney because of their concern to establish a national literary culture. But, suggests Hadfield, this desire for a noble voice 'was designed to kill off a vernacular Protestant literary tradition and replace it with a consciously aristocratic one. To this end, Sidney was instrumental in telescoping, restricting and making more class-bound a varied vernacular poetic tradition and attempting to use the legacy of Surrey to establish a dominant form of national literature' (145). His final chapter examines Edmund Spenser suggesting that Spenser used the figure of Colin Clout to appeal to the common people rather than to Sidney's noble, court culture (which had rejected Spenser's work). For Hadfield, the *Shepheardes Calendar* can be read as a critique of a polemic Protestantism but it also addresses the failure of Spenser's courtly suit to Elizabeth. In this way it utilizes the pastoral genre as a mode for a critical commentary on the English court and national policy, which enables him to articulate larger issues, such as his own identity in Ireland. Spenser's exilic feeling is replicated in *Colin Clouts Come Home Againe* that announces the new English in Ireland as the shepherd nation, 'the guardians of a tradition of English public poetry which is able to stand outside and by-pass the constraints of a purely courtly culture' (189). So while Hadfield begins his book by suggesting the role that poetry played in creating a specific sense of Englishness located in mainland England, he concludes by implying that its definition was fluid and dependent on definitions of target readers and the political sympathies of its writers.

Influence

Hadfield's elaboration of the formation in literature of a national identity has been contested by a number of studies which argue against any sense of national coherency. Some have examined texts such as *I Henry IV* and *Henry V* (in relation to Wales,) or Jacobean masques to question the strength of the Union

(Baker and Maley 2002) and to suggest that any sense of national British cohesion was undermined by the persistence of a profound and compelling sense of disunity. Philip Schwyzer has argued, for example, that King Lear abjures rather than supports a notion of a unified nation since the play ends without the promise of marriage or children, and hence implies a country unable to guarantee its future (Schwyzer 2004). Other critics have suggested that nationalistic myths were, at their best, tenuous. The essayists in Alan Shephard and Stephen Powell's collection link (2005) what they see as the fragility of the mythos of early modern nationalism to a sense of loss wherein the past was perceived as either irretrievable or apocalyptic which, in either case, compromises any clear sense of the future of the nation.

Ania Loomba, *Shakespeare, Race and Colonialism* (2002)

Edition cited: *Shakespeare, Race and Colonialism*, Oxford: Oxford University Press, 2002.

Definitions of national identity were wrapped up not only in concepts of regional difference but also in notions of race and imperialism. (Tokson 1970; Barthelemy 1987; Erikson and Hulse 2000). A number of studies have been conducted on depictions of blackness in relation to nationalism; among them are Hendricks and Parker (1994), Hall (1995), Callaghan (2000), Vaughan (2005) and Iyenger (2005). But by far the most precisely written account of how skin colour was understood in terms of ethnic origin, moral character and sexual chastity has been written by Ania Loomba.

In our account of Bruce Smith's *Homosexual Desire in Elizabethan England* we noted that Smith begins by questioning the received understanding of the categories employed today to define sexualities. A very similar strategy is adopted by Loomba, who begins her lucidly written book by acknowledging the dangers of creating anachronistic readings of race in the early modern period, asking whether we have adequate vocabularies to describe it. She posits the suggestion that race reflects social rather than natural divisions so that it 'historically has been deployed to reinforce existing social hierarchies and create new ones' (3). New markets and colonies during the early modern period led Europeans towards a new cultural openness, Loomba argues, but paradoxically, they also generated an insularity towards that which was 'foreign' in their own nations. Loomba sees the early modern formation of difference as profoundly affecting our own sense of difference today. 'Shakespeare's plays', she claims, 'have been an extraordinarily powerful medium between generations and cultures, a conduit for transmitting and shaping ideas about colonialism and race' (5). She identifies the three main ideas about race in this period: inheritance of classical and medieval ideas, newer cross-cultural ideas due to extended contact during Shakespeare's own times, and other notions of difference based on class and gender that interacted with difference based on race. For her, the crucial point here is not so much the relative distribution of races in Renaissance England, but the representation of those races. She argues that as England was created as a modern nation inter-national webs of filiation were dissolved and a unified imagined community arose in its place, which was instrumental in establishing both modernity and racism in the attempt to shape others in the Europeans' own image. Anxiety about cross-cultural encounters reflected on the inside and outside of the theatrical space: inside, 'outsiders' are transformed into the dominant culture, whereas outside, the English might convert to the cultures of those they live among. So a hardening of racial categories existed alongside an acknowledgement of hybridity.

An explanation of this internally competing intersection of discourses characterizes each of Loomba's six chapters. In chapter one for example, she identifies race as connected variously to concepts of lineage and family, sexuality and concepts of national affiliation. To assert that one belonged to England or Britain was to acknowledge nationalism as a racialized term. But notions of race were complicated by intersections of religion, gender and class. In the figure of the 'race' of Amazons, for instance, anxieties about gender overlapped with anxieties about the foreign and exotic; conversely higher social classes were frequently figured in the literature of the period as being nobler races, a discourse which overlapped significantly with later rationalizations of blackness. Beliefs in the genetic superiority of the male help to explain why no union can be allowed between Caliban and Miranda; Caliban, indeed, condensing attributes of race and of class, being 'an amalgam of location, religion, culture, language, sexuality and physique, all of which are part of the discourse of "race" which was to remain volatile and variable in years to come' (35).

In the second chapter, Loomba suggests that an amalgam of skin colour and religion helped produce notions of skin difference (20). She looks at distinctions between Aaron's blackness in *Titus Andronicus* (which is negatively equated with sin,) and Othello's (which is positively associated with lineage). These conflicting associations reflect the complicated histories of interaction between the West and the East. Such interaction produced anxieties about the influence of the other on the Western body, such as the fear that the adoption of practices such as body piercing and tattoos from another culture would issue in biological consequences: 'once the body is altered by these cultural practices, Nature retaliates by reproducing the effect of these practices and bringing forth monsters at birth' (63).

The other four chapters work out these implications in the plays of *Titus Andronicus, Othello, Anthony and Cleopatra* and *The Merchant of Venice*. With *Titus*, Loomba examines race in the context of ideas of female deviance: 'older stereotypes about barbarism, black sexuality, and evil evoked by Aaron', she claims, 'mediate newer anxieties about nation, religion, race, and femininity' (76). Aaron's blackness is complicated by his status as slave which confirms the servility associated with skin colour, while his irreligious sentiments tag him with the immorality of the Sub-Saharan black in contrast to the North African

Muslim Moor whose lighter skin colour denotes less immorality. In considering the way in which the play deconstructs the overlapping binary oppositions of Rome/Goths and civility/barbarity, Loomba considers the role of Tamora, arguing that her whiter hue is acceptable in her alliance with Saturninus; it is her ambition and relationship with Aaron that establishes her alien status. Tamora, Amazon-like, is threatening because she is older, and sexually desiring; the fatal combination for the Roman state then is Aaron's blackness and her dangerous femininity. In her treatment of *Othello*, she focuses on complications posed by Islam. She notes that Othello's racial identity is uncertain in the play: he appears to be a hybrid of the inferior 'blackamoor' and superior Moor, the sub-Saharan African and the 'turbaned Turk' betraying ways 'in which medieval as well as newer ideas about blacks and Muslims intersected in early Modern England' (92). This interconnectivity between past and present (see Chapter 8) informs Loomba's discussion of *Anthony and Cleopatra*, which she sees as a play which explores the complicated layering of classical past's idea of empire and sexuality with contemporary anxiety about colonial contact. Egyptian culture, she argues, is again represented as a hybrid, including aspects of Greek and Turkish influences, and betrays the English tendency to conflate Egyptians with gypsies. Loomba reads *The Merchant of Venice* as an exploration of connections between commerce and race. She suggests that the complaints in the play about stark economies – Jessica's conversion raising the price of pork, for example – mirrored Elizabethan edicts promising the eviction of 'negars and Blackamoors' from England in 1596 because they consumed what ought to be eaten by white people. 'The links between conversion and inflation', she argues, '. . . underline the play's interest in interweaving sexual and racial exchanges with economic ones' (138).

All of the last four chapters of Loomba's book suggest that issues about race, ethnicity and identity formed a diachronic discourse into which older conceptions of relations between East and West were woven, inflecting the articulation of contemporary debates. In her conclusion, Loomba focused on *The Tempest* again insisting on the circulation of multivalent discourses. She points out the narrowing of critical attention on the New World alone in *The Tempest* whereas the inclusion of references to North African, the Moorish appearance of Sycorax from Algiers, and the possible analogies to Ireland suggest 'the historical interconnections *between* different encounters – the Irish experience, according to some historians prepared the English for their American forays, while according to others, attitudes to Native Americans coloured English opinions about Moors. Thus, the multiple valences of *The Tempest* remind us of the global connections inaugurated by colonialism' (167).

Influence

Loomba's emphasis on the circulating discourses of race, gender and class across transnational lines is characteristic of a number of studies which have attempted to link colonialist preoccupations with internal struggles of domination and control. The British relation with Ireland has been compared to the relation to Bermuda and Virginia, configured as the 'Atlantic world' in which England exerted a variety of improvised powers and articulated fear and curiosity as well as crude, racialized dominance (Bach 2000). The term 'imperium studies' has been coined as a way of foregrounding the powerful political and cultural legacies behind these current fictions of nationhood (Ingham and Warren 2003). Meanwhile, Loomba's sense of the fluid definitions of race in the early modern period is supported by other studies that focus predominately on relations between race and colonialism. Such work suggests that race then was based on lineage, genealogy and social rank as well as skin colour. In their synchronically rich collection, for example, Beidler and Taylor (2005) present essays that critique the concept of hybridity, that examine how the Roman occupation of Britain influenced British attitudes towards the colonization of Virginia; that discuss how the discovery of the 'caucasoid' Kennewick Man parallels early modern claims for prior white occupation of the New World and that consider the dangers posed to European households by Moorish servants, such as the serving maid Zanche in John Webster's White Devil. Similarly, Barbara Fuchs' *Mimesis and Empire: The New World, Islam, and European Identities* (2001) points out imitative concepts of behaviours in say the equation of Islamic Barbary corsairs with English pirates. This leads her to call for further comparisons – between, for example, the English experience in Ireland and the Spanish with the Moriscos – in order to suggest that the manipulation of sameness and difference was a constant preoccupation of the period.

5 Key Critical Concepts and Topics

Nate Eastman

Chapter Overview

Allegory

At its most basic, an allegory is a story with more than one meaning. It can therefore be understood and interpreted at two or more levels. In this sense allegory is similar to (but more structurally intricate than) fable, and is a more general category than the parable; Renaissance allegory includes pictorial texts such as emblem books, and need not always be religiously explicable.

That said, much Renaissance allegory has a religious tenor and is doubtless rooted in understandings of scriptural allegory set forth in Aquinas' *Summa* (thirteenth century), which describes a four-layered allegorical structure where textual objects have simultaneous literal, symbolic, moral and anagogical meanings. Perhaps the most often-quoted example of this is his reading of Jerusalem, which is (literally) a city, (symbolically) the Church Militant, (morally) the righteous soul and (anagogically) the Church triumphant.

But classical allegorical models were perhaps even more influential – especially Prudentius' *Psychomachia* (fourth century), which allegorizes the mental processes of decision making by personifying various virtues and vices. This allegorical tradition has clear descendants in the Morality Play and the Comedy of Humours, as well as a range of other texts where characters are named aptronymically, their names describing their occupations or qualities.

The most famous Renaissance allegories are doubtless Spenser's *The Faerie Queene* (1589, 1596) and Tasso's *Gerusalemme Liberata* (1574), but these draw on a tradition of Medieval allegory including Gilliaume de Lorris' *Roman de la Rose* (thirteenth century), Dante's *Divina Commedia* (thirteenth century), and Langland's *Piers Plowman* (fourteenth century). Renaissance allegory would also deeply influence Bunyan's *Pilgrim's Progress* (1678), and the allegorical elements of the Comedy of Humours and City Comedy would give rise to a late seventeenth and early eighteenth century rash of satirical allegory, including Dryden's *Absalom and Achitophel* (1681) and Swift's *Tale of a Tub* (1704). For an analysis of an extract from *The Faerie Queene* see Chapter 3.

Antimasque

A masquing innovation introduced in Ben Jonson's *Masque of Queens* (1609), in which a short episode thematically contrasts with the masque proper. This episode generally takes the form of a grotesque interlude or introduction. (In this last case it is more properly termed an *antemasque*.) For example, the *Masque of Queens* begins with a dozen witches who testify to their crimes before falling into a dance 'full of preposterous change and gesticulation'. These witches are interrupted and dispelled by the introduction of the masque proper, with its House of Fame and twelve Queens.

It is worth noting that the antimasque is the culmination of earlier Jonsonian experiments with the masquing form. The *Masque of Beauty* (1608), for instance, is a continuation of the *Masque of Blacknesse* (1605) and a deliberate contrast to it; *Hymenai* (1606) makes explicit the Jonsonian idea that the rhetorical and visual splendour of the masque should set forth some central idea. These two Jonsonian experiments converge in the typical antimasque, which uses contrast to explicate this central idea.

Ballad (Ballet)

Ballads have traditionally been understood as the musical accompaniment to a dance (or, in the case of Renaissance ballads for which the music is lost, the lyrical components of the musical accompaniment to a dance). But ballads are generally also stories told through dialogue and action, usually in simple language and with incremental repetition and predictable refrains. The imagery is generally sparse, and the definitions of character (where they exist at all) are often simple.

As opposed to the Old French *Ballade* form occasionally imitated by Gower and Chaucer (three eight-line stanzas rhyming ababbcbc with an *envoi* rhyming bcbc), Renaissance ballads generally comprise quatrains of alternating tetrameter and trimeter, rhyming either abab or abcb. In this respect the first stanza of *The Gest of Robyn Hode* (1515) is typical:

> Lythe and listin, gentilmen,
> That be of frebore blode;
> I shall you tel of a gode yeman,
> His name was Robyn Hode.

For ballads like the *Gest*, which almost certainly existed as part of an oral tradition before they were printed, these formal cues are the clearest differentiation from the more general folksong or from lays such as *Havelok the Dane* or *Sir Launfal*. But not all ballads originated orally. So-called 'literary ballads' were written by poets as they composed them, and are (unlike other ballads) not anonymous; excellent examples of these are Skelton's *Ballade of the Scotyshe Kynge* (1513) or Suckling's *Ballade Upon a Wedding* (1646).

Similarly, 'broadside ballads' were written (generally anonymously) to circulate news of doings in London or abroad; an excellent example of this is *The Long Nos'd Lass* (*c.* 1685), which details the ill-fated courtship of a woman (presumably Tannakin Skinker, a real life gentlewoman with a facial deformity, who was born around 1618 and whose 'visage was perfectly just like a sow'). This broadside ballad, like many others, is probably best conceived as one facet of a durable folk tradition that included other media (such as pamphlets, songs or on and off-stage jokes), but broadside ballads were also often ideologically loaded. *The Long Nos'd Lass*, though it seems an unlikely vehicle for English nationalism, is principally a joke told at the expense of non-English suitors to its eponymous hog-faced gentlewoman.

Bed Trick

This is the clandestine sexual substitution of one person for another. This is generally, although not always, used to compel a man's marriage to the substitute woman, and has a long literary history. The book of Genesis, with which Renaissance audiences would have been thoroughly familiar, tells of Jacob being tricked into wedding Leah after she is substituted for Rachel, her younger sister. Renaissance audiences may have also been familiar with the seduction of Alcmene by Zeus, who took the form of her husband, Amphitryon (and so fathered Hercules on the unsuspecting woman). The bed trick also appears in Arthurian legend and fabliaux.

The most famous Renaissance bed tricks are Shakespeare's, in *Measure for Measure* (1604), *All's Well that Ends Well* (*c.* 1605), and a short biographical anecdote by contemporary law student John Manningham:

Vpon a tyme when Burbidge played Richard III. there was a citizen grone soe farr in liking with him, that before shee went from the play shee appointed him to come that night vnto hir by the name of Richard the Third. Shakespeare ouerhearing their conclusion went before, was intertained and at his game ere Burbidge came. Then message being brought that Richard the Third was at the dore, Shakespeare caused returne to be made that William the Conqueror was before Richard the Third. Shakespeare's name William.[1]

Blank Verse

Blank Verse is unrhymed iambic pentameter, and was introduced by Henry Howard, Earl of Surrey, in his translation of the *Aeneid* (*c.* 1540). During the sixteenth century, it became (and remains) one of the most widely used English verse forms, and was particularly favoured by for drama (beginning with Sackville and Norton's 1561 *Gorboduc*). It was also used for reflective and narrative poems, most notably Milton's *Paradise Lost* (1667).

Blazon

Though the term was generally used to mean 'coat of arms', it also refers to the Petrarchan tradition of describing the parts of a woman's body in poetic detail, creating a catalogue of her physical virtues. Sidney's *Arcadia* (1590) provides an excellent example:

> What tongue can her perfection tell
> In whose each part all tongues may dwell?
> Her hair fine threads of purest gold,
> In curled knots man's thought to hold [. . .] (*Arcadia*, Book II)

After this convention quickly and inevitably tired, it was parodied in the *contre-blazon*, or *antiblazon*, the most famous of which is doubtless Shakespeare's sonnet 130, 'My Mistress' Eyes are Nothing Like the Sun.' (1609), though Greene's *Menaphon* (1598) may present the most memorable:

> Thy teeth like to the tusks of fattest swine,
> Thy Speech is like the thunder in the air:
> Would God thy toes, they lips, and all were mine.[2]

Broadsheets

Also known as broadsides, these were sheets of paper printed on one side and either distributed by hand, much as small-circulation newspapers are in modern cities. These were largely used for disseminating news or like information as well as songs and ballads. Their distribution began in the early sixteenth century and continued into the early twentieth.

Carnival

Originally a feast observed by Roman Catholics before the Lenten fast began and, more broadly, an occasion or season of revels, carnival now more often suggests the symbolic disruption, subversion, or inversion of social authority in a process Mikhail Bakhtin calls 'carnivalization' (in *The Dialogic Imagination*).

Bakhtin suggests that carnival in literature is necessarily subversive, since it subverts authority and introduces farcical alternatives to it; this aspect of his theories, expressed in his readings of *Gargantua and Pantagruel*, are enumerated in *Rabelais and His World*.

Cavalier Poets

Poets of the early seventeenth century are generally broken into two groups: the Metaphysicals (who stylistically follow Donne) and the Cavaliers (who stylistically follow Jonson) – although it is occasionally useful to imagine a third school of poets stylistically similar to Drayton (for instance, Browne, Drummond, Davies, Sandys, Sylvester and Wyther).

The best known Cavaliers are Jonson, Herrick, Lovelace, Suckling, Fane, Denham, Waller and Carew (who is often also numbered among the Metaphysicals), as well as Lord Herbert of Cherbury, Townshend, Cartwright, Randolph, Fanshawe and Graham. The Cavalier poets are also associated with political support of Charles I during the English Civil War, and were generally courtiers (although Herrick is a notable exception).

Cavalier poetry differs from Metaphysical poetry in that it is light, elegant, witty and secular. The Cavaliers also abandoned the sonnet, which until them was the preferred vehicle for love poetry.

Chapbooks

Popular literature sold by pedlars or 'chapmen' between the sixteenth and eighteenth centuries, generally consisting of ballads, pamphlets, tracts and stories from folklore. These were often illustrated with woodcuts and notoriously inexpensive (1–6 *d.*). Two popular (and often reprinted) examples are the romances *Bevis of Hampton* and *Guy of Warwick*.

City Comedy

Also known as 'citizen comedy', this was a type of play popular during the early seventeenth century, and was generally about life in contemporary London. The characters were based around those likely to be found in middle or lower-middle classes (such as innkeepers, apprentices and soldiers). City comedy is also differentiable from earlier comedies in its reliance on more elaborate sets (including stage properties as complicated as storefronts, whose quickly-dropping shutters occasionally brain passing ne'er-do-wells) as well as quick and often intricate pacing. Jonson's *Alchemist* (1610) is an excellent example of the latter.

These plays are generally of two types. One type celebrates the lives of ordinary citizens, as in Dekker's *Shoemakers' Holiday* (1600). The second depicts (and usually celebrates) London as a cauldron of vice, as in Jonson's *Devil is an Ass* (1616) or Middleton's *Chaste Maid in Cheapside* (*c.* 1613). This second type, with its exhibition of domestic vices and various domestic intrigues, might be considered a forerunner to the Restoration Comedy of Manners.

Class

The hierarchical structure, or distinctions between individuals or groups, in Renaissance England is fraught with complexities, but we can arguably consider class during this period in terms of individuals' and groups' social proximity to governing bodies – most notably the Crown, but also, for example, London's Aldermen. While the latter was roughly governed by wealth, occupational prestige, family structures and society membership (principally guilds during the Early Renaissance, but an increasingly diverse set of organizations as the sixteenth and seventeenth centuries progressed), social proximity to the Crown was largely a function of an individual or group's hereditary situation, position in the Church or place in the initially-small-but-ever-growing bureaucracy surrounding the day-to-day functions of government.

Close Reading

Close reading is the careful, detailed and sustained interpretation of a short passage of a text, paying close attention to the syntax, word choice, ambiguities and sentence-level images and tropes. This process took its modern form in I. A. Richards' *Practical Criticism* (1929), and was more thoroughly developed by Richards' student William Empson and by the New Critics. This parallels a similar technique in French literary study (*explication de text*) popularized by Gustave Lanson, and has extensive precedent in explicatory traditions of religious texts.

The end of New Criticism has perhaps overshadowed the fact that good close readings are essential components of any textual criticism, no matter what other methods the critic brings to the text.

Comedy

In his *Apologie for Poetrie* (1595), Sidney calls comedy 'an imitation of the common errors of life [. . .] represent[ed] in the most ridiculous and scornful sort that may be; so that it is impossible that any beholder can be content to be such a one'. He goes on to explain that comedy traffics in 'our private and domestical matters' so that 'in the actions of our life who seeth not the filthiness of evil wanteth a great foile to perceive the beauty of vertue'. Sidney's comedy, in other words, is defined both by its subject matter (common errors of life) and by a social objective (the recognition and reformation of these errors by the audience).

This idea of comedy, and of comedy's reformative purpose, is shared by Puttenham, who in his *Arte of English Poesie* writes that comedy is 'tended altogether to the amendment of man by discipline and example'. While this perceived tendency of comedy to concentrate on the details of everyday life has its critical origins in Aristotle, the idea that comedy is explicitly reformative has been intermittent and (even during the Renaissance) unevenly applied. Among the Romans, for instance, Evanthius, Diomedes and Donatus were in fundamental agreement about comedy's concentration on the everyday (though Diomedes adds that comedy is generally about the romantic seduction or abduction of maidens), but only Donatus suggests that comedy has a moral or didactic quality.

During the Middle Ages, the definitive quality of comedy was that it begins with misfortune and ends with joy; while Johannes Januensis' *Catholicon* (1286) also argues that comedy necessarily deals with the matters of private men and is written in a humble style, Dante's *Epistle to Can Grande* (*c.* 1310) derives 'comedy' from *comos* (village) and *oda* (song), suggesting that comedy is rustic in style rather than necessarily humble; Dante also expands comedy's characteristic improvement of fortune to metaphysical grounds, beginning his *Divina Commedia* (*c.* 1308–21) with *Inferno* and ending it in *Paradiso*. Lydgate's *Chronicle of Troy* (1430) defines comedy in similarly broad strokes, claming that it begins in 'a manner complaynynge, / and afterwarde endeth in gladnesse'. It is worth noting that all these critics of the Middle Ages were discussing poetry rather than drama.

Renaissance comedy is, perhaps unsurprisingly, something of a lumpy mixture of Classical and Medieval comic priorities. Early Renaissance comedies, such as Udall's *Ralph Roister Doister* (*c.* 1553), *Gammer Gurton's Needle* (1566) and Gascoigne's *Supposes* (1566) take as their subjects everyday people, but do not consistently move towards a reformation of the audience; in *Gammer Gurton* and *Ralph Roister Doister*, the movement from misfortune to joy is on farcical terms, if any.

Shakespeare and Jonson, the major writers of dramatic comedy between 1590 and 1630, are similarly diverse in their conceptions of comedy. Shakespeare wrote no extant satirical comedy, so while his comedy generally deals with private persons and improves on some initial misfortune, it makes no clear attempts to reform its audience. It also ranges from the farcical (*The Merry Wives of Windsor*) to the disconcerting (*Measure for Measure* and *All's Well that Ends Well*) to anticipations of later forms like the comedy of manners (*Much Ado About Nothing*).

Jonson's comedy is, in contrast, almost exclusively satirical; while almost all Jonsonian comedy makes some attempt to reform its audience, those attempts are on occasionally baffling terms, and it is often more productive to consider Jonsonian comedy in terms of the vices or foibles it exposes rather than those it tries to reform. This exposure defines the structure of his comedies of humors: *Every Man in His Humour* (1598), *Every Man out of His Humour* (1599) and *The Magnetic Lady* (1632), as well as many of his city comedies, such as *The Alchemist* (1610) and *The Devil is an Ass* (1616). Other notable writers of comedy for this period include John Lyly, Robert Greene, George Peele, John Marston, Philip Massinger, Thomas Dekker, John Beaumont, John Fletcher, George Chapman and Thomas Heywood.

Comedy of Humours

A species of drama that became popular with Ben Jonson's *Every Man in His Humor* (1598) and remained popular through the beginning of the seventeenth century. It is named for its comic structure, in which characters are chiefly defined (and their conflicts chiefly motivated) by a particular passion, trait or disposition associated (sometimes loosely) with the four 'humors' (bodily fluids) of Galenic medicine: blood, choler (yellow bile), phlegm and melancholy (black bile). Characters in a Comedy of Humours were consequently generally sanguine (energetic or manic), choleric (ambitious or bad-tempered), phleg-matic (calm or lazy) or melancholy (creative, depressed or obsessed with tragedy and cruelty). In Jonson, at least, Humorous characters are named aptronymically, as with Knowell, Kitely, and Brainworm in *Every Man in*.

This type of one-dimensional characterization has clear ancestry in both Morality Plays and Allegories (as well as intermediate forms like the Interlude), though Jonson seems to have been the first to significantly elaborate on these personalities or to use the natural tension and conflicts between them to motiv-ate a dramatic plot. Aside from *Every Man in*, other Comedies of Humors include Jonson's *Every Man out of His Humor* (1599) and his forgettable *Magnetic Lady, or Humors Reconciled*, as well as Chapman's *All Fools* (c. 1604), Middleton's *A Trick to Catch the Old One* (1605), and its derivative, Massinger's *A New Way to Pay Old Debts* (1625); the genre was revived during the Restoration by Shadwell, with *The Squire of Alsatia* (1688) and *Bury Fair* (1689).

Country House Poem

A minor verse genre endemic to the seventeenth century, in which the poet extols the good qualities of a friend or patron through praise of his estate's beauties and fruitfulness, as well as the excellence of its domestic economies. Perhaps the most famous of these is Ben Jonson's 'To Penshurst' (1616) which praises the Kent estate of the Sidney family (where Sir Philip Sidney was born). But while Jonson's 'Penshurst' was perhaps most often imitated, the earliest country house poem is Aemilia Lanyer's 'Description of Cookham', which was included as a dedicatory verse with her 1611 printing of *Salve Deus Rex Judaeorum*.

Other examples of the Country House poem include Carew's 'To Saxham' (1640) and Marvell's 'Upon Appleton House' (*c.* 1650–52).

Courtly Love (see Petrarch)

Eclogue

A short pastoral poem (or a pastoral excerpt from a larger work) in the form of a dialogue or a soliloquy. The form, used to describe Virgil's bucolic poems, was revived by Dante, Petrarch and Boccaccio and became particularly popular during the fifteenth and sixteenth centuries. Spenser's *Shepheardes Calendar* (1579) is the most well known example from this period, though Barclay wrote several while at Ely (1515–21) and Pope would later attempt the form.

Elegy

Though modern readers often associate the elegy with mourning for an individual or the lament of some tragedy, the term was more expansive during the late fifteenth and early sixteenth centuries. Subjects were various – for instance, Donne wrote both the elegies *His Picture* and *On His Mistris*, neither of which are poems of mourning in the same sense as, for instance, Milton's *Lycidas* (1637).

Emblem Books

An emblem books is a collection of symbolic pictures and associated mottos. These generally also contain *explicato* (expositions) of the meanings for each picture/motto entry. The most famous Emblem book from this period is almost certainly Quarles' *Emblemes* (1635).

Epic

An epic is a long narrative poem about the deeds of warriors and heroes, broadly and grandly conceived. Epics often incorporate history, folk tales, legends and myths, and are often of national significance, in the sense that they both envision a culture's literary and social priorities on a magnificent scale and imagine a past built both around these priorities and a myth of national or cultural unity.

Unlike earlier epics, which are generally thought to have origins in oral verse forms, Renaissance epics are decidedly literary – either whole cloth retellings of myths or legends, entirely new stories or translations. John Harington's translation of Ariosto's *Orlando Furioso* (1591) probably marks the high point of epic's popularity during the English Renaissance; Robert Greene published his dramatic adaptation of Ariosto (*The Historie of Orlando Furioso*) in 1592, and Spenser published sections of his *Faerie Queene* in 1589 and 1596.

Epic experienced a brief resurgence of popularity in the middle of the seventeenth century, which saw the beginning of Milton's *Paradise Lost* (1667) and Cowley's (unfinished) *Davideis* (1656). The later seventeenth century saw a reduction of the scale and scope of epic even as its trappings were retained; Dryden's *Absalom and Achitophel* (1681) is an excellent example of this briefer heroic form.

Epigram

Coleridge called the epigram

> A dwarfish whole,
> Its body brevity, and wit its soul.[3]

The term itself derives from the Greek for 'inscription', which nicely captures its classical evolution. The epigram was originally an inscription on a monument, but later became a genre in its own right, with Roman authors (most notably Martial) composing extensive collections.

The most famous practitioners of the Renaissance epigram were Jonson, Donne and Herrick, although Isabella Whitney, England's first professional secular poet, wrote dozens of epigrammatic verses that were collected in her *Sweet Nosgay, or Pleasant Poesie* (1573).

Epithalamion

From the Greek 'at the bridal chamber', an epithalamion is sung outside the bride's room on her wedding night. Sappho is commonly credited with inventing the form, which was revived during the Renaissance. In England, the form was exercised by Sidney, Donne, Jonson, Herrick, Marvell, Crashaw, Dryden and, most notably, Spenser (who may have written his for his 1594 wedding).

Folio

From the Latin *folium*, or 'leaf'. This refers to a book made by folding a printer's sheet only once (to make two leaves or four pages). Folios were generally more expensive than quarto and octavo texts, and so were generally reserved for classics and pulpit bibles. Folios are perhaps best known today as comprehensive collections of the works of Jonson and Shakespeare, though the practice of publishing English plays in folio was uncommon in the early seventeenth century and unheard of before that point.

Genre

A form, class or kind of literature deriving from the French. The major classical genres (in roughly descending order of prestige) were: epic, tragedy, lyric, comedy and satire. In the Renaissance, these genres were highly conventional, and authors were often expected to follow the rules that writing in a genre prescribed; this is one reason Sidney called tragicomedy a 'mungrell' – it described a group of plays that did not adhere to classical genre formulae.

History

During the English Renaissance, this refers to a play based on chronicle material (i.e. recorded history) rather than myth, legend or history from non-chronicle (classical or Biblical) sources. Even so, there is often considerable overlap between Histories and Tragedies. Shakespeare's *Richard III*, now considered a History, was titled *The Tragedy of King Richard III* in its first printing (the 1597 quarto) and *The Tragedy of Richard III* in the First Folio (1623); Marlowe's *Dr. Faustus* (*c.* 1588) is fully titled *The Tragical History of Doctor Faustus*. Other plays, such as *King Lear* (1606) present problems of classification because they substantially alter chronicle material and, in the case of *Lear* specifically, self-classify differently in different printings: the 1608 *Lear* quarto is titled *The True Chronicle of the History of the Life and Death of King Lear and His Three Daughters*, while the 1623 Folio simply calls the play *The Tragedy of King Lear*.

Early history plays, such as Bale's *Kynge Johan* (*c.* 1538), Sackville and Norton's *Gorboduc* (1561) and Preston's *Cambises* (1569) have clear ancestors in Moralities and Interludes, combining, for instance, historical and allegorical content. Marlowe's *Edward II* (1593) more fully develops the genre, and by the time of Shakespeare's first tetralogy (*1–3 Henry VI* and *Richard III* (*c.* 1588–*c.* 1591)) the History seems to have been an established genre and popular, perhaps partly owing to the surge of English Patriotism that followed the 1588 defeat of the Spanish Armada.

While with Comedies and Tragedies Shakespeare shares the stage with other luminaries such as Marlowe and Jonson, Shakespeare's Histories dominate the genre. Shakespeare wrote at least ten histories (his second tetralogy, *Richard II, 1–2 Henry IV* and *Henry V* (*c.* 1595 *c.* 1599) along with *King John* (*c.* 1595) and *Henry VIII* (*c.* 1593)). Claims have been made for two more: *Edward III* (1596) and *Sir Thomas More* (*c.* 1592). Other dramatists also contributed to the genre; Fletcher's *Boudica* (1619) and Ford's *Perkin Warbeck* (1634) are typical examples.

Humanism

A Renaissance revival of interest in Classical literature that came largely at the expense of Medieval scholasticism. The long-term effects of this revival were immense, and led to an increasing devotion to classical ideas as the seventeenth century progressed.

This revival was intellectually and philosophically divers, but its tenor was the dignity and nobility of man – an aesthetic inconceivable in Medieval philosophies but well expressed by Hamlet:

> What a piece of work is man. How noble in reason, how infinite in faculty. In form and moving how express and admirable. In action, how like and angel; in apprehension, how like a god. (Hamlet, 2.2.303–06)

Interlude

A short (and in the Renaissance, generally dramatic) entertainment staged between the acts of a play or the courses of a banquet, although the genre's signature is brevity rather than any single species of content; most dramatic interludes are about one thousand lines long, and it is generally accepted that they were performed as court entertainments, in the houses of the nobility, at the Inns of Court or in University Colleges. Unlike other entertainments often staged in these venues, interludes seem to have been performed by professional actors, such as Henry VIII's 'Players of the King's Interludes'.

Additionally, interludes can be usefully divided into two types: the popular, which generally allegorize well-worn religious doctrine, dramatize familiar religious matter and are often cross-categorized as Moralities (e.g. *Mankind* (c. 1465–70)), and the aristocratic or courtly, which allegorizes political wisdom or dramatizes history or classical mythology (e.g. *Fulgens and Lucrece* (1497)) – although (as in *The Play Called the Foure P.P.* (c. 1520–22)) this can be done satirically and with an occasionally inventive ribaldry that recalls the *fabliau*.

Though interludes were exceptionally popular in England from about 1550–1580, they are a comparatively old and pan-European form, similar (if not essentially identical to) the Italian *intermezzi*, the French *entrements* and the Spanish *entremeses*; in England, at least, the interlude became an established form of entertainment during the early fourteenth century. Other notable examples of the interlude include *The Pride of Life* (c. 1300–25), *The Castle of Perseverence* (c. 1400–25), *Hyckescorner* (1512), *Youth* (c. 1518–28), Heywood's *Play of the Wether* (c. 1527), *Thersites* (1537), Udall's *Respublica* (c. 1533), Wever's *Lusty Juventis* (c. 1550) and *Like Will to Like* (1567).

Lyric

While classical lyrics were meant to be sung to the accompaniment of a lyre, Renaissance lyrics are short poems (usually between a dozen and fifty lines) that express the thoughts and feelings of a speaker in a personal way. The breadth of this definition means that there is an immense variety of lyric poetry (sonnets, for instance, are often considered a subset of the lyric form).

Early sixteenth century English lyrics, such as those of Wyatt and Surrey, were heavily influenced by Petrarch and Ronsard. But as the sixteenth century progressed and the lyric increased in popularity, Sidney, Daniel, Shakespeare, Campion, Southwell, Drayton, Donne, Jonson and others developed a decidedly less continental lyrical style. The best known publication of lyrics during the Renaissance is almost certainly *Songes and Sonettes, written by the ryght honorable Lorde Henry Haward late Earle of Surrey* (usually called *Tottel's Miscellany*) (1557), which was reprinted several times during the sixteenth and seventeenth centuries.

Masque

An elaborate form of courtly entertainment, particularly popular during the reigns of Elizabeth I, James I and Charles I in England, as well as in France and Italy (where the masque first acquired its distinctive form). The masque itself combines poetic drama, song, music and dance in a spectacle that roughly approximates modern opera. Like opera, masque costumes were sumptuous and the sets often elaborate; unlike opera, the plot and structure were generally simple, consisting of stylized contests and mythological or allegorical characters, and ending with a dance of masked figures in which the audience joined. Masques were also occasional, and hence saw no repeat performances.

Towards the end of Elizabeth's reign, *Circe* (1581), produced in Paris, had a considerable effect on English masquing and this, combined with the influence of Daniel and Gascoigne, saw the elevation of the English masque's poetic element. During the reign of James I, Ben Jonson and Inigo Jones began a tumultuous partnership that arguably perfected the masquing form, introducing ever more lavish costumes and sets (including stage machinery) that made the masque both more elaborate and more expensive. Jonson's *Oberon*, for example, cost over £2,000 – a phenomenal amount of money at the time, and one that may have disturbed even Jonson, who felt that the increasingly elaborate sets and sumptuous costumes obscured the masques' reformative purposes.

Further development of the masque was cut short by the English Civil War and the closing of the theatres by the Puritans; the last court masque of any note before this was probably Davenant's *Salmacia Spoilia* (1640). This was not the last masque, however (though it may be the last memorable one). Shirley's *Cupid and Death* (1653), Davison's *Masque of Proteus and the Adamantine Rock* (1688) and Congreve's *Judgment of Paris* (1701) joined the masque's slide into obscurity by the beginning of the eighteenth century.

Despite its rapid decline, the influence of masquing tradition on other genres, particularly drama, cannot be overstated. Certainly, Restoration drama benefited immensely from the staging technologies first developed during early Stuart masques, and masques were written by some of the foremost talents of the Renaissance, including Spenser, Chapman, Fletcher, Campion, Beaumont, Middleton and (of course) Jonson. But the masquing tradition bled into other entertainments as well – most notably Milton's *Comus* (1634) which, like Peele's *Araygnement of Paris* (1584), is a stew of pastoral, dramatic and masquing conventions.

Metaphysical Poetry

A term now generally applied to the seventeenth century poetry that exhibits ingenious and complicated metaphors, and more specifically to the poetry of Donne, Carew, Herbert, Crashaw, Vaughan, Marvell, Cleveland and Cowley; these Metaphysical poets are now often understood as a group in stylistic contrast with the Cavalier poets, with John Donne in prominence among the Metaphysicals as Jonson was among the Cavaliers.

While William Drummond is often credited with first labelling poetry as 'metaphysics' in this sense, Samuel Johnson more permanently established the label in his *Lives of the Poets*:

> The metaphysical poets were men of learning, and to show their learning was their whole endeavour; but, unluckily resolving to show it in rhyme, instead of writing poetry they only wrote verses and very often such verses as stood the trial of the finger better than of the ear; for the modulation was so imperfect, that they were only found to be verses by counting the syllables (Murphy 1840; 7)

Johnson received the Metaphysicals' complexity and intellectual artifice less warmly than modern critics, such as T. S. Eliot, Cleanth Brooks and Helen Gardner, who effected a new appreciation for Metaphysical poetry during the early twentieth century.

As a label, Metaphysical Poetry is as slippery and unclearly bounded as oil in a hot frying pan; while it always suggests arresting, original, and intellectually complicated images and conceits, Metaphysical Poetry generally also uses colloquial speech, irregularities of rhyme and meter, preoccupations with mortality and a terse phrasing in constant tension with dialectical argument and paradox.

Narrative

Narrative tells a story. As poetry, narrative has an English tradition comprising epics (such as Harington's translation of *Orlando Furioso*), metrical romances (such as Spenser's *Faerie Queene*) and ballads (such as the anonymous *Gest of Robyn Hode*). Major sixteenth-century narrative poems also include Hall's *Chronicle* (*c.* 1540), Marlowe's *Hero and Leander* (1593), Daniel's *Civil Wars* (1595) and Drayton's *England's Heroicall Epistles* (1597). The end of the sixteenth century saw the scale of narrative verse contract from expansive epics and romances to what might be more properly called epyllia, though Cowley's unfinished *Davideis* (1656) and Milton's *Paradise Lost* (1667) would buck that trend in the seventeenth century.

Prose narrative took several forms in Renaissance England, the most popular of which was in pamphlet form and related sensational non-fiction (such as murder and witchcraft trials, the discoveries of unusual creatures, accounts of travels and adventures or undifferentiated news from afar). Narrative fiction generally imitated these forms, and at times (such as in Nashe's 1594 *Unfortunate Traveller*) was of nearly novel length. Sidney, Nashe, Greene and Deloney's longer prose narratives, along with pieces like Emanuel Ford's *Irnatus and Artesia*, are generally termed *novellas*, and grouped as a genre with Boccaccio's *Decameron* (*c.* 1350) and Guardati's *Novellino* (1467).

Parody

From the Greek for 'beside'. Parody is an imitation of the words, style, theme, attitude, tone or ideas of a work or group of works that makes them ridiculous. This is usually done by exaggerating a work's signature traits, much as a caricature exaggerates a persons most prominent features. As Parody is also generally satiric, its purpose may be to reform as well as to mock.

Shakespeare may be the most well known parodist of the Renaissance, taking on Lyly's euphuism in *Henry IV Part 1* (1597), Marlowe's Bombast in *Hamlet* (1603) and Nashe's style in *Loves Labors Lost* (1595). Pamphlet literature was also ruthlessly parodic; Nashe's *Unfortunate Traveller* (1594) and Francis Godwin's *Man in the Moone* (1638) are two excellent examples of parodies involving popular pamphlet genres (in their cases, travel accounts).

Pastoral

A minor but significant mode of Renaissance drama, poetry and prose that is, by convention, concerned with the romantic pastimes of shepherds. In classical sources, such as Theocritus' *Epyllia* (*c.* 300 BCE), these pastimes include piping contests, improvised songs and conversations on the attractions of fair women. A central figure in the *Epyllia* is Daphnis, who is killed by Aphrodite for being faithful to his nymph wife, Chloe; mourning of Daphnis in the *Epyllia* takes an early form of the pastoral elegy, of which Milton's *Lycidas* is a finely crafted example. Virgil modelled his *Eclogues* (with which Renaissance authors were often familiar) on the *Epyllia*, in the process introducing the pastoral convention of a golden age in which shepherds lived in primitive bliss.

This Virgilian pastoral tradition came to Renaissance England in two ways. The first is through Medieval Mystery plays, such as *The Adoration of the Shepherds* and protocomic Mysteries like the *Second Shepherd's Play* (*c.* 1500) which, though unconcerned with piping contests or romance, use the grammar of Virgilian pastoral in religious drama. The second is through an Italian pastoral tradition, which included works by Petrarch, Boccaccio and the improbably influential Mantuan (1448–1516), who was grammar school material in

Elizabethan England. Barclay's *Eclogues* (*c.* 1516), two of the five of which were translations of Mantuan, were also influential throughout the sixteenth century.

The sixteenth century also saw the rise of more ambitious pastoral works, both in the form of loosely confederated poem sequences and of prose romances. While Boccaccio wrote his *Ameto* in the fourteenth century, Sannazaro's *Arcadia* (1504), a series of twelve eclogues linked by prose, inspired Montemayor's *Diana* (*c.* 1560) which in turn inspired Sidney's *Arcadia* (1580). Spenser's *Shepheardes Calendar* (1579) might be considered part of this sequence of influence but is more closely modelled on Theocritus and Virgil (although it contains strong allegorical elements).

The sixteenth and early seventeenth centuries saw a further development of English pastoral in which the nostalgic attractions of its rustic bliss were worked out in greater detail; the dominant idea of this pastoral is the search for a simpler life away from the social complexities of court and town, and from the inconveniences attendant on civilization, like war, greed and economic necessity. Apart from Montemayor, Sidney and Spenser, significant pastoral poetry includes Marlowe's *Passionate Shepherd to His Love* (*c.* 1590) and Ralegh's response, *The Nymph's Reply to the Shepherd*, (and Donne's response, 'The Bait') as well as Drayton's eclogues (1593). Later notable pastoral poems include Browne's Collections, *Brittania's Pastorals* (1613) and *Shepherd's Pipe* (1614), as well as Milton's 'L'Allegro', 'Arcades' and 'Lycidas', and Marvell's mower poems.

This period also saw the development of English Pastoral drama. While the influence of pastoral is clear in many of Shakespeare's plays (e.g. *As You Like It*), Jonson also worked on at least one entirely pastoral drama, the unfinished *Sad Shepherd* (1641). James Shirley adapted Sidney's *Arcadia* in his 1640 drama of the same name, while Fletcher's *Faithful Shepherdess* (1608) is a typical and well-crafted example of the form. Period masques also show some pastoral influence; the latest of these is Milton's *Comus* (1634).

Patronage

The sponsorship of art, in this case poetry, by a person of wealth and (usually) influence. During the sixteenth and seventeenth centuries, patrons were generally of the nobility, and patronage was a component of many professional writers' incomes. Ben Jonson, often credited as England's first full-time professional writer, owed much of his living to indirect patronage (being paid to write court masques) and to direct patronage (in the forms of stipends and sinecures granted throughout his life). Not all patronage relationships were as successful as Jonson's, however. Robert Greene's career is notorious for its constant seeking of gentry sponsors.

It is worth noting that drama, which could be a profitable enterprise, was perhaps the first genre of English letters to distance itself from patronage relationships, although indirect patronage (in the form of paid court performances of popular plays, as well as occasional dramas) was a substantial part of period theatrical economies.

Persona

The central, first person, speaker of a poem, often conflated by the unwary reader with the writer him- or herself, with whom the persona may or may not share similarities.

Petrarch/Petrarchan Courtly Love

Amour courtois was first used in 1883 by Gaston Paris to describe a set of romantic conventions in literature and song that dated from about the twelfth century. These conventions include the idealization of women by a lover who, struck by the beauty and virtue of a lady, was obedient to her wishes in the hopes that such obedience would ennoble him and make him worthy of her love. The emotional anguish that stems from the narrator's romantic anxieties is highly conventional, and is at the centre of sonnet sequences from Sidney, Spenser and Shakespeare.

Problem Plays

At their most general, problem plays examine a perplexing issue or a moral dilemma, usually in the form of a representative instance of a contemporary social problem. The term originates with F. S. Boas, who in *Shakespeare and His Predecessors* (1896) identified several Shakespearean dramas that, like the dramas of Ibsen, Shaw and Dumas, resolve their central themes in ways that audiences may find unsatisfying, largely owing to the gravity and complexity of the issues at their centres.

Shakespearean problem plays also share rapid and severe tonal shifts, and often suddenly move from violent psychological drama to light comedy. Boas' examples are *All's Well That Ends Well* (1603), *Measure for Measure* (1603) and *Troilus and Cressida* (1602), though later critics have located problem elements in *Hamlet* (1600), *The Winter's Tale* (1605), *Timon of Athens* (1607) and *The Merchant of Venice* (1600).

Protestantism

In England, Protestantism refers chiefly to membership in the Church of England (as opposed to the Catholic Church and non-Anglican denominations), regardless of the Church's religious orientation at any particular historical moment (which was e.g. closer to Catholicism under Henry VII than Edward VI, and of more variable practice and belief under Elizabeth I). During and after

Elizabeth's reign, Anglicanism became roughly synonymous with English political autonomy and social identity, with recusants (especially Catholics) being fined for not attending Anglican services and being gradually and systematically excluded from political office – an issue that was of continual importance but reached revolutionary proportions when it became clear that a Catholic, James II, would succeed his nominally protestant brother, Charles.

Puritanism

In England, this is a catch-all term for non Anglican protestants, who were in practice generally Calvinists but also included arguably non-Calvinist sects such as the Diggers and Levellers. Puritans, like Catholics, endured soft exclusion from state offices and perquisites but, unlike Catholics, were a political and social force of considerable magnitude; their priorities fairly dominated England during the Interregnum.

Quarto

From the Latin *in quarto,* meaning 'in fourth' and often abbreviated 4to. This refers to a book made from printer's sheets folded twice to form four leaves (eight pages), a form in which most pamphlets, as well as many plays and books, were printed. Quartos are perhaps best known for the problems they pose for Shakespeare's editors, who for about twenty plays must reconcile text printed in quarto with that printed in folio. Different versions of the same play can be very dissimilar indeed; this is apparent in the René Weis parallel text edition of *King Lear* (Weis 1993), which prints the two versions on facing pages.

Revenge Tragedy

A form of tragic drama in which a protagonist violently rights a savage wrong. While Aeschylus' *Oresteia* arguably comprises the earliest identifiable dramas of this kind, Renaissance Revenge Tragedies are generally cut to fit a Senecan model; that is, while the plots of many Renaissance dramas are driven by cycles of vengeance, the term 'revenge tragedy' (as developed by twentieth century critics like A. H. Thorndike, Fredson Bowers, Lily Campbell and Ronald Broude) is more exclusive, comprising plays whose plots are not only driven by revenge, but which also feature ghosts, the revenger's madness, and no small quantity of melodrama and bloodshed.

While early plays, such as *Gorboduc* (1561), are essentially driven by a revenge plot, Kyd's *Spanish Tragedy* (c. 1586) is generally considered the earliest revenge tragedy. Its plot is typical of the genre: it begins with a ghost and spirit of revenge who function as a chorus throughout an intrigue in which Hieronomo, knight-marshal of Spain, revenges the murder of his son Horatio through an improbably crafted court play that ends with the stabbing of his son's killers – a process abetted by Hieronomo's either feigned or providential madness, and made necessary by deeply rooted political corruption.

Shakespeare continued Kyd's tradition in the much-maligned *Titus Andronicus* (1594) and the much elevated *Hamlet* (1603), which may have been based on another of Kyd's plays, now lost. John Marston also contributed two plays to the genre: *Antonio's Revenge* (1600) and *The Malcontent* (1604) – a play which is arguably a comedy but features multiple revengers and a complex of disguises. Tourneur's *Revenger's Tragedy* (1607) is the last major play in this tradition.

Throughout its progress, revenge tragedy became increasingly sensational, featuring not only the traditional complement of ghosts and insanities, but rape, incest, adultery, infanticide, cannibalism and a litany of ever more intricate and spectacular murders. It also became increasingly influential, bleeding revenge plots into a range of other dramas (such as Carey's *Tragedy or Miriam* (1613) and Marlowe's *Tamburlaine* (1590)). Other notable Revenge Tragedies include Chettle's *Hoffman* (1602), Chapman's *Revenge of Bussy D'Ambois* (1607), Tourneur's *Atheist's Tragedy* and Fletcher's *The Bloody Brother* (c. 1616). It is also worth noting that the Romantics half-revived the genre in Shelly's *The Cenci* (1819) and in Hugo's *Hernani* (1830) and *Ruy Blas* (1838).

Rhetoric

From the Greek 'speaker in the assembly'. Rhetoric is the art of using spoken and written language persuasively, and classical theoreticians codified rhetorical techniques extensively. Their influence (and especially the influence of Cicero) was powerful enough that, during the Middle Ages, the study of Rhetoric became part of the *trivium*, where it remained throughout the Renaissance.

Romance

Romance, like pastoral, is a genre of drama, poetry and prose. The term likely has origins in the Medieval Latin word *romaince*, meaning 'in the romantic tongue' or, in the context of continental Europe, in the vernacular rather than Latin; in other words, this linguistic distinction was also a cultural one that differentiated popular literature from the scholarly or historical. The content of that popular literature, now the basis for modern scholars' definitions of Romance, involves courtly characters living at some remove from the everyday and whose activities involve improbable, fantastic and extravagant plots of adventure, love and marvel. In Renaissance England, Romance was generally chivalric.

The principle influences on Renaissance Romances came from the continent (in the poems of Ariosto and Tasso) and from Medieval English Romances, such as the fourteenth century's *Havelock the Dane* and *Sir Gawain and the Green Knight*, as well as Malory's *Morte D'Arthur* (1485). Renaissance Romances generally combined these Medieval and Continental traditions with others, such as Allegory and Epic (in Spenser's *Faerie Queene* (1596)), Pastoral (in Sidney's *Arcadia* (1590)) and Comedy (in Shakespeare's *Winter's Tale* (1611)). Greene's *Pandosto* (1588), a source for *The Winter's Tale*, is also a significant piece of prose Romance.

Renaissance Romances are also implicated in a long tradition of Romantic parody. Chaucer, for instance, burlesques the Romance in his *Tale of Sir Thopas*, and English translations of *Don Quixote* were published between 1612 and 1620. Beaumont's *Knight of the Burning Pestle* (1607) is also partly a parody of Romantic conventions (though it also specifically parodies Heywood's *Four Prentices of London* (c. 1592). The attitude of these parodies might be well summarized by William Congreve's preface to *Incognita* (1713):

> Romances are generally composed of the Constant Loves and invincible Courages of Heros, Heroins, Kings and Queens, Mortals of the first Rank, and so forth; where lofty Language, miraculous Contingencies and impossible Performances, elevate and surprize the Reader into a giddy Delight, which leaves him flat upon the Ground whenever he gives of, and vexes him to think how he has suffer'd himself to be pleased and transported, concern'd and afflicted at the several Passages which he has Read, viz. these Knights Success to their Damosels Misfortunes, and such like, when he is forced to be very well convinced that 'tis all a lye (Congreve 2004, 7)

The term is also sometimes used to describe Shakespeare's late plays; when used in this sense it bears similarities to (but is not exactly the same as) the term 'tragicomedy'.

Satire

From the Latin *satura*, or 'medley'. In his *Dictionary*, Samuel Johnson defined *satire* as a poem 'in which wickedness or folly is censured'.[4] While this definition confines the matter closely, it locates the key difference between satire and other parodic or imitative forms: satire is principally and explicitly concerned with reformation. This property of satire is so durable that twentieth-century critic Ian Jack defined it much the way Johnson did. 'Satire', he wrote 'is born of the instinct to protest; it is protest become art'.

While English satire did not necessarily begin with the rediscovery of Horace and Juvenal (since both Chaucer and Langland have arguably satiric elements), the revival of classical texts doubtless contributed to satire's increasing popularity through the sixteenth and seventeenth centuries. There are certainly satiric moments in Erasmus' *Moriae Encomium* (1509) and More's *Utopia* (1516), but later satire likely owes more to Skelton, who married his reformative projects to a seemingly bottomless well of free-floating invective. Drant's translations of Horace (1566s *Medicinable Morall* and 1567s *Art of Poetrie*) were likely also influential, though they certainly speak to a growing audience for satiric material.

There is a clear Horatian influence on the satires of the late sixteenth and early seventeenth centuries. Lodge's *Fig for Momus* (1595) is explicitly Horatian, as is the overwhelming majority of Jonson's drama – in fact, Jonson's drama comprises almost nothing but. In contrast, the satires of Donne, Hall and Marston (particularly 1598s *Scourge of Villanie*) are more pessimistic and bitter, and therefore closer to Juvenal.

It is worth noting that satire became a major form in late seventeenth and early eighteenth century verse, with Rochester, Dryden, Pope and Swift even now best known for their satiric work.

Self-Fashioning

Self-fashioning describes the process of constructing one's identity and public persona according to a set of socially acceptable standards.

Castiglione's *Book of the Courtier* (1528, but translated into English by Thomas Hoby in 1561) is one of the first texts to depict behaviours gentry were expected to adopt, including instructions on how people of the noble class were to dress, speak and otherwise conduct themselves socially. For instance, one was not supposed to act in an affected manner, but present naturalness and nonchalance, or *sprezzatura*. In addition to this, *Courtier* emphasizes the importance of resembling one's master; this presents a key theme in self-fashioning: the conscious effort to imitate a praised social model.

Sonnet

From the Italian *sonetto*, a 'little song'. Renaissance sonnets consist of fourteen lines of (generally) iambic pentameter, but have varied rhyme schemes. Sonnets are usually considered to be of three types: the Italian or Petrarchan sonnet (comprising an octave rhyming *abbaabba* and a sestet usually rhyming either *cdecde* or *cdcdcd*), the Spenserian sonnet (comprising three quatrains and a couplet rhyming *abab bcbc cdcd ee*), and the Shakespearean sonnet (again comprising three quatrains and a couplet, but rhyming *abab cdcd efef gg*).

Generally, the structure of the Italian sonnet involves a turn (or *'volta'*) between the octave and the sestet, whereas the Shakespearean and Spenserian sonnet express different but interlocking ideas in each quatrain, and unite these ideas in the final couplet. But there are notable exceptions; Shakespearean and Spenserian sonnets also often include a logical or tonal shift between their second and third quatrains, effectively mimicking the *volta* structure of the Italian sonnet. Until the early seventeenth century, sonnets were almost exclusively about Petrarchan-style courtly romance.

Sir Thomas Wyatt and Henry Howard, Earl of Surrey, imported the sonnet form to England in the early sixteenth century, with Surrey establishing the

Shakespearean rhyme scheme (*abab cdcd efef gg*), by far the period's most popular. The first major sonnet cycle was Sidney's *Astrophil and Stella* (printed in 1591, though in circulation a decade before), which was immediately followed by Daniel's *Delia* (1592), Lodge's *Phillis* (1593), Constable's *Diana* (1594), Drayton's *Idea's Mirror* (1594), and Spenser's *Amoretti* (1595). These were followed by Shakespeare's sonnets (printed in 1609, but in circulation during the late 1590s), and Lady Mary Wroth's *Pamphilia to Amphilanthus* (1621).

After this point, the sonnet was adapted for subjects other than romance. Those collected in Donne's *Songs and Sonnets* (1635) are a clear if complicated instance of this, perhaps made clear by Milton's adoption of the sonnet as a form for non-romantic occasional verse, an example followed by Thomas Gray, Thomas Warton and William Bowles in the eighteenth century.

Theatres: Globe

(For a general discussion of theatres, see Britland and Munro, this volume, pp 42–47) Evidence suggests that the Globe was a three-storey amphitheatre about 100 feet in diameter which could seat about three thousand, with a forty-foot apron stage complete with a trap door (which could be used to disappear the ghost in *Hamlet*), a stage balcony (sometimes called the 'heavens', which could be used for scenes such as the balcony scene in *Romeo and Juliet*), several back wall doors through which players could enter and exit (along with entering and exiting stage right or left) and a curtained area (or 'discovery space') centred at the back of the stage (where, for example, Polonius could hide to spy on Hamlet and his mother).

The Globe was built in 1599 using timbers from the Chamberlain's Men's earlier residence, the Theatre, which had been built by Richard Burbage's father James Burbage in Shoreditch. When the lease on the land the Theatre occupied expired, the landlord Giles Allen claimed that the building had become his property, so on 28 December 1598 (while Allen was celebrating Christmas outside of London), carpenter Peter Street, supported by the players and their friends, dismantled the Theatre beam by beam, possibly sliding the timbers over the frozen Thames and storing them for the later construction of the Globe.

The Globe was owned by shareholders in the Lord Chamberlain's Men. Two of the six Globe shareholders, Richard Burbage and his brother Cuthbert Burbage, owned double shares of the whole, or 25 per cent each; the other four men, Shakespeare, John Heminges, Augustine Phillips and Thomas Pope, were actors in the company and owned a single share, or 12.5 per cent. William Kempe, then the most famous comic actor in the Chamberlain's Men, was intended to be the seventh partner, but he sold out his share to the four minority sharers, leaving them with more than the originally planned 10 per cent. This shareholding, rather than proceeds from his plays, eventually made Shakespeare wealthy.

On 29 June 1613 the Globe Theatre caught fire during a performance of Henry the Eighth when a theatrical cannon ignited the roof's thatching. According to Henry Wotton's *Letters to Edmund Bacon* (1661) none were injured except a man whose burning clothes were put out with ale.

Tragedy

From the Greek word meaning 'goat song'. While Aristotle defined tragedy as a drama in which misfortune is brought on an individual through an error of judgement, many writers elaborated on this definition before Sidney introduced a moral element to it; tragedy, according to Sidney 'teacheth the uncertainty of this world, and upon how weak foundations gilden roofs are builded'. Diomedes (fourth century CE), for instance, defines tragedy as a narrative of the misfortunes of heroic characters; Isidore of Seville (sixth–seventh century) defines tragedy as sad stories about kings and kingdoms; John of Garland (twelfth century defines tragedy as a poem written in the high style about wicked deeds, beginning in joy and ending in grief; Chaucer, in his prologue to the Monk's tale, gives a similar definition:

> Tragedie is to seyn a certyn storie,
> As olde bookes maken us memorie,
> Of hym that stood in greet prosperitee
> And is yfallen out of heigh degree
> Into myserie, and endeth wrecchedly. (86–89)

Renaissance tragedies beginning with Sackville and Norton's *Gorboduc* (1561) draw unevenly on these definitions; while *Gorboduc* presents a clear error in judgement (the Lear mistake of dividing a kingdom between one's children), many revenge tragedies (such as *Hamlet* or *The Spanish Tragedy*) obfuscate or go without locating errors of judgement in their protagonists; instead, the engine of their characters' misery is wide ranging political and social corruption, as it is in *Romeo and Juliet* (1595).

Indeed, Renaissance Tragedy presents considerable variation. Apart from revenge tragedies (probably the most significant subgenre of Renaissance Tragedy), there are a number of tragedies patterned on Moralities; *Gorboduc* is part of a tradition of political morality that includes Bale's *Kynge Johan* (1538) and Skelton's *Magnificence* (*c.* 1533), just as Marlowe's *Dr. Faustus* (*c.* 1588) is part of the undifferentiated morality tradition typified in *Mankind* (1475). The Renaissance also saw the birth of domestic tragedy with the anonymous *Arden of Faversham* (*c.* 1592), though Heywood's *Woman Killed With Kindness* (1603) better represents the genre.

That said, many Renaissance tragedies fit the conventional pattern of errors in personal judgement leading to falls from high social places. Among these are Preston's *Cambyses* (1569), Shakespeare's *King Lear* (1606), *Macbeth* (1606), *Antony and Cleopatra* (*c.* 1607) and *Coriolanus* (*c.* 1608), Ben Jonson's *Sejanus His Fall* (1603) and *Cataline* (1611), Chapman's *Bussy D'Ambois* (1613), Webster's *The*

131

White Devil (c. 1608), Middleton's *Women Beware Women* (1621) and Middleton and Rowley's *The Changeling* (1622), Massinger's *The Roman Actor* (1626) and Ford's *'Tis Pity She's a Whore, or The Broken Heart* (1633).

Key terms in understanding of Renaissance Tragedy are *catharsis* and *hamartia*. *Catharsis*, from the Greek for 'purgation', originates in Aristotle's definition of Tragedy in Chapter 6 of the *Poetics*. There has been much debate about what, exactly, this term means; the central point of contention is the meaning of Aristotle's 'Tragedy, through pity and fear, effects a purgation of such emotions'. The gist of this seems to be that tragedy has a therapeutic effect, arousing powerful and unpleasant emotions to bring about emotional peace or calm.

Hamartia, from the Greek for 'error', also originates in Aristotle's criticism of tragedy, where it specifically refers to an error in judgement, or a mistake of great magnitude, from which originates the tragic action. This concept greatly influenced A. C. Bradley, whose elaboration of what he termed the 'tragic trait' (later critics called it a 'fatal flaw') of the Shakespearean hero owed a great deal to Aristotle's notion of *hamartia* (Bradley 1904). One key difference between the two, however, is that for Bradley, this flaw is embedded in the character, or psychology, of the tragic hero: for him, character is the single most important aspect of Shakespearean tragedy, from which all of its action derives. This is not true of Aristotle's notion of hamartia, which is unrelated to character, and far less ethically charged (the protagonist does not know what he is doing when he makes his mistake). It is worth noting that hamartia, or indeed the notion of a fatal flaw, is by no means a universal property of Renaissance tragic heroes. While *Gorboduc* begins with a clear error in judgement (the decision to divide a kingdom between two heirs), *Macbeth* and *Hamlet* either complicate the conditions of this error or make it difficult to locate. Most contemporary critics would be unsympathetic to the claim that the fatal flaws of Shakespeare's protagonists cause the action in those plays.

Tragicomedy

This derives from Plautus' reference to his *Amphitruo* as a 'tragico-comoedia' (thanks to its unconventional mixture of gods, kings and servants), and generally refers to a play with both tragic and comic elements. These are of two identifiable types: tragedies with comic endings (in the tradition of Cinthio's *tragedie miste*) and plays marrying tragic plots to comic sub-plots (in the tradition of Guarini, whose *il pastor fido* also draws on a pastoral tradition).

In response to hostile receptions of *il pastor fido*, Guarini penned a defence of his tragicomedy in 1601 (*Compendio della poesia tragicomica*), which roughly corresponds with the development of English theory and criticism of tragicomedy. Both Sidney and Jonson seemed to disapprove of tragicomedy (both called it a 'mongrel' form), though Jonson's unfinished *Sad Shepherd* (1641) was tragicomic. Fletcher, who adapted Guarini in his *Faithful Shepherdess* (1608) defines the genre more neutrally in that play's preface, where

A tragicomedy is not so called in respect of mirth and killing, but in respect it wants deaths, which is enough to make it no tragedy, yet brings some near it, which is enough to make it no comedy[.]

Beaumont and Fletcher, like Shakespeare before them, wrote several tragi-comedies. Shakespearean examples of the genre include *Troilus and Cressida* (1602), *All's Well That Ends Well* and *Measure for Measure* (1604). *Pericles* (1608), *Cymbeline* (1609), *The Winter's Tale* (1610) and *The Tempest* (1611) are sometimes referred to as tragicomedies; other critics prefer the term 'Romance' to describe them; still others reject both those terms in favour of the less prescriptive 'late plays'.

Critical Responses and Approaches to British Renaissance Literature

6

Tita French Baumlin

Preamble

Any starting point for the history of Renaissance literary criticism must be arbitrary. One could begin with the eighteenth century, and Dr Samuel Johnson, or with the Romantics of the early nineteenth century: William Blake's and Samuel Taylor Coleridge's readings of Milton, for example, or Coleridge's of Shakespeare (for an account of the presuppositions of this early criticism, see Bruce, 1998). The late nineteenth century saw the advent of the 'old philology', or the study of the history of ideas in relation to literature, along with broad biographical criticism and the earliest attempts at psychological studies of literary texts. The Swiss historian Jacob Burckhardt, often called the 'father of cultural history', promoted the notion that political and military developments are not the only elements of what is called 'history' – that art, literature and the habits of people in everyday life must be included as well – which ultimately added to the growing emphasis on literature as an academic discipline worthy of study on its own merits. His mammoth *The Civilisation of the Renaissance in Italy* (1860; tr. 1878, 1990) established the view of the Renaissance that many of us (although see Healy, this volume, Chapter 8 for a different point of view) take for granted today: that the age distinguished itself from the Medieval period by its idealization of the self-conscious individual and its emphasis on reason, science and humanism.

And it is also at the end of the nineteenth century that we meet the first literary critic whose views remain influential today, at least among school students and first year undergraduates (although not among contemporary scholars). This was the Oxford professor A. C. Bradley who introduced the study of Renaissance drama from the standpoint of a reader rather than a spectator in the theatre. His lectures, collected and published as *Shakespearean Tragedy* (1904) interpreted Shakespeare's characters as if they were real people whose desires, motivations and relationships are at once humanly cogent and central to the impetus of tragic action in the plays. This insistence on the realism of Shakespeare and the central importance to his tragedies of character (Bradley read the plays as if they were nineteenth-century novels) remains Bradley's lasting legacy and continues to influence many a student essay on the plays. Academics teaching Renaissance tragedies, in fact, spend a good deal of their time trying to disabuse first year students of the notions that Renaissance tragedies can be explained by recourse to consideration of the 'fatal flaw' of their protagonists, a Bradleian notion which has now largely been superseded by other explanatory models, as has the idea of the 'universality' or eternal value of literature. Across the Atlantic at around the same time was the Harvard philologist George Lyman Kittredge, whose works in the early twentieth century standardized Shakespeare in the American university curriculum.

New Criticism to Structuralism

New Criticism
It was out of this atmosphere that the first great textual theory emerged, termed variously, Formalism or 'New Criticism'. The latter name reveals its attachment to Modernism: both sought to reject the traditionalism of the nineteenth century and to make of themselves an 'avant-garde' force in the arts. The importance of New Criticism to the development of literary criticism cannot be overstated, since its insistence on a 'close reading' of the text – its attention to language itself – is the great insight out of which flowed all later approaches to literature (see Chapters 3 and 5). This concentration on the text – the patterns of words and

images, the formal designs of rhythm and rhyme, the devices and recurrent themes, the sounds of the words against the play of denotations and connotations – provided a new way of seeing literature spatially upon the page as well as thematically in the mind. The practice itself still informs much introductory classroom literature instruction.

However, Formalist theory insisted on the text as an artefact whose meaning is largely (though not wholly) independent of any 'context' – whether that be authorial intention, biographical experiences, history or anything outside the text. It situated itself as a rebellion against the biographical and personality-driven criticism dominated by Bradley and Kittredge. The literary work must be taken as an independent thing: its meaning is to be discovered through close reading of the text. A landmark New Critical work was Cleanth Brooks' treatment of John Donne's poem 'The Canonization' in *The Well-Wrought Urn* (1947). Brooks' moves line-by-line through the poem, considering the controlling metaphors and deciding on the speaker's intended meaning. Brooks ultimately argues that the speaker praises his lover and their personal religion of love, repudiating the world of politics and wealth that seems to obsess the speaker's silent listener. While this reading may seem compelling, other readings might come to very different conclusions. A biographical reading, for example, might take into consideration Donne's elopement with Ann More, and find in 'The Canonization' an ironic expression of Donne's own reversals of fortune at this time in his life, when falling in love brought him scandal and financial ruin. New Critical hostility to the biographical, character-driven criticism which pre-dated it, and against which it explicitly or tacitly pitched itself can be observed in L. C. Knights' famous essay: 'How many children had Lady Macbeth? An essay in the theory and practice of Shakespeare criticism' (1933; rpt. 1946). Knights' spends the entire article stating the premises of the New Criticism – its call for attention to the words and rhythms and imagery – and examining the theme of evil in the text of *Macbeth*. The title question – 'How many children had Lady Macbeth?' – he never addresses. This is presumably a parodic jibe at critics such as Bradley, for whom, unlike Knights, such a question might conceivably have seemed legitimate.

There were various applications of such studies of imagery. Caroline Spurgeon's *Shakespeare's Imagery and What It Tells Us* (1935) and Derek Traversi's multi-volumed *An Approach to Shakespeare* (1938), identified patterns of imagery in order to speculate on how the 'great mind' of the author worked. Other Formalists argued that the 'organic unity' of the work should be at the heart of the demonstration, and that a literary work should not be interpreted according to its imagery but vice versa – that the imagery should be analysed in its relationship to the larger organic whole that has its own artistic integrity within it. Within this tradition, C. S. Lewis (1942), G. Wilson Knight (1930; 1931) and others argued that Renaissance dramas are best read as poems, since the contexts of dramatic audience and characters' motivations distract from the organic unity of the poetic icon that is the play, and since it is the playwright's 'visionary whole', the 'atmospheric suggestion', the 'poetic-symbolism' (Knight 1930, 11), and indeed the 'poetic splendours' (Knight 1931, 24) to which readers most deeply respond.

Early Historicist Criticism

Next came a reformulation of historicist criticism, in response to New Criticism, attempting to use many of the insights of New Criticism in a broader contextualization of meaning. For example, when Hamlet speaks of himself as a 'distracted globe' in Act 1, scene 5, the image calls to mind not only the crazed, fragile, crystal bulb that the New Critic might examine but also the more universal sense of the macrocosmic spheres of the 'Elizabethan World Picture' – the phrase adopted by E. M. W. Tillyard (1943) to describe the Renaissance system of cosmology. Such traditional historicists sought to reconstruct everything that could have had an impact upon the literary work – contemporary law books, educational manuals, rhetoric textbooks and, most of all, the vast store of Classical works that the Renaissance venerated – though any such text must be known to have been within the author's physical grasp or must be demonstrated (usually through word-links) to have been likely known by the author. Now was the heyday of ferreting out every source and analogue for British Renaissance literary works, the pinnacle of which may be Geoffrey Bullough's multi-volume *Narrative and Dramatic Sources of Shakespeare* (1957–75). Significant works of this traditional historicist criticism include Rosemond Tuve's *Elizabethan and Metaphysical Imagery* (1947), which argued for close readings of seventeenth-century poetry to historicize textual allusions; and C. S. Lewis' *The Allegory of Love* (1936) which explored Medieval courtly love and applied it to Spenser's poetry.

These texts are still useful for understanding conventional aspects of the British Renaissance; current critical theory, however, would hold not only that the emphasis on authorial intention was a flawed element of this approach but also that the vision of history itself was flawed. A case in point is *The Elizabethan World Picture* (Tillyard 1943), whose assumption of a singular 'picture' betrays the book's conviction that all Renaissance individuals subscribed to the same set of beliefs to which one dissented. As Annabel Patterson puts it, traditional historicists presented 'a particularly idealized view of Elizabethan society and literature' and a 'naïve view of "history" as an unproblematic category of the factual' (1992, 186). Still, a mastery of the concepts presented in Tillyard's little book remains useful to an understanding of the age; Tillyard clearly describes the 'orthodox' or 'conventional' belief system contested by dissenters like Copernicus and Galileo. (see Chapter 1)

Structuralism

Some mention here of the relatively brief appearance of Structuralism may clarify the development of today's methodologies' distinctive emphases on textuality. In British Renaissance studies, the most significant Structuralist critic was the Canadian Northrop Frye, whose landmark work *Anatomy of Criticism* (1957) initiated 'archetypal criticism' and did much to displace Formalism as the major force in criticism at the time. Frye's conception worked in two directions – analysis *into* the work in order to identify the figures and themes that connect to the system of myths and rituals throughout world cultures; analysis *across* literature to identify 'modes' of literature (comic, tragic, ironic) and genres, in terms of mythological strata and collective social needs. He influenced many critics who took genre criticism and character criticism into new directions that reached into distant myths to demonstrate the connectedness of human expression and imagination.

Rhetorical Criticism

A reaction to Formalism may be charted in a resurgence of the 'Chicago School' of American criticism, which looks to Richard McKeon for the genesis of what was called the New Rhetoric. This branch of literary criticism focused on the language of the literary work (hence owing its origins to the insights of New Criticism) but turned its lens more deeply into Aristotelian questions of how rhetoric's 'spell' is maintained over the reader. Donald Leman Clark's *Milton at St. Paul's School: A Study of Ancient Rhetoric in Renaissance Education* (1948) and Sister Miriam Joseph's *Shakespeare's Use of the Arts of Language* (1947) explored Milton's and Shakespeare's presumed educational experiences, based on the typical Early Modern grammar school's (see Chapter 1) training of pupils in some two hundred classical figures of speech, and also exhaustively catalogued the authors' uses of them in their works. However, beginning in the 1970s, critics examined rhetorical devices in order to determine larger thematic issues about the function of language in human relations, in creativity and so on, since language, after all, is the writer's medium. Critics such as Richard Lanham (in *The Motives of Eloquence: Literary Rhetoric in the Renaissance*, 1976) began to ask: how did the British Renaissance culture view human language itself? How do these views of language work in the world of a given literary piece? How does language function for a literary artist? What might this work be suggesting about the ways that language functions? Such a critic may see the author as a self-conscious user of language, who conveys to a reader the complexities inherent in human language, which is his own medium and the 'thing' that distinguishes humanity from both the beasts and divinity, according to Renaissance writers' most prized sources – the *Bible*, but also the Greek and Roman rhetorical texts so prized by Renaissance culture. For the Greek philosopher Isocrates, for example, language was the force that lifted humankind above the beasts and made community possible; the Roman rhetorician Quintilian ascribed the power of rhetoric to the *'bonus vir dicendi peritus'* (the good man who has been taught the skill to speak); Elizabethan Thomas Wilson promised that learning the skills of rhetoric would make of a man 'halfe a god' (1553, 9).

As applied to English Renaissance poetry, Rhetorical Criticism encompasses numerous traditions and methods. In its simplest expression, it applies the stylistic vocabulary of Ciceronianism – the 'schemes and tropes', as codified in the pseudo-Ciceronian *Rhetorica ad Herennium* (and subsequently imitated in Erasmus' *De Copia*, 1512, and George Puttenham's *Arte of English Poesie*, 1589) – to literary texts. Or it might explore the confluence of style, rhetorical aim and literary genre. O. B. Hardison's *Enduring Monument: A Study of the Idea of Praise in Renaissance Literary Theory and Practice* (1962) surveys the development of *epideixis* – the rhetoric of praise and blame – in the classically based genres (ode, verse epistle, epigram) favoured by such poets as Ben Jonson.

Throughout the Tudor-Stuart age, the problematic status of the Bible *as literature* proved worrisome to poets, who sought either to Christianize the classical genres or to affirm the literary-stylistic excellence of Scripture itself. 'There are not so eloquent books in the World as the Scriptures', Donne preaches (*Sermons* vol. 2: 170–71): numerous studies of the scriptural echoes, structures and voices recurrent in Spenser, Donne and Milton were produced during this period, such as Thomas Kranidas' *Fierce Equation: A Study of Milton's Decorum* (1965) a seminal study of the classical-Ciceronian doctrine of *decorum* – that is, of the 'dynamic unity' of style with structure and genre with voice. Or, rhetorical criticism might seek to identify a text's 'linguistic epistemology', in particular its attitudes towards the nature (and possibility) of truth and the powers of language to express the same. Thomas O. Sloan's *Donne, Milton, and the End of Humanist Rhetoric* (1985), for example, maintains that Donne's poetry is characterized by epistemological scepticism (which assumes that truth is contingent and, thus, changes with time, audience, occasion and circumstance), and therefore consistently presents 'both sides' of complex arguments – a Ciceronian-humanist rhetorical habit that accounts for the contradictory attitudes filling his *Songs and Sonets*.

Psychoanalytic Criticism

Freudian Psychoanalysis

Although any strand of psychology may be applied to literature, the most influential for literary criticism has been the psychoanalytic analyses of critics versed in the theories of Sigmund Freud and his followers. Such critics hold that the development of the psyche hinges on the self's growing awareness of its differentiation from its parents and its fantasies as it both attempts to separate itself and battles against separation. A psychoanalytic approach to a piece of literature will often incorporate the concept of the 'Other': the Other being that which pre-exists the psyche, that which brought one into being but which also always eludes one's understanding and which consequently one fears and tries to master. For Jacques Lacan, who, later, extended and developed his own strand of post-Freudian psychoanalysis (see below) the Other is a complex interrelationship of the unconscious, the parents and the 'symbolic order' of social reality, dominated by language and the 'law of the father'. (In fact, many different strands of literary criticism have now also adopted the term, though they interpret 'Other' in varying ways: for Feminist Theory, the Other is Woman, that which society has thrust out; for New Historicism it is the subversive force that must be contained, that is, kept estranged by *and* incorporated into the power structure all at the same time; for Deconstruction, the Other is the inferior yet primary part of the most basic binary of all and so on.)

Freud's basic proposition that the unconscious mind is the primary motivating factor in human behaviour, originally found its applications in literary criticism (up through the 1960s) in the following ways. First, since dream interpretation was a major aspect of psychoanalysis, any dreams in literature became subject to analysis; and second, characters' behaviour was subjected to psychoanalysis according to Freud's notions of the ego, the superego, the id and the complexes that result from childhood trauma and repressed sexual desire. A simple Freudian character analysis might emphasize repression, for example: in Thomas Middleton and William Rowley's *The Changeling* Beatrice-Joanna's transformation from 'lady' to a licentious 'whore' might be held to issue from her repression of violent sexual desire, which results in the split (indicated, perhaps, by her hyphenated name?) in her behaviour and eventually, her tragic downfall (Daalder 1999). In this older school, the critic sometimes acted as analyst to the author, and the literary work became the author's fantasies. Ernest Jones (1910; 1949), for example, takes Freud's own suggestion that *Hamlet* represents the expression of Shakespeare's own Oedipal complex (1900, 299) and develops the argument that Hamlet's famous delay in killing Claudius (until Gertrude herself is dead) is because Claudius has completed Hamlet's own fantasy to kill Gertrude's husband and marry her himself.

Later Freudian critics saw a fundamental problem with this simpler approach, for it misrepresents the analytic situation in a fundamental way: analysis is done in conjunction with – and in a large part by – the client, not only by the analyst him or herself. The analyst enables the client to interpret, and an analysis done without the client is likely to be more revealing of the analyst than anyone else. For this reason, contemporary Psychoanalytic critics tend to take as given a conception of culture and proceed by exploring literature as 'collaborative fantasies'. For them, characters are not so much projections of the author's psyche as they are manifestations of the psyche of the culture, as if the author is transcribing the collective's dream. Such a critic, according to Stephen Orgel (1986), should acknowledge that she/he too is implicated in the fantasy she/he describes, since any psychoanalysis is a collaboration between analyst and client and also because the analyst in this case is a member of the very culture she/he is 'putting on the couch' and therefore is analysing her/himself as much as any other aspect. Still other writers have chosen to use psychoanalytic insights selectively. In *John Donne: Life, Mind and Art* (1981), for example, John Carey ascribes Donne's distinctive literary personality to the trauma of his apostasy: Donne's conversion from Catholicism to the culture's dominant

Anglicanism opened a psychic wound from which the poet never fully recovered and to which his poetry continually returns.

Lacanian Theory

Another branch of Neo-Freudian theory emerged in the later twentieth century in the work of Jacques Lacan. Like Freud, Lacan held that the formative stages in human development depend upon entry into a symbolic realm, but unlike him, the crucial development of the child's psyche is for Lacan intricately involved with the development of language and the psyche's perception of the place of language in the whole symbolic system. According to Lacan, boys and girls enter into and deal with language – the 'Symbolic Order' – in fundamentally different ways (an aspect that attracts some Feminist critics while repelling others). In fact, Lacan proposes that the unconscious itself is structured and functions like language. Of those theoretical claims which have proved especially fertile for literary criticism, his notion of the 'Mirror Stage' is one of the most salient. This is a highly complex account of a developmental passage in which occurs the infantile formation of the Ego; and during which the mother becomes the first image of the Other for the infant: an experience that is self-affirming and alienating, at the same time. Kathryn Schwarz (2000) applies this theory to Book III of Spenser's *Faerie Queene*, when Britomart sees the image of her beloved Artegall in her magic mirror. Spenser's poetic narrative of Britomart's experience replicates Lacan's description of the simultaneous desire, identity and alienation in this 'Mirror Stage'. Schwarz uses this aspect of Lacanian Theory to examine the ideas of 'normal' female identity in British Renaissance culture – especially domesticity and its social and political dimensions – in relation to Britomart's warrior ethos, her masculine armour and the Amazon myth. Also fruitful has been the Lacanian notion of 'desire', the simultaneously biological/symbolic/imaginative/rhetorical energy that pulses through Renaissance sonnet tradition, fuelling the frustrations of the Petrarchan lover. As demonstrated by essays in Valeria Finucci and Regina Schwartz's collection *Desire in the Renaissance: Psychoanalysis and Literature* (1994), it is in the fictive, quasi-narrative realm of the sonnet sequence that the wounded, narcissistic, playfully self-deceptive Lacanian 'subject' of Sidney and Shakespeare can best be glimpsed.

On the other hand, Lynn Enterline's *The Tears of Narcissus* (1995) is grounded in Julia Kristeva's work on the infantile/preoedipal phase. Kristeva describes this psychological realm of instinctual experience and terms it the 'semiotic', in which the sounds and rhythms underlying language – similar to the motilities of the (maternal) human body – predominate over the (masculinist) meaning in words. Yet the child must leave its mother's breast to enter into the 'Symbolic Order', ruled over by the Law (and language) of the Father. Individual selfhood, subjectivity and identity rest upon this abandonment of the maternal/material/ semiotic for the masculinist spirit/logos, that is, for language as meaning, rather than as motility. Enterline argues that narcissism and melancholy in British

Renaissance literature are particularly masculinist phenomena in self-reflective male characters who blame their frustrations on female figures (especially mothers): bound still to the semiotic, their language fails – in effect, their self-expressions contain within them a semiotic content that exceeds the capacities of masculinist spirit/logos.

Reader-Response Criticism

Reader-Response Theory grew out of the developing study of hermeneutics and phenomenology; the application of such inquiry, in the literary sphere, resulted in an increasing interest in a basic question: what does it mean to 'read' – that is, to 'experience' – a text? Some, such as Wolfgang Iser and Louise Rosenblatt, concentrate on searching for elements in the text that control the reader's response. Some Renaissance critics, such as Norman Holland, delve more deeply into readers' psychological patterns of reading, combining Reader-Response with Psychoanalytic criticism; Holland's approach in fact, uses literature to lead readers into psychoanalyses of themselves (*The Dynamics of Literary Response*, 1968; *5 Readers Reading*, 1975), with the pedagogical intent to 'know one's self' through reading literature while Stanley Fish's later theoretical work proposes the existence of 'interpretive communities' of readers, predictable groups into which readers' interpretations may fall. Fish, who is probably the most influential Reader-Response theorist and critic in the field, argues that meaning, or controlling devices, are not located in the text at all. For Fish, what the text 'does' to a reader is more accurately a matter of what the reader 'does' to the text. His landmark text, *Self-consuming Artifacts* (1972), articulates the Augustinian theory of reading as a moral exercise: to misinterpret is in fact to demonstrate the weakness of the fallen intellect and to come, as a reader, to understand one's need to rely on God. Renaissance poetry thus is experienced as an entrapment of the reader to teach humility and proper reliance on Divine reason. In Fish's treatment of George Herbert's poetry in *The Temple*, for example, the poet's hymns of praise ultimately prove themselves to belong to the Divine, for, 'although [the poem or hymn] may appear to be the invention of our brains, [it] is in fact the result of God's "kindlings" ' (1972, 193). As such, the reader's experience is that of 'a surrender . . . of initiative, will and finally of being' (193). But further, 'To the extent that this surrender is also the poet's, it requires the silencing of his voice and the relinquishing of the claims of authorship, and therefore an undoing of the poem as the product of a mind distinct from the mind of God' (158). The poem 'consumes itself' as we read it.

Deconstruction

What we now call 'Deconstruction' may be said to have begun in the field of English literature in 1976, with Gayatri Chakravorty Spivak's translation of Jacques Derrida's *Of Grammatology* (1976). Many of Derrida's theories depend on his own critical applications of Heidegger and the field of phenomenology, ultimately exploring the complex relationships among the mind, the world and language. In its most basic terms, a Deconstructive reading of a text does not seek to find some system of meaning which would 'make sense of it' – but, on the other hand, a Deconstructive reading is not simply *destructive*, either; rather, it seeks to undo the text, or at least, to undo the sense of a governing authority inhabiting the text, to show that what we thought was 'The' meaning of the text turns out to be only one of a set of continually oscillating, indeterminate meanings. Deconstruction tries 'to tease larger systemic motifs out of gaps, aberrations, or inconsistencies in a given text . . . because it is aware that language, especially written language, is reflexive rather than representative; it folds back on itself in very interesting and complex ways that produce meanings that proliferate beyond an author's conscious control' (Crowley 1989, 7–8) and issue in *aporia*, a blockage or blind spot where the text undermines its own rhetoric or authority. Typically, a Deconstructive reading might proceed by probing and undoing what seem to be clear binary oppositions in a text: presence and absence, for example, or writing and speech. Jonathan Goldberg's *Voice Terminal Echo: Postmodernism and English Renaissance Texts* (1986) pioneered the application of Deconstruction to early modern literature; a more recent example is Peter C. Herman's *Destabilizing Milton: 'Paradise Lost' and the Poetics of Incertitude* (2005), which finds moments of *aporia* throughout Milton's literary canon.

Feminist Criticisms

Here we encounter a problem in terminology, since different kinds of 'Feminist' reading can result in multiple and radically different interpretations of any given work. So diverse are the different kinds of feminist readings that many now feel that the term 'Feminist criticisms' better describes the multiplicity of the field. In its early years, feminist criticism sought to answer: what happens to 'the feminine' in this work? This question resulted in two basic approaches to British Renaissance literature, though this is admittedly an oversimplified division. The first held that since Renaissance authors were predominantly male, and writing in a patriarchal culture, their female characters tend to reflect that perspective, being portrayed as either male-fantasy figures or as destroyers of masculinity who receive 'just' punishment (in the context of that culture) for their sins. Female figures in Renaissance literature, such criticism held, are either dangerous to or supportive of the proper, 'right' and 'good' order of the world of the work, and their respective punishments or rewards thus ultimately reinforce the reigning attitudes about women in the Renaissance culture. An early work of this category is Marilyn French's *Shakespeare's Division of Experience* (1981), which argued that Shakespeare presents female characters who are perfect constituents of their culture or who are rebellious or evil, but none who are merely human, as he does with male characters. The second approach was quite different; it maintained, to the contrary, that the period saw the appearance of some authors who were remarkably 'ahead of their time', who questioned the reigning assumptions about femininity in their own day or celebrated women who did not conform to the prescriptions for proper behaviour. The conventional view was that women were defective physically and, therefore (through the 'doctrine of correspondences'), flawed mentally and morally; however, some authors were what might be called 'proto-feminists' (or 'early' feminists) willing to portray and celebrate in their works strong, unconventional women who behaved against the grain of their culture's expectations and are admirable for that independence from the dominant cultural mores of their time. From this viewpoint, these British Renaissance authors subversively criticized the limitations placed on women in their culture and subtly advocated more social freedoms for women at the time. Perhaps the most important work of this earliest phase of Feminist criticism of British Renaissance literature was *The Woman's Part: Feminist Criticism of Shakespeare*, a pioneering collection of articles focused on Shakespeare's female characters edited by Carolyn Ruth Swift Lenz, Gayle Greene and Carol Thomas Neely (1980). Margaret W. Ferguson, Maureen Quilligan, and Nancy J. Vickers' groundbreaking collection *Rewriting the Renaissance* (1986), combined feminist criticisms with insights from Marxism, deconstruction and psychoanalysis to analyse the structures of power in the state and the home, and to explore examples of actual and fictionalized women in the history, literature and art of the period. Not only do the essays in the collection demonstrate the ways that women were marginalized in the home, the community and the state, but they explore evidence of various women's means of breaking the rules and circumventing the strictures placed upon them in the patriarchal world of Renaissance Europe.

Another phase of Feminist Criticism has since ensued that centres on combining Feminist Theory's insights with subsequent strands of critical theory. As Materialist/Feminist critic Kathleen McLuskie argued in 1989, what is 'the female experience' if not a culturally determined one? How can even the designation of 'feminine' be understood apart from culture? (See Gender Studies and 'Queer Theory' section below.) Nowhere is the dense interconnection of larger questions of 'culture' with ostensibly more circumscribed ones of 'gender' more apparent than it is in the Renaissance construction of ideal womanhood, which prescribed for female behaviour three interlocking 'cardinal virtues': chastity, obedience and silence. If a woman spoke, therefore, that breaking of her silence pointed not only to her disobedience, but also to her lack of chastity. Hence there was a sexual dimension to language use, and indeed many women were physically punished for being outspoken or were slandered as promiscuous for doing so. The behaviour manuals of the time period pointed out that it was only prudent to silence a woman, given the consequences of Eve's conversation with the serpent; and the proscription on female speech had roots in Aristotle, as well as in interpretations of the Bible. Clearly, linking silence to chastity and obedience was a way of limiting women's influence in public as well as domestic fora (see Chapters 1, 2 and 7). This cultural insight opened up many avenues for literary criticism, allowing the insights of Rhetorical Criticism to inform those of Feminist criticism, which extended this sensitivity to language use to examine fictional characters as well as to writers in the period. The late decades of the twentieth century also saw the reclamation of women Renaissance authors, whose works had been suppressed from publication when they produced them, or were vilified, ignored or quickly forgotten, when published. Feminist criticism of these women authors' works has become a major strand of British Renaissance literary criticism, noticing how the authors utilized and often subverted male authors' models, wrote about specific subjects of feminine concerns, or constructed defences of different aspects of female experience, such as authorship, for example.

Perhaps a simple and illustrative contrast of oppositional feminist readings of an author may be seen in the following views of Edmund Spenser's female characters in Book III (the allegory of chastity) of *The Faerie Queene*. Stevie Davies (1985) finds that Spenser's characterizations of Britomart and Amoret were informed by the age's Platonic 'Idea' of woman that was being modelled and even mythologized in the person of Queen Elizabeth. Britomart, the 'warrior-maiden' who rescues fellow damsels in distress, is an especially positive emblem of woman's equality with man – 'an inclusive image of perfection, touching all the female and all the male characters in the book in her mirroring of nature' (Davies, 6). On the other hand, Susan Frye argues that the two characters make visible the two definitions of chastity that concerned the late sixteenth century: Queen Elizabeth's definition (virginity, dramatized in the character of Britomart), and the culture's definition (possession by a male, visible in Amoret, who is held captive and threatened with rape by Busirane). Ironically, Britomart is forced to watch the captivity and torture of Amoret, providing an odd occasion in which one symbolic Elizabeth must watch another version of herself being violently assaulted in a presumed cautionary tale about the need for male protection. Since Busirane is something of a poet (as well as a magician), Frye argues that the sadistic male torturer and would-be possessor is a misogynistic figure of Spenser, himself.

Marxist/Materialist Criticism

The Marxist critic of British Renaissance literature reads from a standpoint of the economic conditions in the period – economic forces, modes of production and social classes – that is, the social constructs and the power struggles and ideologies that 'form and inform' societies. For the Marxist critic, society is controlled by those who own the means of production at any given time. In the Renaissance, the ruling class was the aristocracy: the means of production remained in large part bound to inherited land rights in the form of the feudal estates over which the aristocracy held sway. The peasantry, who worked on that land, were governed and (with some temporary rebellious exceptions) controlled by their aristocratic masters. However, the period also saw the rise of a new class, whose wealth came not through inherited land rights, but via trade. This mercantile class would in later centuries develop into the bourgeoisie; growing in power and self-confidence, it increasingly challenged the dominance of the aristocracy until, at the end of our period, outright conflict erupted in what for some Marxists would be best described as the English Revolution (other critics might call it a Civil War) (see Chapter 8 for a critique of such a Marxist position).

For the Marxist critic, everything in a culture proceeds from its economic base: human beliefs and values derive from material conditions, and other 'values', such as religious beliefs, or conceptions of virtue, for example, are fictions (ideologies) constructed so as to support and maintain the dominant class in its position of supremacy, legitimizing the ruling class by making its norms appear just and natural. These are complex and sometimes internally contested concepts, but broadly speaking, ideology, for the Marxist critic, is at least as powerful as force: a conviction that 'God has chosen us to rule and has endowed us with superior virtues so that you will be taken care of' is likely to be at least as efficacious in maintaining the status quo as a violent quelling of a rebellion. Marxist Criticism often seeks to expose the way in which ideologies operate in literary texts to legitimize the dominant (or hegemonic) power, and to mystify structures of oppression or articulations of resistance.

There are several variants on Marxist approaches, but one of the most influential has been Fredric Jameson's theory of the 'Political Unconscious' (1981) which borrows from Freud in positing that a culture has an unconscious need to reconcile the social contradictions present in it, and so creates through its art imaginary or fantasy solutions to these otherwise irreconcilable paradoxes. Through its literature (as well as other systems of symbolism), a culture tries either to resolve or to forget the social problems caused by the economic system at hand. Notable Marxist interventions in the field of Renaissance literature include Richard Halpern's *The Poetics of Primitive Accumulation* (1991), which argues that English Renaissance literature must be read in the context of Marx's observation that Sixteenth-century England was a site of the 'pre-history' of capitalism, where the process of 'primitive accumulation' dispossessed the feudal agrarian classes of their means of production and gradually forced them into more modern modes of 'employment'. Halpern examines humanist educational practices in the Tudor age as a locus not only of this transition from feudalism to capitalism but also of the renegotiation of class relations as the economy shifted. Also notable as Marxist treatments of the period are Jonathan Dollimore's *Radical Tragedy*, described in detail by Christopher Orchard in Chapter 4 of this volume (and sometimes defined as 'Cultural Materialism'); and Christopher Hill's *Milton and the English Revolution*, which is covered in Thomas Healy's concluding essay at the end of the handbook.

Although it is often defined more specifically by each of its practitioners, Cultural Materialism is most broadly distinguished from Marxism by its concern with the more physical, material items of economic production and their effects on class structures. These material products analysed by the Cultural Materialist literary critic may very well be the objects or 'stuff' that the labouring class characters produce in the literature – for example, the textiles women produce with distaff and spindle – but they may also be the cultural 'artefacts' (plays, poems, paintings, pictures) which appear in the literary works or even the dramas and books/texts themselves as cultural artefacts or material 'products' of the Renaissance. Such critics often seek to understand texts as historical processes, continually developing products of specific social formations, not merely simple outgrowths of the economic base. An early work in this vein was *The Politics and Poetics of Transgression* (1986) by Peter Stallybrass and Allon White, which addressed among other things the interrelation between categories of 'high' and 'low' culture, hierarchies of class and notions of the body. Certain genres or authors, for example, were in the Renaissance conceptually related to consumption by specific classes (as they are now: think of soap opera and opera, for example). Stallybrass and White were especially interested in examining the ways in which these complex and interconnected rankings might be undermined or transformed in certain circumstances. 'High' culture may be generally correlated with the aristocratic, the rational and orderly, and the classical body; and 'low' culture associated with – for instance – the peasantry, the irrational and disorderly, and the ugly or unwieldy body. But such binary dichotomies may be collapsed in certain circumstances or situations, most notably the carnival or fair, wherein oppositions intermix and become hybridized in figures which are grotesque and transgressive. Stallybrass and White drew upon the work of the Russian cultural critic Mikhail Bakhtin, whose work on the dialogic and on Carnival was very influential for critics of the 1980s and 1990s, and who remains a key figure in literary discourse today: other scholars who used his concepts include Jean-Christophe Agnew, in his *The Market and the Theatre in Anglo-American Thought 1550–1750*, and Michael D. Bristol's *Carnival and Theatre: Plebeian Culture and the Structure of Authority in Renaissance England*.

New Historicist Criticism (Cultural Poetics)

The lines between Cultural Materialism, and what is called Cultural Poetics, or more usually New Historicism, are blurry ones: these categories, it should be noted, overlap. But New Historicist criticism has, along perhaps with feminism, been the most influential theoretical approach of all in our field; indeed, it was out of Renaissance Studies that New Historicism emerged, with the publication, in 1961, of Stephen Greenblatt's *Renaissance Self-Fashioning* (described in detail by Christopher Orchard in Chapter 4). The popularity of New Historicism derives in part from its interdisciplinary nature, which is appealing to scholars and readers; its re-visioning of the historical era, furthermore is often thought to produce elegant views of the complexities of Renaissance culture.

Although it shares some characteristics with Marxism, New Historicism is influenced primarily by Michel Foucault and in particular, by his vision of power. For Foucault, Marx reduces power to economic exploitation, while it should better be understood as a 'rationalization' and complex use of discourse by conventional institutions in order to 'discipline' society and create notions of 'normality' to be accepted by all levels of the social structure (Best 1995, 115). In other words, where Marx sees deliberate oppression of the lower classes, Foucault emphasizes how the institutions 'produce' people and their ideas of identity, how all persons (even those in the governing institutions) rationalize their actions to believe they are creating the common good; and where Marx finds that labouring classes are regulated according to the needs of the ruling class, Foucault sees all social spheres – even the human body itself – disciplined by the power structures under which they exist (116). Two basic applications of British Renaissance New Historicism exist in today's books and journals: the complex methodology that was called 'New Historicism' by its inventor, Stephen Greenblatt, in the early 1980s; and a broader method of 'Localizing' or 'Local Reading' as it was originally coined by Leah Marcus (1990) – reading the literary work according to the specific cultural or political climate in the geographic location of the author and the narrowest time-span at the time of the work's composition (for example, Marcus analyses Jonson's *The Devil is an Ass* in the context of James I's speech before the Star Chamber of 20 June 1616 [1989, 85–105]).

Insisting upon basic instabilities of self, history, language (and therefore literary texts), Greenblatt's method (influenced by Foucault and cultural anthropologist Clifford Geertz) takes political power to be a matter of complex negotiations among groups identified as 'empowered' and 'powerless'. Those who wield power often court the favour of the powerless in various subversive ways, and vice versa: the social community, then, is comprised of complex strands of social energy that circulate among the various negotiating individuals or groups. At some point in a New Historicist exploration, the very terms 'empowered' and 'powerless' become unstable, since there is a constant oscillation between them. What appears to be political 'power', then, is actually a manifestation of an illusion, a theatrical feat, which inscribes a certain link between the monarchy and the theatre. This explains, Greenblatt argues, why Elizabeth and James loved the theatre so much. Not that this kind of negotiation is altogether conscious, however, in terms of the participants or the literary authors. The New Historicist often locates examples of these 'circulating energies' in literary works by analysing the nuances of works that were hitherto seen to be un-literary – such as pamphlets, local histories, behaviour manuals, medical records, court testimony, travelogues, letters, memoirs and so on – and applying them to the literary work at hand, whether or not the author could have had any knowledge of them. Then the literary work, in turn, may be seen to have effects on the circulation of that social energy, through further published works, through the powerful literary coteries or through the theatrical stage.

An example of this oscillation may be charted in the spectacles of public executions during the Elizabethan age. While a conventional analysis might come to the conclusion that public executions were held in order to deter crim inals in the crowd or to reassure law-abiding citizens that the crown was protecting them, Greenblatt (1988) notices the theatricalized aspects of executions: they were held on scaffolds that looked like stages, where the participants knew the 'script' and the 'audiences' knew their proper responses. Further, this 'staging' produced other rebels in the audience who no doubt vowed rebellion against the authority who brutalized their fellows before their eyes. Here the oscillation of energy foregrounds itself, for the monarchy's deliberate public 'staging' of executions produced the rebellion that it needed to consume in order to display its power. It is no wonder, Greenblatt argues, that Elizabeth loved the 'legitimate' theatre and subsidized it to keep it in operation, even in the face of mounting Puritan opposition.

Other exemplary New Historicist books include Leonard Tennenhouse's *Power on Display* (1986), which contributes the argument that genre and the totality of an author's canon can be analysed according to political developments rather than the customary biographical/psychological arc of a lifetime. In this case, Shakespeare's generic shifts are scrutinized in light of Elizabeth's versus James' reigns and the politics of gender. Tennenhouse most notably rescues comedy for New Historicist analysis and contributes his thesis that Shakespeare's 'strong women' were fashioned according to the monarch at the time of composition: his 'strong female characters' are rewarded with happiness during the Elizabethan age (Portia, Rosalind, Viola) and tend to be murdered (Cordelia) or vilified (Lady Macbeth, Regan, Goneril, Volumnia) in the misogynist reign of James. Like Greenblatt, Tennenhouse argues that Shakespeare's own middle-class identity and his writing for the public stage made his works both valuable for the monarchy's public display of its power (as the playwright sought to curry favour with court and patron) and objects of suspicion (as the playwright sought to please his audiences). Nancy Armstrong and Leonard Tennenhouse extend this investigation of the writer's cultural currency in *The Imaginary Puritan* (1992) to examine the notion that 'modern humanism began in writing and continues both to empower and to conceal the power of intellectuals' (27). Using Foucault's proposition that late-seventeenth-century writers became self-aware as authors and shapers of their cultures, they focus on Milton's *Paradise Lost* (1667) as a crucial point of transformation not only for the English culture – from the Renaissance aristocratic and patriarchal hierarchy to the middle-class-dominant marketplace of the Modern world of print capitalism – but also for Milton, himself, into that new creature, the writer, whose influence is shown to span the centuries and the Atlantic. A contradiction, of course, lay in the fact that so much of *Paradise Lost* displays Milton's spectacular Renaissance humanist education, which had been grounded in a classical pantheon of texts fit for the aristocratic mind of a previous century, but the poem solves this through its final emphasis, which falls on Milton's Puritan ethic of industry, conscience and morality that governs Adam and Eve's expulsion from Eden into their sacred mission of populating and civilizing the earth.

While most initial New Historicist criticism centred on Shakespeare, Donne and Jonson, all of whom wrote for patrons, audiences, aristocrats and others in obvious positions of power in the social structure of the period, Michael C. Schoenfeldt's *Prayer and Power: George Herbert and Renaissance Courtship* (1991) was perhaps the first to prove that New Historicism could illuminate the poetry of an apparently non-political devotional poet. Aiming to unite the sacred, poetic and political concerns of the culture, Schoenfeldt draws on a varied selection of material from Herbert's age to 'reconstruct a Herbert at once worldly and saintly, sophisticated and seraphic, whose sincere devotional motives are entangled in and enriched by the manipulative tactics of supplication that he practiced in the social world' (12). Perhaps the most intriguing reading in the book is Schoenfeldt's interpretation of 'Love (III)' – as 'a culmination of two kinds of behaviour which the [courtesy manuals] of Herbert's culture subjected to increasing regulation: table manners and sexual conduct' (15).

Postcolonialist Criticism

Edward Said's *Orientalism* (1978) is said to have begun Postcolonialist studies by examining how constructing the East and Middle East in a particular kind of exoticized way helped Western Europeans to colonize those areas. Another landmark work, Gayatri Chakravorty Spivak's 'Can the subaltern speak?' (1988), brought the theories of Marx and the Italian Marxist writer Antonio Gramsci to bear on the British colonizers' response to the Indian practice of *sati* (a widow's immolation of herself on her husband's funeral pyre). Postcolonialist critics working in the Renaissance use post-colonial theory to reconceptualize the history of Europe's imperialism in the New World, re-evaluating such concepts as 'nation', and 'native'; raising questions about the roles of language in attempts to enforce or resist the powers of colonization; and examining the ways in which the production and consumption of literature (modes of writing and reading it) were influenced by imperialism (O'Connor 2005, 297–98). Some scholars broaden the category to the more inclusive 'Ethnic Studies', a term which better allows attention to the range of ethnic encounters experienced by sixteenth and seventeenth century travellers, who met the indigenous people of the Americas (in their New World explorations) or the Africans, Moors, Turks and Asians in the course of their search for new trade routes. As a demonstration of the wide-ranging interests of British maritime commerce and conflict, Daniel Vitkus' collection *Piracy, Slavery, and Redemption* (2001) offers seven captivity narratives from Englishmen captured on the Barbary Coast (North Africa). These narratives supply a fascinating view of diplomatic relations between England and Islamic cultures during this period and provide invaluable details about the economic, religious and commercial practices of the Islamic captors, and the effects that captivity in this region of the world had upon the Englishmen. Nabil Matar's research on England's relationship with Turks (*Islam in Britain 1558–1685*, 1998; *Turks, Moors, and Englishmen in the Age of*

Discovery, 1999) provides groundbreaking evidence of bidirectional movement between Britain and the Ottoman Levant, as British merchants and soldiers travelled east and stayed as captives, slaves or free partners of Turkish pirates, then returned to Britain, sometimes as secretly converted Muslims. The impact of this cultural undercurrent in British drama is one of Matar's most provocative explorations: because the economic and cultural attractions of the Islamic regions had drawn these travellers to begin with, the English stage began to present hostile images of Islam, to compensate for the threat to the status quo that these eastern cultures presented. Combining Postcolonialism with Feminist critique, Ania Loomba identifies the literary treatment of race and ethnicity with that of gender (1989, 1996) and of sexuality and religion, (*Shakespeare, Race, and Colonialism* 2002), specifically arguing that modern colonization occurred alongside the development of capitalism (1998), and that the later ideologies of 'race' that emerged during colonization were not strong during the seventeenth century.

Concepts of Nationhood have been scrutinized in relation not only to New World exploration but also to England's relationship with Ireland and other parts of the British Isles during the sixteenth and seventeenth centuries (see Chapter 4). Willy Maley (*Salvaging Spenser: Colonialism, Culture and Identity*, 1997; *Nation, State and Empire in English Renaissance Literature: Shakespeare to Milton*, 2003) examines literature according to the 'new British historiography' – that is, that the concept of 'Britain' was in many ways invented during the Renaissance – and analyses not only Ireland in relation to concepts of Nationhood in English literature but also Scotland and Wales. Maley reveals how the literary works of previously assumed Anglocentric writers such as Spenser, Shakespeare and Milton actually participated in greater dialogues about broader British issues and identity, ultimately demonstrating that colonization began in the British Isles rather than abroad.

Applications of Postcolonialist theory to British Renaissance literature may be said to occur in three basic categories: (1) those works that are quite obviously 'about' colonialism; (2) works that are 'related' to colonialism, such as utopian narratives (e.g. works by Thomas More, Thomas Elyot and Edmund Spenser) and speculations about the nature of races that might exist in unknown regions of the globe; (3) literary works dealing with issues of race and ethnicity. Because of its implicit links with New World exploration, Shakespeare's *The Tempest* is probably the work from the British Renaissance that is most scrutinized from the first perspective listed above. This play has a rich history of criticism related to England's imperialism in the New World: Octave Mannoni's (1950) controversial psychology of the 'Caliban complex' proposed that the colonized native comes to desire the attention of the colonizer – Caliban in the play stages a revolt not because he wants freedom but because he feels abandoned by Prospero, according to Mannoni. In later decades, these theories were condemned as being precisely the sort of excuses that had been used to justify imperialism; further, Mannoni had ignored Caliban's ownership of the isle through his mother Sycorax. Ania Loomba (1989) argues that the historical obliteration of matriarchies by the patriarchal society is implied in the displacement of Sycorax by Prospero, who excuses his own actions by thinking of her as a black witch who bore an illegitimate son to the devil. Similarly, the Eurocentric view of indigenous people is figured in the play in Caliban's characterization as monstrous, rebellious and sexually violent. But Miranda teaches him English, which ultimately he subverts into his means of cursing his oppressors – a pattern demonstrated in imperialism, when the colonizers force their language on the natives to gain obedience but find it eventually turned into a medium of protest against them.

In studies of race and ethnicity, characters such as Cleopatra and Othello provide much ground for exploration, as does Marlowe's *The Jew of Malta*. Peter Berek (1998) argues that Marlowe's play may be seen as a drama about the presence of the 'Marrano' (a Jew who was allowed to reside in England based on willingness to convert to Christianity) in England during the crucial period following the Reformation, when the culture was inventing a national identity (130). Such Jews were always 'foreign, exotic, or "other" ', since England's doors had hitherto been closed to them; however, in the Marrano's conversion lurked an anxiety-producing fluidity of identity that emerged on the English Renaissance stage in characters such as Marlowe's Barabas and Shakespeare's Shylock – and not, as Berek shows, in contemporary discussions of *real* Marranos. Thus, argues Berek, much anti-semitism of subsequent British ages may have been influenced if not produced by such early renderings of Jewishness on the English stage (159). Conversely, James Shapiro (*Shakespeare and the Jews*, 1996) brings together exhaustive research to show that England had a veritable 'obsession with Jews' (88) that would tend to run contrary to the tiny number of them that resided in England by the sixteenth century. Shapiro argues that the English culture used these 'Jewish questions' to answer English concerns about the stability of their nation, religion and society, during a particularly unstable period of British history, since the defining nature of Jewishness in England at this time was instability (1).

Gender Studies and 'Queer Theory'

Gender Studies have taken over, it seems, where Feminist Criticism logically leads: patriarchy marginalizes not only women but any persons whose concepts of gender and gendered behaviours do not fit into the orthodox notions of 'normality'. Further, in granting elder males supreme dominance, any radical patriarchy (such as existed in the British Renaissance, where primogeniture was combined with male supremacy) disenfranchises younger males and, in effect, distorts cultural concepts of masculinity and even the psychologies and behaviours of individual men (who come to believe in their own godlike supremacy) to monstrous proportions. The applications of Gender Studies in this broader sense of sexual politics than the label 'Feminist criticism' might allow are quite varied. Alan C. Shepard's *Marlowe's Soldiers: Rhetorics of Masculinity in the Age of the Armada* (2002) is one such example: Shepard examines the rigid codes of masculinity and warfare that governed the English culture during the 1580s and 1590s and finds that Marlowe's plays rehearse various messages about 'playing the soldier' in the 'theatrics of masculinity' (3) on Marlowe's stage. For example, Shepard argues, there is an apparent endorsement of the glories of the warrior in *Tamburlaine* that is undercut by Tamburlaine's and his men's anxiety about the artifices of war and manhood (36).

Queer Theory seeks to destabilize identity categories as the mainstream culture knows them, where the basic ideas of the shapes and behaviour of human minds and bodies received from Enlightenment philosophy were seen to be 'essential' – that is, where identity and rationality were thought to be fixed traits inherited at birth. Male/female, heterosexual/homosexual, socially accepted/socially outcast: these 'essentialist' binaries are rejected by Queer Theory, along with even the notions that there are only two kinds of sexuality, heterosexual and homosexual (and that only the former pertains to families), and two genders, male and female. Individuals can be bisexual, autoerotic, transgendered or outside binary gender and sexual constructs entirely. For Queer Theorists, such notions of identity are merely 'constructed' by those structures of power and knowledge in society that try to keep 'good' and 'bad' values clearly demarcated. That which is understood linguistically and materially as sexuality and gender (as well as race and class) are always already available for contests of will and power. Therefore, accepting a variety of identities, behaviour and bodies enables humans to reconstruct themselves and communities in ways that are unbounded by limiting, oppressive categories into which most people simply do not fit. Alan Sinfield (2005) argues that, in fact, it is the very instability of hierarchies in social and political relationships that attract, repel and govern human fantasies and literatures. Queer Theory seeks to 'queer', or 'make peculiar or strange', *both* the dominant categories of identity *and* the minority/oppressed categories of identity while simultaneously valorizing difference, opening up possibilities for being in the world. As Jonathan Goldberg points out, 'queering' the literature of the Renaissance does not mean looking for homosexual themes; it means *freeing* the texts from an assumed heterosexual reading (1994: Introduction).

Eve Sedgwick's *Between Men: English Literature and Male Homosocial Desire* (1985) was a landmark work of Queer Theory, defining her newly invented term 'homosocial' as a system of 'male friendship, mentorship, entitlement, rivalry and hetero- and homosexuality' (1) that ultimately finds its deepest bonds in the domination of women. In fact, Sedgwick argues, a fear or hatred of homosexuality often accompanies these homosocial male relationships. She argues that the 'triangulation' in Shakespeare's sonnets examines the male-to-male relationship of the early sonnets that is then made seemingly dangerous and unstable by the woman's potential subversion of the masculine bond. Howard Marchitell's analysis of sado/masochistic domination in Jonson's *Volpone* (1991) examines the servant/master relationship of Mosca and Volpone and also Celia's position in the male homosocial community. Ultimately, Marchitell finds that Jonson extends the domination and sadism towards his own audiences whom he 'continually wooed and simultaneously reviled' (288).

Important contributions have been Jonathan Goldberg's collection of essays *Queering the Renaissance* (1997), the book that brought Queer Theory into Renaissance studies, and Alan Bray's *Homosexuality in Renaissance England* (1982), which provides groundbreaking historical research about the existence, numbers and cultural practices of the London 'molly houses' (male brothels). Mario diGangi in *The Homoerotics of Early Modern Drama* (1997) argues that, because of the taboos of the time and therefore the limited evidence available to us about same-sex relationships, our modern concepts of sexual identity and sexual orientation do not correspond with those of the Renaissance and, therefore, a more useful examination of the literature of the age should focus on homoeroticism and the distinctions between 'orderly' and 'disorderly' expressions of male-to-male friendship and love. Valerie Traub's *The Renaissance of Lesbianism in Early Modern England* (2002) contributes a literary study as well as a social and cultural history of women via a vast collection of texts – not only drama and poetry but also anatomy and medical books, midwifery manuals, pornography, theological books, marital conduct manuals and travel books – to analyse what scholars long considered even more elusive and 'impossible' than male homosexuality in the period. Her findings indicate that behaviour disruptive to the social norms of the time (transvesticism, for example) was branded criminal. Love between women was thought to be licit because 'technically chaste' (52) early on but, increasingly in the late seventeenth century, was presented as perversion or at least in need of social discipline in the form of 'companionate marriage' (265).

Postscript

This, then, concludes what can only be a partial overview of the approaches that have been taken to the rich literature of the early modern period. Are any of these approaches more valid or more useful than any other? Can a given critical theory be applied to all literature? Some would say 'Yes', arguing that critical approaches are allied with political stances and that, therefore, the critic's duty is to provide students with consistent political readings that give them alternative choices to their culture's messages, allowing them to question the 'status quo'. Others argue that more valuable is the presentation of a plurality of critical approaches, so that the individual student may choose viewpoints consistent with his or her own ways of thinking. Still others point out that, practically speaking, specific pieces of literature seem to 'open themselves' more readily to certain theories than others: for example, the Lacanian approach fits well within the sonnet tradition because sonnets tend to be about desire and selfhood; feminist theory may have a natural affinity with Shakespearean comedy; Marxist analyses may prove especially useful to account for the tensions in – say – Revenge Tragedy. At the end of the day, though, you, like the critics you read, should adopt the approach that you like best, and believe in most. For that sense of interest and intellectual commitment is what is likely to generate the most convincing, and most compelling, readings of the texts that you want to understand.

Changes in the Canon

Joshua B. Fisher

In his diary entry for Monday 26 August 1661, Samuel Pepys offers the following brief account of the day's play-going experiences: 'thence to the Theatre, and saw *The Antipodes*, wherein there is much mirth, but no great matter else'.[1] Pepys' succinct assessment of Richard Brome's 1636 play provides a useful starting point for a discussion of the literary canon and its development in the late twentieth and early twenty-first centuries. The 'great matter' that Pepys fails to find in the play is at the heart of conventional definitions of the literary canon, itself concerned first and foremost with the lasting and impacting artistic merit of literary works. To be fair, Pepys was often notoriously difficult to please when it came to theatre and popular drama was at this point rarely considered for its literary merit, with the exception of folio publications of works by Shakespeare, Jonson and Beaumont and Fletcher earlier in the seventeenth century.[2] In addition, the canonical works in Pepys' time were almost exclusively limited to ancient Roman and Greek as well as biblical authors, although the idea that 'modern' authors could also merit inclusion was increasingly gaining favour. Yet even to this day, Brome's work often continues to be met with the kind of dismissive response voiced by Pepys. Left out of most anthologies of literature and drama from the early modern period, *The Antipodes* and Brome's other work is infrequently performed and seldom taught in university curriculum save for the occasional special topics course or graduate seminar.[3]

While few today would dispute that *The Antipodes* is a non-canonical work, recent reception of Brome's play is part of a larger development that is re-shaping the parameters and strictures of the conventional literary canon. Far from recognizing no 'great matter' in Brome's life and works, Richard Cave at the University of London and his fellow editors of the online Richard Brome Project have this to say about the author and his works:

> The distinctive feature of Brome's dramaturgy is the highly inventive forms of theatricality through which he promotes his stringent satire of Caroline society, the politics of trade, the commercialism of court life, the surreal nature of a world governed by an absolutist monarch, and the moral vacuity of forms of drama achieving fashionable success within such a society. Most of Brome's plays need contextualizing within the theatrical, political and social history of their time.[4]

According to the editors, online publication enables this kind of contextualizing by interlinking searchable early texts (both print and manuscript) with modern editions, commentary, annotations, pictorial resources such as maps, glossaries and other resources. The editors' assessment of Brome's significance and their defence of the Richard Brome Project offer a remarkably telling indication of the ways in which attitudes towards the value of early modern literature and of canonical versus non-canonical works have changed in recent years.

Perhaps the most significant word in the above description is *contextualizing*, since, as we will see below, attending to the historical, cultural and social contexts of early modern literature has become a key focus of literary inquiry and has significantly transformed the valuing of literary texts from the period. For Pepys, the play offers little of value beyond some humorous diversions. Yet for the editors of the Richard Brome Project, Brome's work serves as a kind of social transmitter or conductor that is at once a window into and a product of early modern socio-cultural forces and institutions (including the theatre, the court, trade and commercialism). As such, the play becomes valuable not exclusively for its aesthetic or even its diverting properties, but rather as a productive entity in the enterprise of understanding and negotiating early modern culture. While this does not necessarily change the status of Brome's play as a 'non-canonical' work in the conventional sense of the literary canon, it does indicate the significant transformations that are currently taking place in the perceived value and usefulness of early modern literature. Thus, the question of inclusion in or exclusion from the canon is often eclipsed by the question of what texts will prove most productive and conducive in the project of illuminating and interpreting early modern culture and its practices.

Having highlighted this profound shift in the perceived value of early modern literature and its interpretation, it is necessary to emphasize that the canon in its conventional sense is neither dead nor irrelevant. Rather, as numerous scholars and theorists have pointed out, the canon is malleable and ever-changing. As will be explored below, in recent years a number of representative works by traditionally marginalized and sometimes dissident voices (women, minorities, cultural outsiders) have found their way into the canon. In other cases, attending to these voices has highlighted the boundaries between canonical and marginal or non-canonical works. While this sometimes involves challenging the integrity and the viability of canonical texts within academic curricula and institutions, rarely is this a complete refutation of the evaluating mechanisms on which the canon is predicated. In other words, even when the canon is being challenged directly, it is usually in the interest of serving an alternative or supplemental conceptualization of the canon.

Take, as a brief example, the seminal collection of early modern women's autobiographical writing *Her Own Life* edited by Elspeth Graham, Hilary Hinds, Elaine Hobby and Helen Wilcox in 1989. While this collection and others like it were prompted by concerns about the absence of female voices from the conventional canon and sought to forge a separate path outside canonical works, the collection simultaneously worked to broaden and expand notions of the canonical to include both women writers and literary genres conventionally deemed non-canonical such as private diaries, epistolary correspondences and spiritual confessions.

In such cases, the current shift in literary value from the largely aesthetic to the largely productive has invigorated marginal and non-canonical works while potentially devaluing the category of the canonical at least within the traditional meaning of that term as 'great' literature. Yet this does not mean that those works traditionally included in the canon are necessarily being excised from curriculum or scholarly study. Rather, as we will see, the emphasis on contextualizing works within historical and cultural frameworks has reinvigorated the canonical status of familiar texts, albeit on new terms that do not necessarily privilege the aesthetic superiority of the work nor the distinctive 'genius' of the author. This also means that a conventionally non-canonical play like Brome's *The Antipodes* is increasingly given scholarly attention (in criticism and even in the classroom) alongside canonical works such as Shakespeare's *The Tempest* and Marlowe's *Tamburlaine* in the interest of illuminating cultural considerations (early modern conceptions of self and other, travel encounters, representations of power and the imagination, etc.) Rather than single-handedly dismissing Brome's play as necessarily inferior to Shakespeare's and Marlowe's on formal and aesthetic grounds, scholars increasingly emphasize the significance of traditionally marginal texts and materials to elucidate cultural practices and understanding. Not simply providing background or supplement to canonical works, texts such as *The Antipodes* become completely implicated in the production and interpretation of early modern culture.

What then can this mean for the canon and its future? What are the implications for studying texts in the classroom and in scholarship, particularly with regard to the apparent divide between cultural and formalist considerations? Should we conclude (as many who lament the cultural changes taking place have) that the very integrity of an established literary hierarchy is threatened when works such as Brome's play are included in scholarly discourse and classroom curriculum? Or should we take the position that many cultural critics have in questioning the very relevance of an established literary hierarchy? Does the privileging of cultural and historical considerations over aesthetic ones amount to an unrelenting 'assault on the literary masterpieces' as lamenting critics including Alvin Kernan have charged? Or can the aesthetic aspects of a text (its status as a thing of beauty) actually be enhanced when that text's distinction as a material object in a particular cultural time and place is considered? Before exploring these issues more closely, it is useful to focus on how these ideological changes have come about over the past few decades. By first examining how the modern literary canon took shape, we will be able to recognize that cultural factors including politics, religion and the growth of the consumer market have always played key roles in the very development of the canon.

Canon Definitions and Developments

In all of its meanings, the word canon is associated with the idea of measuring value. Canon derives from the ancient Greek *kanon* (**κανόνας**) meaning a ruler or measuring rod. This word perhaps stems from the word *kanna* meaning reed (and the cognate term cane) – the standard measuring device for carpentry and other trades in the ancient world. The word's other ancient meaning, as a list, often overshadows the notion of a canon as a standard by which quality or value can be determined. This most likely results from the use of the term, starting in the fourth century CE, to designate authorized scriptural texts and to distinguish these from apocrypha. While the idea of an authoritative list is certainly central to the biblical canon designating official scriptural books, laws and saints, it is important not to lose sight of the notion of canon as a standard of measure when considering the literary canon and its impact. In fact, even as the idea of the literary canon was taking shape in Europe during the medieval period, the biblical, patristic and classical works that found inclusion there were recognized as a standard by which aesthetic, spiritual and intellectual values could be measured. In addition to recognizing the authority of the scriptural canon, readers during the middle ages acknowledged the canonical status of *auctores*, patristic and classical writers who were considered worthy of study in medieval schools and universities.[5] Such value stems from the writer's *auctoritas*, a claim to truth that could only be sanctioned by the church. For this reason, contemporary medieval writers were by and large prevented from seeking inclusion in the literary canon as *auctores*.

Most scholars identify the fourteenth century as a significant turning point in the development of the literary canon. Poets such as Dante, Petrarch, Chaucer and Gower were highly conscious of their positions as self-promoting authors, at once cognizant of their literary predecessors and confident in their abilities to establish themselves as significant writers in their own right. Such efforts played a key role in transforming the canon into a more malleable entity concerned not only with literary preservation but also with questions of literary value, including the assessment of 'modern' writers as potential *auctores*. While the economic, social and religious changes taking place in the fourteenth century are too complicated and extensive to outline in the present discussion, suffice it is to say that economic mobility, the flourishing of patronage support systems for the arts, early religious reform placing emphasis on individual devotion, and other such factors played important roles in the promotion and preservation of contemporary works within the late medieval canon. In England, for example, the self-promoting authorial efforts of Geoffrey Chaucer (*c.* 1343–1400) as well as his reception as the 'father' of English poetry in the fifteenth century and beyond helped to transform the canon into a 'living, plural, and heroically autonomous tradition' (Ross 1998, 44) in which contemporary authors could be ranked alongside ancient classical authorities.

Along with the rise of print and the influence of humanism by the sixteenth century, the English literary canon in the early modern period arguably became even more dynamic and subject to the self-promoting concerns of individual courtiers, scholars and writers within a distinctly rhetorical culture (see Chapters 1 and 2). According to scholars such as Trevor Ross, the 'rhetorical' culture of early modern England prioritizes a uniform and ubiquitous evaluative community that assesses texts and individuals based on their ability to conform. Where an 'objective' culture (such as the one that takes shape in England by the eighteenth century) places emphasis on the reception of texts as distinct objects to be consumed by discriminating and autonomous readers, a rhetorical culture emphasizes the production of texts to the extent that they will be capable of *re-producing* through verbal power the distinct values and ideals of the cultural community. So, for example, writers (including canonical ones such as Edmund Spenser, Sir Philip Sidney and Ben Jonson) 'wrote not for an autonomous audience but in the service of social relations' (Ross 65), particularly those social relations that would confirm the writer's and the work's allegiance to the specific values and standards of the community. In this system, canonization arguably has less to do with the unique virtues of a particular work of art and more to do with that work's effectiveness in representing and circulating 'a restrictive order of polite values' (Ross 65).

At the same time, as a result of the rise of print during the late sixteenth and early seventeenth centuries, literary works increasingly came to be seen as objectified commodities and this potentially overshadowed their relevance as instruments of social relations and transactions. Thus, many authors worked to enforce clear distinctions between literary works (both in print and manuscript) and the innumerable printed materials that potentially threatened the integrity of a closed system of social relations between author, text and reader that had characterized an exclusive (coterie) manuscript culture throughout the Middle ages and into the early Renaissance. Lyly's terse admonition that 'bookes be stale when they be printed, because they be common'[6] reflects the 'stigma of print' that many writers in the late sixteenth and early seventeenth centuries espoused (see the Introduction to this volume). Yet the distinction is not so much concerned with all books in print as it is with those 'innumerable sortes of

Englyshe bookes, and infinite fardles of printed pamphlets'[7] that potentially undermine an integral literary canon by blurring the lines between a distinct evaluative community and the more general and indiscriminate readership to which printed works would often be subjected. A pamphlet published in 1591 by an author identified only by the initials R. W. voices this kind of anxiety about the influx of printed materials:

> We live in a printing age, wherein there is no man either so vainly, or factiously, or filthily disposed, but there are crept out of all sorts unauthorized authors, to fill and fit his humor, and if a man's devotion serve him not to go to the Church of God, he neede but repayre to a Stationers shop and read a sermon of the [devil's] . . . every red-nosed rimester is an author, every drunken mans dreame is a booke . . . in a word, scarce can a cat looke out of a gutter, but out starts a halfpenny Chronicler, and presently *A proper new ballet of a strange sight* is endited.[8]

Promoting a distinct and autonomous literary tradition for England in the early modern period involved attempting to draw clear distinctions between the common printed texts of 'unauthorized authors' and those works which upheld 'the universalism of values authoritatively set out in the writings of the ancients' (Ross 1998, 151), thus aligning concerns for self-promotion and personal distinction with the stability of canonical authority and precedent. In turn, this move towards autonomization, stimulated by an increasingly competitive marketplace of print in the seventeenth century, arguably underscores a gradual but profound shift from a rhetorical to an objective culture.

By the eighteenth century, an emerging cultural emphasis on probabilistic knowledge ushered in by the rise of the new science and its embracing of contingency arguably led to a shift from a rhetorical culture to an objective one, from 'valuing persuasion by seduction to valuing persuasion by evidence' (Ross 151). Many scholars have suggested that this shift plays a crucial role in the reconceptualizing of the canon from the eighteenth century to the early twenty-first century, most notably in terms of giving shape to essentialized notions of value that have fuelled debates about the canon up to the present day. Prioritizing the experiential gives rise to 'an ideology of the aesthetic', a fusing of perception and cognition that 'sublimely overwhelms the reader in an inexhaustible tide not of rhetoric but of representation and knowledge . . .' (Ross 158). Emphasizing the aesthetic in turn perhaps helps to resolve the potential paradoxes inherent in literary value by promoting a belief in literature's inherent ability to convey as well as conform to essential truths. In a society increasingly concerned with the refinement of manners through the consumption rather than the production of cultural commodities, literary texts were infinitely reproduced through elaborate editions as well as through analysis and critical commentary in an effort to drive the process of acculturation. Discussing the rise of literature anthologies in the eighteenth century, Barbara Benedict explains how this culture of consumption transforms the role of the reader 'from that of a collaborative participant in forging literary culture to that of a recipient of commodified literature who reads poetry to train his or her moral response' (Benedict 1996, 6).

As England became a society increasingly driven by commodity consumption through the eighteenth and nineteenth centuries, the idea of a 'pure poetry' characterized by aesthetic value worked to distinguish literary representation from the countless commodities within the marketplace that would otherwise threaten to debase the status of literary works. Such efforts range from the 'transporting Passion' that Joseph Addison ascribes to Milton's *Paradise Lost* and its impact on readers to Immanuel Kant's efforts to define the aesthetic experience as an emotional rather than a rational one to Matthew Arnold's objective approach emphasizing the 'high seriousness' and 'high truth' attainable by literature. Such criticism worked to distinguish art from the interests and pressures of an increasingly commodified culture while simultaneously treating the act of reading literary texts as the consumption of 'cultural capital' capable of cultivating taste and shaping moral autonomy.[9] By the middle of the twentieth century, the view of canonical literature as upholding a romanticized and universal aesthetic value was thoroughly in place. Following the Arnoldian view that literature (particularly poetry) is capable of conveying universalized 'truths', critics from T. S. Eliot and the Leavises to the mid-century New Critics and more recent scholars such as Harold Bloom, Alvin Kernan and Frank Kermode assert the steadfast and essential authority of the literary canon.[10]

While this trajectory from a rhetorical to an objectivist culture is one way to understand the factors that have shaped the modern literary canon, it is important to recognize that more particular and localized aspects of a given culture also play key roles in determining whether or not texts find inclusion in the canon. Take, for example, the case of early modern English dramatists. While writers such as Thomas Middleton, John Webster and Thomas Dekker can be included alongside William Shakespeare, Ben Jonson, and Francis Beaumont and John Fletcher as canonical, this has not always been the case. Nor have the works by the former writers been so extensively incorporated into the canon as have those of the latter. Most would explain this discrepancy by pointing to the apparent aesthetic superiority of work by Shakespeare and Jonson (perhaps less so for Beaumont and Fletcher), but other important factors must be identified here.

Following Shakespeare's death, the majority of his works were gathered together and published (many for the first time) by fellow actors and company shareholders John Heminges and Henry Condell. By the time of the Great London Fire of 1666, when countless singular copies of plays and other diffuse texts went up in flames along with most of the city, Shakespeare's folio had seen several editions and was safely secured in numerous printed copies. So too was the fate of Jonson's work secured after his revolutionary gesture of including most of his plays among his collected *Workes of Benjamin Jonson* published in folio form in 1616. And Beaumont and Fletcher's unpublished plays were easily obtained from their theatre company, The King's Men, and printed together in a 1647 folio edition.[11] In contrast, as Gary Taylor has recently emphasized in the introductory section of *Thomas Middleton: The Collected Works* (2007), playwrights including Webster, Dekker and especially Middleton wrote for multiple theatre companies and lacked the posthumous support for folio publications. Neither friends and family members nor scholars collected and published the plays following these writers' deaths. Thus, numerous unprinted and singular copies of plays and other writings failed to survive the tumultuous years of the English civil war, the Restoration (when nostalgia for Elizabethan drama favoured Shakespeare, Beaumont and Fletcher, and a handful of others more amenable to Restoration manners and political ideologies) and the Great Fire. Taylor estimates that about one-half of Middleton's plays were lost as a result (Taylor and Lavagnino 2007, 25–58).

While this factor speaks less directly to the question of canon inclusion than it does to the mere survival of plays, it does underscore how the process of canon formation entails more than simply selecting from a predetermined list of literary texts. As Taylor explains, while the modern English literary canon was taking shape in the century and a half following Middleton's death, Middleton's extant writings were largely being forgotten and ignored. Even though Middleton as well as Dekker, Webster and other seventeenth century dramatists found their way into the canon eventually, such inclusion was often limited to a handful of representative works.[12] Thus, one might say that the canonical status of writers such as Shakespeare and Jonson is not entirely unrelated to the presence of cohesive folio editions of their work either within their own lifetimes or shortly thereafter. By the time that the modern literary canon was taking shape within the eighteenth century consumer marketplace, the comprehensive textual presence of writers such as Shakespeare was well established.

Born out of this emerging consumer culture of the eighteenth century, the literary canon was fostered by the institutionalization of English literary study as an academic discipline in the nineteenth and twentieth centuries. Literary anthologies, critical discourses, and course syllabi tended to promote the hierarchical ordering of canonical works and highlighted the canon's distinct role as an agent of both cultural preservation and change (at least to the extent that the canon can be revised and updated to reflect changing cultural values while always upholding the distinction between 'high and mighty' and 'mean and contemptible' works).[13] Yet it was in the realm of academic study that the authority of the literary canon significantly came under scrutiny, thus initiating the so-called 'culture wars' that would radically transform and re-shape attitudes towards the canon (and towards the theoretical and cultural stakes of literary study) by the end of the twentieth century. In the late 1980s, institutions such as Stanford University modified their great books programs, thereby posing a direct challenge to the authority of the traditional canon on the grounds that all but 'dead, white, European males' had been excluded. Writers representing diverse backgrounds based on gender, class, race, religion and sexuality were now given voice alongside (or in some cases in place of) more traditional canonical writers. Immediately, controversy arose on campuses and among cultural pundits, newspaper editorials and academic journals both defending and lamenting such decisions to overhaul traditional great books programs.[14]

Key questions in the debate included the following: Should college and university literature courses incorporate non-canonical authors? If so, how many canonical authors should be excised in order to accommodate the new voices and perspectives? Should the canon be preserved, carefully expanded and revised, or eliminated completely from academic curriculum? Intense and heated responses came from both sides of the debate during the late 1980s and continued through the 1990s. Traditionalists such as William Bennett, Lynn Cheney, Allan Bloom, E. D. Hirsch and Alvin Kernan lamented the 'assault' on humanistic tradition and condemned 'radical' critics who question the literary canon in terms of its ability to 'mak[e] permanent statements about absolute truths' (Kernan 1990, 70). On the other side of the debate, multiculturalists as well as a wide range of Post-Structuralist theorists employed historical and cultural modes of criticism to challenge and oppose the image of the conventional literary canon as the transcendent articulation of universal human truths and concerns.[15] Taking on the question of canon-formation directly in *Contingencies of Value*, Barbara Herrnstein-Smith argues that 'works cannot become canonical unless they are seen to endorse the hegemonic or ideological values of dominant social groups [i.e. white, Eurocentric males]' (Herrnstein-Smith 1988, 51). Such assertions led many traditionalist critics to charge that their radical adversaries were using the canon debate and embracing cultural pluralism to undermine the conventional hierarchy of academic institutions (both the university and the curriculum). Yet critics such as John Guillory have been instrumental in reminding us that the grounds of the 'culture wars' are not so clear-cut, particularly with regard to the stakes of canon reformation.

Calling attention to the distinction between the canon as an 'imaginary totality of works' and the syllabus as a finite and malleable iteration of that totality, Guillory emphasizes how the canon works as cultural capital. The process of selecting works for inclusion in a syllabus is not so much about the representation of individual authors as it is about the distribution of texts that embody particular cultural currency and this in turn reflects how the canon itself registers as a barometer of cultural values. 'Changing the syllabus cannot mean in any historical context overthrowing the canon, because every construction of a syllabus *institutes* once again the process of canon formation' (Herrnstein-Smith 1988, 81).

Guillory's distinction between the 'imaginary' canon and the syllabus provides a cautionary corrective for each side of the canon debate. For those seeking to expand, reform or even reject the conventional canon, Guillory's argument demonstrates that a pluralistic curriculum cannot create a pluralistic society and that canon reformation must be understood not so much as a product of inclusion and exclusion of individual works and authors but rather as a process of distributing cultural currency. As such, 'the totality of the canon as an imaginary list is always in conflict with the finite materiality of the syllabus, the fact that it is constrained by its institutional time and space' (Guillory 1993). Choosing to include a 'marginal' author on a class syllabus does not equal overhauling the canon, although as we will see, re-thinking syllabi and curriculum can play a key role in re-conceptualizing the very idea of an authoritative canon. For traditionalists attempting to preserve a singular and stable canon, Guillory's discussion reveals how canon formation can be an imprecise process and not simply a matter of identifying and preserving the 'great' works. As Susan VanZanten Gallagher describes it, 'Although the biblical canon was intentionally formed in a series of church councils, it is a deceptive namesake for the literary canon, which never was identified by any formal deliberation of dead (or live) white males. The literary canon is a baggy monster, a fluid movement of ebbs and flows, ins and outs – imaginary, therefore, as opposed to concrete' (Gallagher 2001, 54).

Recent work investigating the cultural stakes of the canon-forming process (including Guillory as well as historically focused critics such as Ross) have helped to refute the idea that those who scrutinize canon-formation through the lens of cultural and historical priorities are solely interested in undermining the authority and integrity of the traditional canon. Given that the development of curriculum and syllabi play a key role in shaping the 'imaginary' or theoretical canon, any argument that would seem to favour abolishing the canon makes no sense. As Gallagher argues in defence of canon reform, within the context of the classroom, some kind of 'pedagogical' canon would always exist. 'As long as we continue to teach literature, pedagogical canons will exist, and as they change, so will the imaginary canon. Part of our pedagogy, then, includes our contribution to the ongoing construction of the imaginary canon' (Gallagher 2001, 56). This statement could be modified by recognizing the relationship between pedagogical and imaginary canons as a symbiotic one, where each plays a key role in the construction and transformation of the other.

What then does this mean for developments in the canon of early modern literature during the late twentieth and early twenty-first century? Has the emphasis on pluralistic and multicultural voices meant that lesser known and marginal writers such as Robert Daborne, Ann Dowriche and Margaret Cavendish are *replacing* writers such as Shakespeare, Milton and Spenser in classrooms and scholarship? Does the inclusion of such voices within the space of the pedagogical (or even 'imaginary') canon help to re-think the place of traditionally canonical authors without necessarily *displacing* them? Or, as critics such as Allan Bloom have cautioned, do such non-canonical voices signal a move towards relativism that would undermine the very foundations of our cultural heritage?[16] To explore these issues, it is useful to examine four distinct case studies that reflect changes to the canon over the last few decades. These include the following categories: (1) Women Writers, (2) Outsiders and 'Others', (3) Cheap Print and Ephemera and (4) Documentary and Source Materials. Each category reflects a range of texts and materials that have come to be incorporated into the canon or which have helped to re-shape the parameters of canonicity by complicating distinctions such as canonical versus marginal and elite versus popular. While these categories are by no means representative of all of the changes to the canon over the past forty years or so, they are among the most significant.

Women Writers

Long after Virginia Woolf's famous elegy lamenting the absence of writings by a hypothetical 'Shakespeare's sister' (Woolf 1929), most scholars continued to support the assertion that women indeed 'did not have a Renaissance of their own' (Kelly-Gadol 1977). With several notable exceptions including Aphra Behn, Katherine Philips and Anne Finch, most sixteenth and seventeenth century women writers found very little representation in the literary canon from their own century until well into the twentieth. Even by the 1970s, as critics and students began to take up Joan Kelly-Gadol's famous question concerning whether women had a Renaissance of their own, many tended to re-affirm that women's writing found little purchase in the seemingly hostile, patriarchal environment of early modern England (Kelly-Gadol 1977). Indeed, much of this first wave of feminist criticism emerging in the 1970s and 1980s concerned itself with representations of women in male-authored works (Eve in *Paradise Lost*, for example) rather than with writings by women[17] (see Chapters 4 and 6).

Developing out of a number of important colloquia and conferences held during the mid to late 1980s on the topic of early modern women writers, the Society for the Study of Early Modern Women proved hugely important to the expanding presence of women writers in literary canons both theoretical and pedagogical. Perhaps most significant of all were the inaugural publication of two major series of writings by early modern women. The first, *Women Writers in English 1350–1850* (General Editors Susanne Woods and Elizabeth Hagemen) includes six major volumes each edited by an individual scholar and presenting the work of one early modern writer. These include Anne Askew, Lady Eleanor Davies, Aemilia Lanyer, Rachel Speght, Lady Arabella Stuart and Anna Weamys. The texts are based on the Brown Women Writers Project and are published 'to make available a wide range of unfamiliar texts by women' (Woods and Hageman 1993–2003, ii). The second, larger series, *The Early Modern Englishwoman: A Facsimile Library of Essential Works* (General Editors Betty Travitsky and Patrick Cullen) includes twelve facsimile volumes of works in both print and manuscript for the purpose of 'remedy[ing] one of the major obstacles to the advancement of feminist criticism of the early modern period, namely the unavailability of the very texts upon which the field is based' (Travitsky and Cullen 2000, vi). The series includes works by major writers such as Mary Sidney Herbert and Mary Wroth as well as less familiar figures such as Eleanor Davies and Alice Sutcliffe.[18]

Writing in 2008, it is difficult now to fathom that the works of many of these writers were deemed 'unavailable' less than a decade ago. Any quick perusal through early modern literature anthologies published by Norton, Longman or other major presses will reveal a well-represented selection of early modern women writers, especially Anne Askew, Elizabeth Cary, Mary Sidney Herbert, Elizabeth I, Mary Wroth, Aemelia Lanyer, Margaret Cavendish, Katherine Philips and Aphra Behn, among others. In turn, numerous scholarly essays and monograph studies are devoted to early modern women writers and their cultural, literary and historical significance. Not simply serving to illuminate more thoroughly established canonical writing (mostly by men), early modern women's writing provides crucial insights into a wide range of issues, from identity construction in domestic as well as political spheres to the development of emerging genres (the country house poem, for example, has important examples by female as well as male writers).[19]

Several compelling recent examples will help to illustrate these developments. Queen Elizabeth I's *Collected Works* (2000) edited by Leah S. Marcus, Janel Mueller and Mary Beth Rose, has made available for the first time, a modern, scholarly edition of the queen's poetry, speeches, private letters and other writings (Marcus, Mueller and Rose 2000). The collection has had the effect of putting Elizabeth I squarely on the literary map as numerous scholarly essays, critical studies and classroom syllabi focusing on Elizabeth's writings have subsequently emerged.[20] Lesser-known and long forgotten writers have also found their way into this expanding canon. Contributing to recent interest in the discussion of recusant Catholic identities in early modern culture, the writings of Mary Ward have proven particularly illuminating. As David Wallace discusses in his recent article 'Periodizing Women: Mary Ward (1585–1645) and the Premodern Canon', Ward stands as a key figure in her radical gesture of embracing Jesuit ideology and establishing an active apostolate for women (including fellow Englishwomen) on the European continent. Perhaps more importantly, Ward's use of the saint's life model to tell her spiritual story links her writing to earlier medieval writers such as Margery Kemp and Julian of Norwich. Such associations, according to Wallace, 'prompt us to rethink issues of periodization and what the bounds of properly "English" concerns might be' (Wallace, 2006). In another study of largely overlooked voices and genres, Kristin Poole explores the literary subgenre of mother's advice manuals and underscores the significance of writings such as Dorothy Leigh's *The Mothers Blessing* (1616) and Elizabeth Jocelin's *The Mothers Legacy to her unborn Childe* (1624) (Poole 1995). According to Poole, the particular narrative strategies of mothers offering advice and guidance to their unborn children provide a window into 'literary interactions among Jacobean women outside of the court'. More significantly, writers of mother's advice handbooks 'share a common strategy of creating a space of public privacy, a space which hinges between the worlds of the home and the "worlds eie" (to use Elizabeth Jocelin's phrase)' (Poole 1995, 72).

Beyond text-based editions and scholarly works, early modern women writers have a strong canonical presence in classroom curriculum at the undergraduate and graduate levels. Initially in the late 1980s and early 1990s, separate graduate seminars or upper-level undergraduate courses might be devoted to 'early modern women's writing'. While these kinds of courses still exist today, women writers have become thoroughly integrated into introductory survey courses as well as upper-level period and genre courses. Finally, on-line and electronic editions of women writers continue to expand the accessibility as well as the variety of early modern women's writing. Perhaps in the not-too-distant future, writers such as Mary Ward and Elizabeth Jocelin will find their way into collections such as *The Norton Anthology of English Literature*, further transforming and expanding the canonical scope.

Outsiders and 'Others'

While writing by women has arguably been the single most important development in the early modern literary canon in the past few decades, the investigation of geographical and cultural space particularly with regard to boundaries between 'self' and 'other' has also had a significant impact on re-shaping the canon. Fuelled by New Historicist and Cultural Materialist concerns with the fashioning of early modern subjectivities, (see Chapters 4 and 6) the exploration of English literature dealing with encounters abroad as well as with boundaries between 'self' and 'other' in terms of geographic, racial, religious and other social difference has led to the incorporation of travel narratives and other encounter literature (both imagined and factual) into the canon. These include works describing voyages to the Americas and the Far East as well as texts ranging from factual defences of colonial enterprises abroad (such as Ralegh's *Discovery of Guiana* and Hakluyt's massive *Principle Navigations*) to characterizations of foreign 'others' in the more imagined space of plays, poems and pamphlets (such as numerous 'Turk plays', broadside ballads and conventionally canonical works including Shakespeare's *The Tempest*).

The current focus on early modern conceptions of difference stems from seminal critical studies on the topic (mostly dealing with the eighteenth century and later periods), including Benedict Anderson's *Imagined Communities*, Mary Louis Pratt's *Imperial Eyes*, and Edward Said's *Orientalism* (Anderson 2006; Pratt 1992; Said 1979). In general terms, each of these studies makes a strong claim for the development of institutions of nationalism and colonialism by the eighteenth century, which in turn fosters powerful distinctions of racial, national, religious and cultural difference between English and 'other'. Addressing the question of how these kinds of identities begin to take shape in the earlier period of the sixteenth and seventeenth century, many scholars have argued that distinctions of difference in early modern England were in the process of becoming and were therefore less established and clear-cut than they become in subsequent periods. In his recent study *Traffic and Turning: Islam and English*

Drama 1579–1624, for example, Jonathan Burton builds on responses to Said's *Orientalism* (most prominently work by Nabil Matar, Emily C. Bartels, Richmond Barbour and Ania Loomba, among others) to argue that plays from the period represent both Islam and Muslim people in diverse ways ranging from the reproachful to the laudatory (Barbour 2003; Bartels 1992; Loomba 2003; Matar 1999). By incorporating lesser-known and traditionally marginal dramatic works such as Daborne's *A Christian Turn'd Turk*, Massinger's *Renegado* and Wilson's *Three Ladies of London*, Burton is able to scrutinize more thoroughly the range of English notions of Islamic 'others'. The fact that these kinds of works have increasingly found their way into recent anthologies and modern editions (including Daniel Vitkus' *Three Turk Plays* and Anthony Parr's *Three Travel Plays*) as well as class curriculum attests to the growing presence of marginalized voices within the space of scholarship and pedagogy (Vitkus 2000; Parr 1995). In addition to dramatic works, travel narratives by Sir Thomas Roe, William Biddulph, William Lithgow, Sir Henry Blount, Thomas Coryate and numerous other writers offer a mosaic of cultural representations pertaining to relations between the European west and the Ottoman east (Parker 1999; Vitkus and Matar, 2001). While these works are not necessarily afforded canonical status, such invigorated scholarly and critical attention does suggest a significant shift in the valuing of literary texts from the aesthetic to the culturally useful (as the initial example of Brome's *The Antipodes* demonstrated).

Even plays not directly concerned with encounters between the Christian west and the Ottoman east have been interpreted through the cultural lens of east/west relations. Take, for example, Jane Hwang Degenhardt's recent work on Dekker and Massinger's largely forgotten play, *The Virgin Martir* (1620). Degenhardt convincingly argues that the play (along with numerous pamphlets and woodcut images from the period) appropriates and reconfigures the tradition of medieval Catholic martyrdom as a means of resisting the threat of 'turning Turk' (i.e. converting from Christianity to Islam) (Degenhardt 2006). Degenhardt's analysis thus explores the powerful and intertwining resonances of two distinct cultural outsiders in seventeenth-century Protestant England: recusant Catholics and Ottoman Muslims.

In turn, many scholars have begun to expand on the question of how English identity comes to be defined during the early modern period, thus paving the way for investigations of distinctions between Welsh, Scottish, English and Irish identities that comprise the 'Atlantic Archipelago' (to borrow from a recent collection of critical essays investigating this topic) (Schwyzer and Mealor 2004) (see this volume, Chapters 4, 6 and 8). Writings in native Gaelic, Welsh and Scots languages have thus found their way into the canon, as evidenced by recent collections such as *The Penguin Book of Renaissance Verse* (edited by David Norbrook) which includes a number of representative poems by Scottish, Welsh and Irish writers of the period in their native languages (Norbrook 1993). This focus on archipelagic identities extends to more firmly established works in the canon as well. Take, for example, recent scholarship and pedagogy exploring the diverse, national identities represented and scrutinized in Shakespeare's *Henry V* (Schwyzer 2004; McEachern 1996; Helgerson 1992). Along similar lines, it is difficult to see works such as Shakespeare's *The Tempest* or Spenser's *The Faerie Queene* as disengaged from the broader discourses of colonialism, nation-building and cultural expansion strongly voiced in the numerous texts usually deemed non-canonical or of less value than canonical works.

Cheap Print and Ephemera

Traditionally, the distinction between elite and popular (as well as canonical versus non-canonical) writing would relegate to positions of marginal or inferior status nearly all examples of early modern cheap print: broadside ballads, chapbooks, pamphlets, quarto-sized playbooks, jestbooks, single illustrated broadsheets to be hung on walls and the like. While much of this material continues to reside squarely outside the 'imaginary' as well as pedagogical canons, recent critical developments contesting the elite/popular binary within early modern culture as well as increasing interest in the material conditions of textual production and reception have expanded the opportunity to consider cheap print and ephemera within canonical spaces. Again, it is instructive to turn to recent literary anthologies and collections to see evidence of these developments. *The Penguin Book of Renaissance Verse*, for example, contains several anonymous broadside ballads as well as appropriations of the broadside form by more established poets such as Richard Corbett and Sir John Suckling (Fisher 2003). *The Norton Anthology of English Literature* includes political pamphlet writing by Gerard Winstanley among others. Norton's website for the anthology also includes a wide range of resources, including links to chapbook versions of the Faust myth which may have helped to shape Marlowe's *Dr. Faustus* and excerpts from travel pamphlets detailing voyages to the 'New World'.[21]

More importantly, recent critical attention to early modern print culture as well as social class formation has helped to bring cheap print into the centre of scholarly and pedagogical conversations. Important work by Margaret Spufford, Tessa Watt, Adam Fox, Sharon Achinstein and others during the last three decades has called attention to the ways in which broadsides, chapbooks, pamphlets and other cheap print participates in the processes of early modern cultural production while elucidating material and social practices. Craig Dionne and Steve Mentz's recent essay collection *Rogues and Early Modern English Culture* builds on Arthur Kinney's seminal work in the 1980s compiling and editing rogue pamphlets. This distinct subgenre of cheap print consists of inexpensive printed handbooks written by authors ranging from Robert Harman, Robert Greene and Thomas Dekker to anonymous hack writers that expose readers to the illicit practices, manners of speaking (cant) and clandestine secrets of the underground rogue culture. While Kinney himself views the rogue literature as significant in that it reveals 'nothing less momentous than the birth of the novel in England', Dionne and Mentz (along with many other recent scholars) view the material in terms of its socio-cultural relevance in the early modern period. As they explain in their introduction, 'Since the late 1990s, there has been a suggestive convergence of revisionist-historicist and poststructuralist accounts of the underworld literature as a site of discursive and ideological *contest*, where the making of culturally inscribed social differences – class, race, gender and nation – are written in and through this experimental hybrid form of faux journalism' (Dionne and Mentz 2004, 15).

Along with rogue pamphlets, new and vigorous scholarly and pedagogical attention has been directed towards pamphlet and chapbook literature more generally. These range from plague pamphlets such as Thomas Dekker's *The Wonderful Year* (1603) and Dekker and Middleton's *News from Gravesend* (1604) to domestic travel writing such as John Taylor's *The Pennilesse Pilgrimage* (1618) and prose works intertwining diverse literary genres including Thomas Nashe's *The Unfortunate Traveller* (1594). *News from Gravesend*, for example, follows *The Wonderful Year* in detailing the horrible impact of the most recent bout of plague in London. Dedicating the pamphlet to 'Nobody', Dekker and Middleton remind readers that wealthy patrons who would otherwise support the work have vacated the city as a result of the plague. In fact, as Robert Maslen argues in his recent introduction to the pamphlet in *Thomas Middleton: The Collected Works*, the pamphlet utilizes the description of the plague and its devastating impact to scrutinize the conventional social hierarchy: 'the pamphlet anatomizes the social diseases of seventeenth-century London as minutely as it scrutinizes the physical symptoms of pestilence' (Maslen 2007, 128). Turning away from the 'semi-feudal' institution of patronage, the 'medium becomes the message' as Dekker and Middleton effect their critique of the privileged classes by presenting their critique within the democratic and accessible pamphlet form. Such strategies prove particularly revealing for materialist critics concerned with complex interrelationships between texts and cultural spaces in early modern England. Seen in this light, cheap printed materials such as rogue and plague pamphlets shed their status as curiosities of an inferior, popular literature, instead playing key roles in helping to illuminate early modern cultural values and practices and to contextualize more traditionally canonical works in their social frameworks.

Documentary and Source Materials

While the category of documentary and source materials is certainly the least literary of any of the 'case studies' explored in this chapter, it is important nonetheless to discuss these as significant contributors to the reconceptualizing of the canon and of literary value more generally. Once generally restricted to the realm of historians, documentary sources including probate wills, letters, diaries, account books, conduct manuals, commonplace books, records of civic pageants and processions, proclamations and speeches have begun to assume positions of importance and relevance within literary studies. Once again, the recent focus on cultural and historical contexts plays a crucial role in elevating the perceived value of these kinds of materials. Literary anthologies and collections increasingly include supplemental resources (both on-line and printed) including documentary materials that help to situate texts in a particular cultural context. Critics and teachers frequently use documentary and source materials to supplement and invigorate literary texts, but documentary materials do not necessarily always occupy a subordinate position in relation to dominant literary works. Some texts, such as the diaries, sermons and other writings compiled in Elspeth Graham's collection *Her Own Life* stand as significant literary texts in their own right, in addition to shedding light on topics as diverse as early modern marriage, religious faith, sexuality and political activism. Several items included in the collection such as the visionary writing of Anna Trapnel, the diary of Ann Clifford and Margaret Cavendish's autobiographical *True Relation of My Birth, Breeding, and Life* have made their way into the literary canon (Graham et al, 1985).

Recognizing documentary sources as autonomous literary texts can be exemplified by looking at the case of civic pageant and procession records. Take, for instance, R. Malcolm Smuts' recent edition of *The Whole Royal and Magnificent Entertainment* compiling three distinct published accounts by Dekker, Jonson and the London joiner Stephen Harrison of James I's hugely elaborate and costly coronation entry procession into the city of London on 15 March 1604. Smuts is quick to acknowledge that this compiled edition constitutes an 'ideal reconstruction' of the event and its accounts while reminding readers that the huge crowds, noise and ephemeral nature of the event would certainly complicate any opportunity for a singular, unified and cohesive account. Examining these descriptions of the procession and pageants reveals important considerations about the social makeup of early modern London while reflecting changes in court values and priorities. As Smuts explains, Dekker's *The Magnificent Entertainment* 'looks back to inherited medieval forms of public display and allegory; but it also anticipates the development of a cosmopolitan, classicizing and relatively exclusive court culture under the early Stuarts' (Smuts 2007, 221). Smuts also identifies how the pageantry's over-arching emphasis on 'the king's power to impose peace not only on his people but on nature itself' anticipates many Jacobean masques and panegyrics while underscoring public devotion to the king. Indeed, much recent scholarship has focused on accounts of royal processions, Lord Mayor's shows, and other kinds of civic pageantry, both as a window into early modern cultural practices and values and as literary works in their own right.

Other kinds of materials such as wills and account books similarly help to understand early modern cultural practices and values, thus invigorating the discussion of conventionally canonical texts from innovative and hitherto unrealized perspectives. Wendy Wall's recent *Staging Domesticity: Household Work and English Identity in Early Modern Drama*, for example, utilizes historical sources on wet-nursing, butchery, laundering, medicine, sewing, cookery and other practices to illuminate representations of the domestic sphere in well-established canonical plays including *Gammer Gurton's Needle*, Shakespeare's *A Midsummer Night's Dream* and Francis Beaumont's *Knight of the Burning Pestle* (Wall 2002). Similarly interested in the relevance of material culture to literary works, Adam Max Cohen's recent study *Shakespeare and Technology* explores how discourses of technological innovations (including early modern scientific and technical writing on the clock, the compass, the printing press and gunpowder) find their way metaphorically into the poetic imagination of Shakespeare (Cohen 2006). Here again, expanding the canon to incorporate conventionally marginalized voices reinvigorates rather than threatens the cultural and aesthetic evaluation of traditionally canonical works.

Conclusion: E-Canons and Beyond

Nevertheless, it is the last category briefly discussed that gives perhaps the greatest cause for alarm among those still lamenting the 'damage' done to the conventional literary canon as a result of cultural criticism and pedagogy over the past several decades. If private letters, diaries and account books can be valued on par with more traditional literary works, then what happens to the distinctions of 'greatness', 'originality' and literary merit that apparently make literature worth studying and talking about in the first place? Will university English majors taking courses that replace traditional canonical works with these other materials be as adequately prepared for graduate study and the workplace as those taking a more traditional course of study? It can be argued that these kinds of concerns are often over-stated and for the most part tend to misread the current critical and pedagogical developments taking place. The fact of the matter is that very few universities have replaced their traditional curriculum with materials usually deemed non-canonical or marginal. When these are present, they frequently work to illuminate important aspects of canonical texts and cultures and to raise important questions about how standards of evaluation come into being. When a more conventional canonical work is replaced or excised from the curriculum, there may be a risk that students are exposed to a smaller range of canonical texts than they were before, (see Chapter 8) and in North America, for example, less adequately prepared for GRE and departmental exit exams, but there is also the positive benefit of expanding one's cultural and critical horizons.

More importantly, the proliferation of materials on the Internet and within web culture generally ensures that the question of access to materials both canonical and marginal is no longer very relevant. If the syllabus stands as a practical articulation of the canon (at least as this applies to pedagogical concerns), then the expanding Internet and its myriad of on-line editions (both edited and facsimile), linkable lists and other resources promise to transform the parameters and stakes of the canon even more radically. Electronic resources such as Early English Books Online (EEBO) make access to primary printed materials incredibly easy (as long as one's institution has a subscription to the expensive database).[22] Numerous other resources are readily available to the general public, providing students and scholars with immediate access to primary texts and materials. Such resources include the Voice of the Shuttle Renaissance pages, Project Luminarium, The Richard Brome Project, Brown University's Women Writers Online and the early modern ballad project at the University of California, Santa Barbara's Early Modern Center.[23] Exactly how electronic resources and the increasing innovation of web-culture will continue to transform and expand the canon is yet to be seen. However, even now it is difficult to conceive of the canon as a solitary, unified and static entity when the accessibility of so many electronic resources and e-text editions can only promise to further shape, expand and transform the study of early modern literature and culture in years to come.

Mapping the Current Critical Landscape: Returning to the Renaissance

Thomas Healy

8

Chapter Overview

The Sense of the Past

'All things runne round', the antiquary William Camden observed, expressing the early modern period's characteristic understanding that desirable changes were never entirely new, but occurrences that in some manner replicated what had gone before (Camden 1637, 199) Originality was largely witnessed as disturbing or even dangerous in sixteenth- and seventeenth-century Britain. Whether in social, legal, religious or aesthetic practices, innovation was preferably portrayed as a restoration of better previous circumstances that had been damaged or tarnished by time. For instance, the far-reaching social and cultural shifts attendant on England's establishment of a slate-sanctioned Protestant Church were founded in the contemporary imagination on an ideal of return to the purity of early Christianity. On virtually a weekly basis, Protestants affirmed their break with Rome in Thomas Cranmer's version of the fourth-century Nicene Creed, proclaiming that 'I believe one Catholike and Apostolike Churche', namely the Church of England.[1] It is towards the end of the eighteenth century that our current understanding of 'revolution' as a tumultuous break, an ushering in of decisive changes, of the spark that ignites the new, begins to occur.

There is an interesting irony, therefore, that critical approaches to these centuries' writing over the last few decades have been dominated by models that tend to celebrate their fractures and radical breaks with previous accounts. Predicated largely on the late twentieth-century's anxiety about 'hegemony' – the perception that the Enlightenment's legacy was epistemologies that functioned as instruments of social, political and intellectual control – theoretical models from current linguistics, philosophy, anthropology, psychoanalysis, political science and other disciplines were deployed in literary studies to re-examine the writing of early periods. While this critical energy generated an enthusiasm that has proved inspirational for scholarly enquiry, there has more recently been a growing sense that it also possessed considerable naivety. Miranda-like, criticism of Renaissance writing proclaimed: 'O wonder! How many goodly creatures are there here . . . O brave new world' and only recently has Prospero's rejoinder 'Tis new to thee' started to be heard as a corrective (*The Tempest*, 5.1). For instance, explorations of Renaissance texts as playfully unstable linguistically, politically or sexually were frequently represented as critical breakthroughs resulting from engagements with late twentieth-century post-structuralist deconstruction. Critics focussed on their own adaptations of these models to produce textual analysis that was unconcerned whether the texts' writers shared any of these perspectives, and, indeed, often celebrated the critics' detection of issues that were hidden to the culture the texts first circulated in. In contrast, current investigators situate such textual instability emerging from the period's own understandings of rhetorical play, notably the trope of *serio ludere* (to play seriously), leading to more nuanced and located analysis of both the texts and the culture they participated in.

My argument in this essay centres round a perception that twenty-first-century critical tendencies over the writing of the sixteenth- and seventeenth-century Atlantic archipelago (as England, Scotland, Ireland, Wales and their English-speaking dependencies have inelegantly come collectively to be called) increasingly involve a sense of 'return', a process of relocating the era's own categories for understanding literary, social and political developments. Far from discovering convenient parallels with current models for understanding the present, this engagement with the past's own self-representations can generate models for understanding that appear alien to current sensibilities, indicating cultural environments which do not easily 'map' onto our own. If 1980s and 90s New Historicism engaged with Renaissance texts through a chiastic circulation between past and present, a different historicism is gaining prominence; one that witnesses the past's dissimilarity from the present as a feature which unlocks its own critical energy, often provoking a challenge to familiar categories and organizations of knowledge. For instance, although by no means universally acclaimed, a sense of Renaissance writing as subject to history (in its broadest sense) (see Kerwin's Chapters 1 and Baumlin's Chapter 6, this volume) is leading scholars to challenge imagined continuities of human experience; questioning whether such ostensible human fundamentals as cognitive and sense experience are not also somehow culturally conceived. Many critics of the

1980s and 90s assumed that gender was the driving force behind Renaissance models of identity but more recently, Michael Schoenfeldt has argued that 'the belly' rather than 'the genitals' dominated sixteenth- and seventeenth-century ideas about character (Schoenfeldt 1999). Far more than sexual drive, it was the food that we necessarily ingest that was perceived as the force determining what we are. Could our bodies, our digestions, govern this invading substance and turn it to health? Are we necessarily a product of what we eat and, thus, need to impose a strict sense of diet upon ourselves? For the period, these questions loomed centrally over a construction of an individual's identity, over social relations, and over humanity's interactions with the divine.

Such a perspective challenges traditional psychoanalysis which tends to conceive issues of identity tied to constants in the human psyche. For the psychoanalytic models – principally Freudian, Jungian and Lacanian – which have notably influenced literary criticism (see Baumlin, this volume, Chapter 6), historically located and culturally specific accounts act to mask or repress a more or less universal psychological reality. Equally, too, this new attention to history challenges less theoretical explorations which also assume that modern readers and earlier authors somehow 'experienced' the world similarly despite a gap of four to six hundred years. In examinations such as Schoenfeldt's, current readers of earlier texts discover a less familiar culture, one that asks them to reconsider their own self-construction and location in history and challenges their perceptions of their own cultural locations. Where New Historicist criticism openly invited readers to discover a semblance of their current preoccupations in the past, recent investigations that do not seek such continuities challenge the certainties of a reader's own outlook, causing the present as well as the past to seem less familiar.

This trend is significant because the majority of twentieth-century critical activity started from a perspective that celebrated Renaissance writing because it exemplified élite standards of civility and eloquence which the present would do well either to emulate or, latterly from the 1980s, to question. In contrast, recent critical inquiry suggests discontinuities or unexpected resonances with the past which confront comfortable senses of either literary or cultural connections. A good illustration of criticism's awkwardness over the relation between past and present that emerged during the 1980s surrounds the use of the term 'early modern' in favour of 'Renaissance' and it is worth reviewing how this trend developed.

What's in a Name? From 'Early Modern' to 'Renaissance'

By the early 1980s, many literary critics were becoming uneasy that the study of English literature of the period 1500–1660 had become almost exclusively focussed around a relatively small number of male, mostly socially elite, writers from Sir Philip Sidney through to Milton, with a few honorary earlier inclusions, notably Wyatt. The limitation of this canon was particularly highlighted by the growing re-discovery of women writers. In much of its post-Second World War manifestation, literary criticism had focussed on issues of taste. The academic study of Renaissance writing was founded on arguing a writer or a text's timeless and universally applicable capacities, or 'greatness', as a self-contained literary artefact. Unfairly dismissing – or more usually just ignoring – the literary qualities of poets such as Isabella Whitney, Aemilia Lanyer, Mary Sidney or Katherine Philips, what started to become notably difficult for conventional literary criticism was acknowledging that these women writers might employ language differently from males in order to convey distinctive female visions, ones that articulated literary values that did not always comfortably map onto male dominated cultural assumptions (see Kerwin's Chapter 1, and Britland and Munro's Chapter 2, this volume). Readers – and it is important to recall that women readers are the majority among students studying the Renaissance today – increasingly wanted to explore earlier women writers in order to consider how such female literary agency operated, not least because examining such differences helped illustrate women's social constructions.

The response from with the academy was rarely accommodating. In many instances, traditional criticism's curt dismissal of the literary value of writing that did not immediately adapt itself to its norms began to appear little short of preposterous. While claiming to be unbiased towards gender in its evaluation of literature, such criticism exposed itself as fiercely predicated on male assumptions. At the University of London in the mid 1980s, I vividly recall how numerous senior male academics arose at academic board to denounce a modest proposal to introduce a women's writing paper as an option on the English syllabus, employing as they did so rhetoric that suggested that such a move was an underlying assault upon civilized values. This incident illustrates how the issue of 'taste' in the academic study of English was shifting from being passively, but almost unanimously, imagined as predicated on the indoctrination of students into norms of gentility to, instead, a clamorous instrument of regulation that attempted to prevent literature being examined from perspectives that highlighted texts as offering varying social or political mirrors onto their age.

A new generation of scholars began seeking a re-appraisal of a literary criticism that had imagined authors and their writing as autonomous, as somehow easily transcending their age, and which envisaged the ideal of literature as the provision of civilized pleasure for a similarly autonomous readership, past or present. A new critical orientation towards exploring literature's role in examining social issues began questioning fundamental assumptions about the Renaissance, including the period's nomenclature. Posing the question, 'Did Women Have a Renaissance?', the title of Joan Kelly-Gadol's seminal 1977 essay illustrated how the term 'Renaissance' had begun to seem unsuited to describe the totality of European culture between 1400 and the mid-seventeenth century (see Kerwin, this volume, Chapter 1) (Kelly-Gadol 1977). In addition to women's writing, literary critics were also showing increasing interest in popular literature, autobiography, enthusiastic devotional prose from socially marginalized groups, and other expressive forms that did not neatly map onto traditional pre-conceptions about literary language as *eloquentia*. Increasingly, the term 'Renaissance' was becoming understood as applicable only to certain cultural practices, notably centred around Humanism's educational ideals.

Twentieth-century preconceptions about the 'Renaissance' had largely evolved from Jacob Burckhardt's mid-nineteenth-century formulations, celebrating a movement based on what Burckhardt declared as the Italian genius for self-creation (Burckhardt 1990). In English literary criticism, this prompted accounts about England's Renaissance as a slow process of cultural 'awakening' to this southern European, classically inspired, vitality, a phenomenon that was argued as only properly beginning to be manifest in the British islands from the 1580s. C. S. Lewis' characterization of mid-sixteenth-century writing as part of a literary 'drab age' awakening to a golden one reinforced a sense of late Tudor writing gaining its vigour from the influence of classically-inspired French and Italian literary dynamics (Lewis 1954). By the 1980s, however, art historians as well as literary scholars were increasingly uncomfortable about defining cultural progression in northern Europe as founded simply on its embrace of Italocentric models. Much persisted in English and other Atlantic cultures that did not embrace these models. Gothic embellishment, a continuing preference for elaborate textures instead of classical simplicity in both the plastic and literary arts, a continuing employment of medieval, vernacular-inspired, alliteration and rhyme instead of a whole-heartedly adoption of Latinate forms: all these testified that both elite or popular sixteenth-century Britain imagined its own cultural dynamism in ways that differed significantly from the nineteenth century's retrospective stance.

Increasingly from the 1980s, scholars were noting how the era appeared comfortable with a cultural hybridity, where Italianate classical models readily co-existed with native traditions. A striking instance of this is offered by the London printer John Wolfe's 1588 trilingual edition of Castiglione's *Il Cortegiano*, in which the Italian is printed in parallel with Hoby's English version and Chapuis' French one (see Wyatt 2005, 196). Unlike modern dispositions in translation to try and reproduce as accurately as possible the language of a text's original state, a practice that witnesses the translated version as a type of client to the original, Tudor readers appear to have perceived original and translation existing in a concurrent symbiotic relation (see Adlington, this volume, Chapter 3). Parallel texts encouraged comparison and observation of different effects between languages and the differences of meaning these could generate. Wolfe's edition adopts a format designed to encourage this type of comparative reading. In this practice, Hoby's English text would not be irrelevant to a reader possessing good Italian but offered its own elucidation of Castiglione's work. Just as the period employed literary imitation to demonstrate both similarities with and differences from earlier models, so translation and original were envisaged to be accomplishing different designs, with the English text seeking 'to naturalise' *The Courtyer of Count Baldessar Castilio*, as Hoby entitled his version, within the English courtly milieu. A similar aim might be employed with translations from the Classics, such as Golding's 'englishing' of Ovid's *Metamorphoses* (see Lyne 2001). Rather than indicating a crude grasp of Ovid's manner directed towards those unable to read Latin, Golding likely assumed his readers would be familiar with Ovid's Latin, allowing them to encounter a sense of English difference within what might be termed 'a politics of imitation'. This sense of the period's readers engaging with different versions of the texts both concurrently and comparatively is a feature that has wide implications for our understanding of the era. Annabel Patterson, for example, has demonstrated how the contending accounts of history recorded in sixteenth-century chronicles prompted an independence of judgement among readers in which she perceives the origins of liberalism (Patterson 1994). Other scholars have noted how poets and dramatists often significantly revised work without any expectation or desire that one version would supersede another but that both would simultaneously circulate.

With the recognition that such literary issues were linked to wider social and cultural ones, therefore, it came to seem inappropriate to present English's absorption of 'Renaissance' ideals as merely focussed on stylistic and generic phenomena, such as sonnets' adaptations of Petrarchan techniques. Significantly, English literary differences might now also be observed as acquiescing in desires to articulate a national community, ones linked to Reformation urgings about a return to native purity. As Spenser proposes in E. K.'s introduction to the *Shepheardes Calendar*:

> For in my opinion it is one special prayse, of many which are dew to this Poete [that is the author of the *Shepheardes Calendar*], that he hath laboured to restore, as to theyr rightfull heritage such good and naturall English words, as have ben long time out of vse and almost cleane disinherited. Which is the onely cause, that our Mother tonge, which truely of it selfe is both ful enough for prose and stately enough for verse, hath long time ben counted most bare and barrein of both. Which default when as some endeuoured to salue and recure, they patched vp the holes with peces and rags of other languages, borrowing here of the french, there of the Italian, euery where of the Latine, not weighing how il those tongues accorde with themselues, but much worse with ours: So now they have made our English tongue, a gallimaufray or hodgepodge of al other speches (Spenser 1989, 16).

Just as the English Church's emphasis on its restoration of early Christianity was its principal defence for its break with Rome, so E. K. too seeks the restoration of 'good and naturall' English to its 'rightfull heritage' as part of the *Shepheardes Calendar*'s dynamic. Far from breaking with its medieval inheritance, notably Chaucer, sixteenth- and seventeenth-century English writers generally sought to emphasize their continuity with this past. Yet, beyond E. K.'s claim about English returning to its inheritance as a proper literary language by dispensing with 'the patchings' from other languages, is his extraordinary assertion that the principal languages of the Renaissance – French, Italian and Latin – 'il … accorde with themselves', let alone with English. Spenser's poem quickly became one of the most celebrated of its era and scholars' new attentiveness to its insistence on English's inherent superiority and the cultural and religious 'deficiency' of Romance languages illustrated the need to reconsider traditional ideas about the Renaissance in England as emerging from the country's recognition of Italian and French superior cultural accomplishments.

Literary criticism, thus, began to move towards thinking about the 'Renaissance' as the 'Early Modern'. The term appeared more inclusive, embracing all cultural practices and not only those of the elite. Further, Renaissance had always been problematic in terms of period definition. In continental Europe, the Renaissance was often portrayed as ending with either the French sack of Rome in 1527 or with the advent of the Counter-Reformation in the 1560s, both dates occurring before most perceived the English movement substantially began. Continental scholars of both literature and the visual arts tended to define the arts of the later-sixteenth and early-seventeenth centuries as belong to the Baroque, a sense of period style that English-centred criticism has never felt entirely comfortable with. The term 'Early Modern' allowed a wider range of dates: as early as 1400 and continuing well into the eighteenth century. It was already well-established in History, where it principally indicated the social and economic changes that effected many parts of both southern and northern Europe moving away from feudalism, without signifying specific aesthetic practices. While it must be acknowledged that there have never been any hard and fast definitions of how Early Modern differed from Renaissance (and many scholars frequently use the two almost interchangeably), generally within English Studies it was employed as a type of short-hard to indicate a particular approach to the analysis of its literature, where the critical focus was on what literature articulated about the period's wider cultural imagination. Acting as a particular type of window onto the wider early modern world, literary texts became increasingly scrutinized as repositories of evidence about how witnesses at specific historical moments responded (or wished to respond) to what they felt were their era's pressing issues: intellectual, political, social and religious.

Desperately Seeking Modernity

Yet, literary criticism's employment of 'Early Modern' also carried with it largely unexamined teleological assumptions. Although it enabled easier linkages with writing formerly held to be late medieval, the critical momentum driving it has overwhelmingly sought to establish continuities with the Enlightenment and, thus, with modernity and post-modernity. Even when focussed on 'alternate' histories of previously marginalized figures, the drift of examinations has tended to seek the origins of current similarly marginalized figures or groups now claiming wider attention. A good example of this trend is

Christopher Hill's 1977 influential study *Milton and the English Revolution*. Here is a book by a leading historian that explored Milton's links to what Hill described as 'popular heretical culture': the various Protestant groups that pursued unorthodox theological and social programmes. While Hill acknowledges that these groups and figures were motivated by independent readings from the Bible – and that their perspectives developed from a combination of enthusiasm for fulfilling what they perceived as God's designs matched with a high anxiety about the consequences of ignoring or mistaking these – his main drift is to explore their social and political agendas isolated from their dominating religious one. For Hill, Milton needed to be reconnected to a radical popular tradition instead of being celebrated (or sometimes loathed) as the apogee of English Renaissance *eloquentia*. Crucially, though, Hill's Marxist conception of an English revolution is a very modern one, a period that ushers in innovatory social alteration. He portrays the English Civil War's conflicts as stemming from Parliament's deliberate, energetic toppling of previous social and political institutions. Hill's reading of the events of 1640–60 largely ignores the Protestant dynamic that sought to further the Reformation, returning England to an imagined prior condition of religious purity. Instead, he promotes a view that sees the period's actions emerging from attempts to establish an English republicanism that entailed a repudiation of previous class divisions. Hill maintains that the English Revolution's popular heretical culture was predicated on 'fierce popular hostility to gentry and aristocracy and to the monarchy which protected them' (Hill 1977, 93). For him, the 1640s unleashed a movement directed towards social equality, one that seemed more about redistributing wealth and land than establishing a religious moral commonwealth secured on its belief that it was complying with God's designs for humanity. Hill sees the period as a moment in which 'for the first time in English history . . . ideas of the radical underground could be freely preached, discussed and criticized: they could even be printed' (*ibid.* 93). Understandably, therefore, Hill is more excited that Milton found precedent in English heretical culture for some of his broadminded ideas surrounding divorce than over his approval of its intolerant sectarianism regarding religious truth. He presents Milton's virulent anti-popery, for instance, as largely emerging from a rhetorical anger whose target is essentially Stuart absolutist politics rather than concerns about tyrannical monarchy aligned with the Satanic supernatural.

Milton and the English Revolution was an extremely important book and energized many subsequent wide-ranging, sophisticated and well-researched reappraisals of Milton. Hill's promotion of the importance of seventeenth-century popular marginal writing for Milton forged a view of a socially and politically engaged writer, providing a fresh historicized context through which to read both Milton's poems and prose. Yet, the book's impression of Milton and popular heretical culture as a foundation for later liberal and republican traditions mixed with an assault on class in English political life is achieved by downplaying the significance of the period's perceptions of the supernatural in favour of secular social agendas. Hill's Milton is placed in a free-thinking, non-conformist tradition that appears surprisingly comfortable with mid-twentieth-century oppositional Marxist perspectives. It is true that Milton appears not to have held orthodox Calvinist views about pre-destination, but his uncompromising rigour in defining those in a position to espouse genuine Christian liberty betrays his powerful idea of exclusivity surrounding the issue of who are the proper participants of a godly commonwealth. The early modern Milton that Hill forges tends to wear a familiar democratic garb for current readers. It is unclear how easily this construction rests with Milton's own view, for example, of the readers of *Paradise Lost* as 'fit audience . . . though few' – a community that recent investigations into the period's Protestant sensibilities demonstrate as highly illiberal.[2]

During the 1980s and 90s as literary criticism under the headings of 'New Historicism' and 'Cultural Materialism' sought out alternate 'discursive contexts' in which to situate their examinations of texts, it was becoming clear that such contexts were often assemblages of diverse materials from the past that were selected by critics as part of a narrative of how 'we' became modern. Perhaps no more telling example of this has been the question of subjectivity and interiority that developed from Stephen Greenblatt's seminal *Renaissance Self-Fashioning* (1980). The book is a declaration of the period as defined by a dramatically different sense of human identity emerging – as Greenblatt asserts at its start, 'my starting point is quite simply that in sixteenth-century England there were both selves and that they could be fashioned' (Greenblatt 1980, 3). The influential critic Catherine Belsey was even more emphatic in declaring that 'the inner space of subjectivity . . . came into being in the Renaissance' (Belsey 1988, 85).

Such claims prompted heated responses from medievalists. Lee Patterson argued that to privilege early modernity as the origin of subjectivity was to deny 'historical consciousness and a sense of individual selfhood' to earlier periods, a stance that Patterson's own *Chaucer and the Subject of History* demonstrated as untenable (Patterson 1990, 93; Patterson 1991). David Aers claimed that early modernists employed 'systematic amnesia' towards the Middle Ages, turning it into a: 'homogeneous and mythical field which is defined in terms of the scholars' needs for a figure against which "Renaissance" concerns with inwardness and the fashioning of identities can be defined as new' (Aers 1992, 181, 192). Such assaults condemned New Historicism for having little new about it; suggesting it was effectively a continuation of Burckhardt's view of the Renaissance as the glorious freeing of humanity from the constraints of medieval superstitions. For Lee Patterson, this tendency forged a 'gigantic master narrative by which modernity identifies itself with the Renaissance and rejects the Middle Ages' (Patterson 1990, 92)

Past vs Present?

In contrast, to the Greenblattian/Belsey origin of modern subjectivity, current historicist examinations of subjectivity and identity during the period –

especially those exploring the impact of Protestantism's obsession with the individual as a witness to a Christianity unfettered from reliance on Church authority – have tended to indicate the opposite of liberated, self-fashioning people, discovering instead a culture fearful of their consciences becoming prey to treacherous Satanic urgings (Johnstone 2006). This has considerable implication in literary examinations, as Renaissance writers' presentations of character appear less a transition from models founded on emblematic static types to those of vivid psychologically complex realism, than illustrations of writers reflecting their culture's preoccupation with ideas of human nature emerging from a *pyschomachia*, an internal conflict within the 'self' (both psychic and somatic), in which various passions and humours contend for domination of a highly fractured being.

Thus, some of the critical implications of the Renaissance as early modernity are gradually being replaced by a different form of historicist criticism that tries to bring the period's own categories for understanding to bear on texts. Yet, this has exposed divisions within the academic community. One aspect of approaching early modernity as the precursor to the modernity of our own time is that it proved highly attractive in teaching. For students of literature frequently unconvinced about the need to engage with texts written four or five hundred years ago, or reluctant to pursue historical environments that appear to bear little on their own lives, it was stimulating to employ a critical model that encouraged explorations of early texts as repositories for issues that excite the present. It provoked readings of these early texts as engaging with repressive social and political situations in which literature discovered textual strategies for voicing opposition, ones that echoed with the approaches of writers confronting modern oppressions. New Historicism, especially, offered an attractive argument about subversion and containment which proposed that we can only witness 'subversion' in the past because it poses no threat to our current environment: one where institutions rapidly seek 'to contain' subversions if they are envisioned as genuinely undermining current values (Greenblatt 1988, 21–65). So, while at their moment of origin, Shakespeare's plays may not have appeared subversive to state power (Shakespeare's own culture had mechanisms to contain this threat), their subversive potentials now appear to us. The logic of this argument suggests that if we cannot see true subversive potentials in recent cultural creations, then we might redeploy these dissident past texts to engage current situations with genuinely radical potentials. The mechanism was in place to argue that studying past texts historically might liberate us from our anxieties about a repressive cultural hegemony. Suddenly, these texts of four or five hundred years ago gained credibility not only for still possessing negotiable intellectual currency but for actually surpassing the possibilities offered by the present's own writing for confronting and challenging existing cultural paradigms. The result was that plays such as *Othello*, *Hamlet* and *The Tempest* emerged as loadstones of early modern literary syllabi, examined as addressing issues of psychological, racial and

class-based displacements. Though none of these plays enjoyed huge reputation in their own era (Shakespeare's *Henry VI* trilogy appears to be his most
frequently revived plays before 1640), they have now became so central, to
what Renaissance/early modern literature is seen to consist of, that in some
cases entire undergraduate and graduate courses have been devoted to
Hamlet.

Increasingly, therefore, early modern studies frequently seemed to have
become a mirror image of those previous generations who declared a work's
'greatness' to depend on how it reflected the critics' own prescriptions of literary value. Criticism now extolled texts whose cultural capital or histories
mapped onto various current social preoccupations in conveniently familiar
manners. Stephen Greenblatt's recent biography of Shakespeare is notably
revealing of this arrangement (Greenblatt 2004). Written ostensibly to show how
aspects of Shakespeare's life may have turned into his art, Greenblatt's book
uncritically assumes that the small number of plays it addresses must have been
the points where Shakespeare's life and art especially intersected. Yet, the plays
that he selects to focus on are conveniently those that are currently most regularly taught, performed and critically written about. Greenblatt observes *Hamlet*
(a play in which Shakespeare 'perfected the means to represent inwardness') as
linked to the writer's trauma attendant on losing his son Hamnet (Greenblatt
2001). But the substantiation for this rests on Greenblatt's (and other current
critics') citing of *Hamlet* as one of the founding texts of modernity. We are
confronted with the odd spectacle in which a critic claims discovery of something of the interiority of Shakespeare's actual life based simply on his own
assessment of a play.

Hamlet further helps instance an increasing division within the critical examination of sixteenth- and seventeenth-century literature. There has been a notable growth in interest in what is broadly called the 'history of the book': the
recognition that the material forms texts circulated in contributed significantly
to how their content was established and understood. Editorial examination of
playtexts from the period 1580–1640 has found increasing evidence of authorial
collaboration in many and has highlighted the often substantial differences in
the versions of plays that exist in multiple editions. Previously, modern editorial policies largely operated on principles of 'reclaiming', as far as possible, a
singular authorial text – witnessing a literary work as possessing a definitive
form (often imagined existing in some idealized state in an author's mind) that
editors tried to isolate from varying corrupted printed and manuscript versions.
Now, though, scholars recognize that writers frequently envisaged their texts
much more provisionally: open to change and transformation in the way they
circulated and in the ways authors themselves altered varying versions. This
phenomenon was exaggerated with plays, where acting companies frequently
commissioned additions and alterations in revivals, often from entirely different
writers. The most recent scholarly edition of *Hamlet* offers three texts, the quarto
of 1603, the quarto of 1604–05 and the Folio of 1623 (Shakespeare 2006). As with

the Oxford edition of *King Lear*, which offers two texts, what is apparent is that searching for a definite version of these tragedies is impossible. Even where there is only a sole surviving text of a play, this now has to be seen as possessing a provisional quality around claims that it represents an author's unmediated vision. For instance, the first printed and sole surviving text of Marlowe's *Jew of Malta*, one of the most frequently performed plays of the period, is 1633 and it is improbable to imagine that it is an undiluted copy of the play Marlowe launched forty years earlier.

This position makes claims about Shakespeare life based on evidence extracted from *Hamlet* – which version or all? – seem even more open to accusations of being little other than fabulous speculation. Further, it also illustrates a practical problem within the academic community. Students, critics and readers generally seek a single text to base their examinations around. Even with frequently studied plays such as *Hamlet, Lear* or *Doctor Faustus* that are readily available in different versions, most readers will commonly restrict their inquiry to one text. Thus, there is a growing gap between a critical industry in which multiple versions of texts are rarely acknowledged, and the scholarly understanding of textual history that points to more protean conceptions of what a playtext or poem should be understood to represent, an outlook that often challenges the basis around which critical readings operate. Here, too, I am deliberately ignoring the advent of performance studies which explore dramatic productions at different historical moments outside the Renaissance as a subject beyond the scope of this essay: Shakespeare on film is a twentieth- and twenty-first-century phenomena, not a sixteenth and seventeenth-century one, and though revealing about directors, audiences and mass culture, it is only tangentially connected with either Renaissance or early modern studies.

To conclude this piece, I would suggest that critical approaches to the literature of the period 1485 (the beginning of Tudor reign) to 1689 (James II's deposition) that was written in the North Atlantic archipelago are becoming notably fragmented. On one side there are innovatory studies posited on the idea of returning to the period's own conceptual categories to explain what its writing is attempting: a desire to restore the 'shaping fantasies' and cultural organizations that prompted these texts at their originary moment rather than imposing on them later generations' models for understanding cultural events. Foremost in this design is a readiness to witness this period's literature as dissimilar to the present, anchored in histories and ways of understanding history that are profoundly different to the epistemologies used to engage with the current environment. Such approaches impose on this writing's current readers an obligation to grapple with concerns and become involved in historical specificities that often don't carry any immediate resonance with their own experience. Candidly, for many readers, whether students or professionals academics in English Studies, the demands of such investigations, predicated on acquiring unfamiliar knowledge about both literature and history, often seem disproportionately complex to the nature of the textual encounters that such readers seek. Through internet resources, such as *Early English Books Online*, many students and academics now possess daily access to compendia of information for both literary and historical investigation that are beyond almost every scholar's dream a generation ago. Yet, seemingly paradoxically, the depth and breath of writing 1485–1689 that is regularly taught on undergraduate programmes in English is shrinking in most institutions, in part because the sheer scale of what appears required in order to master literature in history can seem overwhelming. The critical revolution that is posited upon returning to the period's own conceptual structures will, therefore, possibly end up becoming the province of the few, potentially forfeiting the period's wide appeal among students.

In contrast, yet resulting from the same milieu, a new critical 'presentism' is manifesting itself, rejecting the historical placing of texts and insisting that they be experienced within the context of current cultural preoccupations. To date, the focus of this presentism has been Shakespeare, his plays constituting the only group of early texts that have widespread public life and which circulate, in highly amended ways, through film, television and the stage (Grady and Hawkes 2007). The creative producer of a production of *The Tempest* that wishes to highlight post-colonial issues may have little interest in early Jacobean views of the non-European world, witnessing these as little more than antiquarian baggage. Pedagogically, too, in recent years there has been a shift in many British schools from teaching English literature as fundamentally a critical discipline training students in the close reading of texts to a creative discipline in which literary contexts present opportunities for students' own imaginative self-expression. Such training is unlikely to encourage large number of university students studying English to engage with unusual cultural and intellectual environments. Yet, presentism seems to do little more than ask readers to witness literary texts as critical fabrications, inventive visions of what texts articulate based on selective analysis linked to the critic's immediate cultural preoccupations. Further, the writing that resists a ready absorption into this milieu – linguistically, generically or because of subject matter – becomes more likely to be ignored. The implications of ignoring history to extend the appeal of the period's literature among a wide constituency may encourage readers to engage with a diminished number of texts, ones selected principally on the basis of the ease with which they apparently engage with current preoccupations. If reading any literary text is ultimately an encounter with both the strange and familiar, the educational task that confronts those involved with sixteenth- and seventeenth-century literature is enabling readers to grasp the opportunities offered by writing that is initially perplexing as much as it is to interrogate that which seems apparently recognizable.

Appendix: Teaching, Curriculum and Learning

This chapter is available as an online resource aimed primarily at teachers. It offers ideas on how to introduce students to some of the material covered in this volume, from theoretical concerns (such as ideology, for example, or presentism) to generic issues such as allegory, romance and satire, to textual matters such as editing. It can be found at www.continuumbooks.com/resources/9780826495006.

Chapter Overview

'Teaching Renaissance Literature', Susan Bruce, Keele University.

'Introducing the Idea of Allegory: The Faerie Queene', Hugh Adlington, University of Birmingham.

'*Volpone* and Satire', Susan Anderson, Leeds Trinity and All Saints.

'Editing Shakespeare Project', M.G. Aune, California University of Pennsylvania.

'Inspection Functions Ceaselessly': Using Foucault to Consider Surveillance, Prisons and Contagion in *The Duchess of Malfi*. Catherine Bates, Keele University.

'Ideology, Romance, Folklore and Paintings', Susan Bruce, Keele University.

'Teaching the *Rape of Lucrece*: That was Then, This is Now?' Jane Grogan, University College Dublin.

'Breugel's *Dulle Gret and Jonson's Bartholomew Fair*: Level Two Core Module', Kaley Kramer, Leeds University.

'John Donne and Renaissance Anatomy', Eric Langley, University College London.

'Introducing the Renaissance by Reading Pictures', Milena Marinkova, Leeds University.

Notes on Contributors

Hugh Adlington is a Lecturer in English at the University of Birmingham. He has published numerous journal articles and book chapters on early modern literature, religion and politics. He is a volume editor of the forthcoming Oxford Edition of the Sermons of John Donne.

Tita French Baumlin is a Professor of English at Missouri State University. A PhD in Shakespeare, Early Modern drama and rhetorical theory, she was editor of the scholarly journal *Explorations in Renaissance Culture* for ten years and co-author of *The Instructors' Manual for the HarperCollins World Reader* (HarperCollins, 1994). She has published *Ethos: New Essays in Rhetorical and Critical Theory* (Southern Methodist University Press, 1994; co-edited with James S. Baumlin) and *Post-Jungian Criticism: Theory and Praxis* (State University of New York Press, 2004; co-edited with James S. Baumlin and George H. Jensen). Her most recent book *Perpetual Adolescence: Jungian Analyses of American Media, Literature, and Popular Culture* (co-edited with Sally Porterfield and Keith Polette) is forthcoming from SUNY Press. Her essays on *Venus and Adonis* and *The Taming of the Shrew* have been reprinted in volumes of *Shakespearean Criticism*, and numerous articles on Shakespeare and related subjects have been published in such journals as *College English, Studies in English Literature, Papers on Language and Literature, CEA Critic, Rhetoric Review* and *Renascence*.

Karen Britland is an Associate Professor in the English Department at the University of Wisconsin-Madison where she teaches early modern literature, especially Shakespeare. She is also particularly interested in early modern women's writing and theatrical performance and has published a book about women and Stuart court theatre, entitled *Drama at the Courts of Queen Henrietta Maria* (Cambridge, 2006).

Susan Bruce is Head of the School of Humanities and Professor of English at Keele University. She is the editor of *Three Early Modern Utopias* (Oxford University Press, 1999), *King Lear* (Palgrave, 1997) and, with Valeria Wagner, *Fiction and Economy* (Palgrave, 2007). She is the author of essays on diverse topics, including Amenábar's *The Others*, Rochester's poetry and Siegfried Sassoon's prose, as well as several publications on the teaching of English Literature.

Nate Eastman is an Assistant Professor of English at Earlham College whose research interests include famine, gluttony and seventeenth-century competitive eating. He lives in Richmond, Indiana, scant miles from the largest RV dealership in North America, and has most recently authored 'Shakespeare and the Great Dearth'.

Joshua B. Fisher is an Associate Professor in the English Department at Wingate University. He has published on the literary appropriation of broadside ballads in the early modern period. His current project explores notions of textual and cultural translation in relation to the shaping of early modern English nationhood.

Thomas Healy is Professor of Renaissance Studies and Head of the School of English at the University of Sussex. He is the author of books on Crashaw, Marlowe, and Theory and Renaissance Literature and editor of a number of collections, most recently (with Margaret Healy), *Renaissance Transformations: The Making of English Writing, 1500–1650* (2009).

William Kerwin is an Associate Professor of English at the University of Missouri-Columbia where he teaches Shakespeare, early British poetry and Irish literature. His publications include *Beyond the Body: The Boundaries of Medicine and English Renaissance Drama* (University of Massachusetts Press, 2005) and *Brian Friel: A Casebook* (Garland Publications, 1997).

Lucy Munro is a Senior Lecturer in English at Keele University. Her publications include *Children of the Queen's Revels: A Jacobean Theatre Repertory* (Cambridge University Press, 2005) and editions of *Pericles* for *William Shakespeare: Complete Works*, ed. Jonathan Bate and Eric Rasmussen (Palgrave Macmillan, 2007) and Edward Sharpham's *The Fleer* for Globe Quartos (Nick Hern Books, 2006). She has also published essays on subjects including *Coriolanus*, female pirates, 1630s tragicomedy, the reception of early modern comedy in print, and children in film versions of *Richard III*.

Christopher Orchard is an Associate Professor of English at Indiana University of Pennsylvania where he teaches undergraduate and graduate classes in Shakespeare, Renaissance literature and transatlantic studies. He has published articles on Milton and Civil-War literature and the poet Geoffrey Hill. He is currently writing two books, one on the use of marital tropes as signifiers of political dissent in Milton's divorce tracts and polemic literature of the 1640s and 1650s, and the other on the theory of the circularity of knowledge and its application in research writing classes.

Rebecca Steinberger is an Associate Professor of English at Misericordia University and Chair of the English Department. She teaches courses on Shakespeare, Irish Drama, Restoration and Eighteenth Century British Literature, and the Gothic Tradition. Her publications include *Shakespeare and Twentieth-Century Irish Drama: Conceptualizing Identity and Staging Boundaries* (Ashgate, 2008). Currently, she is writing a book project titled *Panic on the Streets of London: Cultural Conflict in the City*.

Notes

Introduction

1 Ben Jonson, 'To My Book-seller'. Consulted at Chadwyck-Healey's *Literature Online* your college library may subscribe to this resource. If not, you can find the poem at www.luminarium.org/sevenlit/jonson/bookseller.htm.

2 A cleft-stick is a stick, split down the middle, which was used to carry bundles of papers and the like.

3 The word, like the concept it denotes, is now archaic; OED has: 'One who resorted to London in term, either for business at a court of law, or for amusements, intrigues, or dishonest practices.'

4 Bucklers-bury was a street in London populated by apothecaries and grocers.

Chapter 2

1 It is important to recognize that the term 'romance' can be applied both to prose and to drama, and has different meanings in either case (see Chapter 5).

2 See *The Courtier of Count Baldessar Castilio ... Done into English by Thomas Hoby* (London, 1561), sig. (3A)1r.

Chapter 3

1 The text of the Arden Shakespeare Third Series version of *King Lear* is a conflation of Q1 (1608) and F (1623). F is now thought to be a revision of Q, not a separate play. F omits several lines from this scene, and Q renders line 5 as 'Ay, honoured love'.

2 Alternative designations for 'one' hill include Mt Moriah, where Solomon built the Temple; or Wartburg, where Luther translated the Bible; or Wittenberg. An alternative designation for 'no hill' is Canterbury, seat of the English Church.

Chapter 5

1 *Diary of John Manningham, of the Middle Temple, and of Bradbourne, Kent, Barrister-at-law, 1602–1603: And Of Bradbourne, Kent, Barrister-at-law, 1602–1603.* March 1601/02.

2 E. Arbor, ed. (London: A. Constable & Co, 1895).

3 Reprinted in Craig William's *Martial: Epigrams, Book II.* New York: Oxford University Press, 2004, 7.

4 David Crystal, ed., *A Dictionary of the English Language.* (London: Penguin Classics, 2007), 529.

Chapter 7

1 Samuel Pepys, *The Diary*, vol. 2 (1661), ed. Robert Latham and William Matthews (London: Bell & Hyman, 1973), 162.

2 Jonson's *Works* (1616) initiated the practice of including dramatic works in expensive folio publications alongside more serious poetic writing. Shakespeare's *First*

Folio (1623) was published posthumously by fellow King's Men Henry Condell and John Heminge and the first folio of Beaumont and Fletcher's plays was published in 1647.

3 Traditional scholarship has until recently largely ignored Brome, although he is often mentioned because of his employment as Ben Jonson's manservant. As representative of conventional criticism surrounding Brome, take for example the following entry from *The Cambridge History of English and American Literature* (1907–18):

> 'Brome's sketches of London life are varied, minute, careful, spirited, and yet they displease; they cannot be read continuously without weariness, and are extremely coarse. Some critics have been pleased to decide that Brome describes life from the groom's point of view, and have ascribed his coarseness to his want of education and humble origin. The truer explanation is that he uses Jonson's manner without Jonson's full-blooded, massive humanity, without his satiric intensity, without his intellectual power; so that the Jonsonian scenes in Brome, his numerous efforts to describe the humours of London life, repel or tire the reader'. (IX, 8).

4 *Richard Brome Project*, http://www.shef.ac.uk/hri/projects/projectpages/rbrome.html

5 The etymological roots of the word 'author' are directly linked to the term auctor and to the Latin word 'augere' which itself means 'to originate or increase' (*OED*). As 'founders' of authoritative knowledge and texts, auctores were recognized as serving a father-like function.

6 John Lyly, 'To the Gentleman Reader', in *Euphues: The Anatomy of Wit* (London, 1579).

7 William Webbe, *A Discourse of English Poetrie* (London, 1588).

8 R. W., *The Epistle to Martin Mar-Sixtus* (London, 1591).

9 For Joseph Addison's remarks on *Paradise Lost*, see *The Spectator*, No. 279, Saturday 19 January 1712. On Immanuel Kant's discussion of the aesthetic, see especially *The Critique of Judgment* (1790). For Matthew Arnold's examination of 'poetic truth and beauty', see *The Study of Poetry* (1888).

10 See especially T. S. Eliot, 'Tradition and the Individual Talent', (T. S. Eliot 1922); F. R. Leavis (1936); René Wellek and Austin Warren (1942); Cleanth Brooks (1947); Alvin Kernan (1990); Harold Bloom (1994) and Frank Kermode (2004).

11 This instance of securing an enduring literary legacy through printed compilation is especially striking. Francis Beaumont's representative contributions in the 1647 folio are relatively minimal and Fletcher collaborated with Philip Massinger on many of the included plays. But the fact that the folio's title attributes the work collectively to Beaumont and Fletcher has ensured their enduring collaborative legacy.

12 Indeed, the massive *Thomas Middleton: The Collected Works* stands as only the third such collection of Middleton's dramatic and non-dramatic writings, the last having been published in 1886. Gary Taylor refers to the 2007 volume as 'The Middleton First Folio', to Middleton as 'our other Shakespeare', and to the cadre of nearly 70 editors contributing to the volume as 'the republic of Middleton' (58). Clearly, an effort is underway to re-cast Middleton as a literary heavy-weight in the canon of early modern literature.

13 For a discussion of distinctions between 'high and mighty' and 'meane and contemptible' works, see Thomas Healy, *New Latitudes: Theory and Renaissance Literature* (London: Hodder & Stoughton, 1992).

14 For a useful discussion of Stanford's revised great books program, 'Culture, Ideas, and Values' (CIV) and its impact, see Alison Schneider, 'Stanford Revisits the Course that Set off the Culture Wars', *Chronicle of Higher Education*, May 9, 1997), http://www.stanford.edu/group/areaone/reference/Chronicle_article.html

15 The May 1968 student uprisings in France and the publication of Michel Foucault's *Archaeology of Knowledge* (Paris: Gallimard, 1969) the following year played formative

roles in post-Structuralist movements prioritizing the re-evaluation of literary traditions within a cultural framework. For representative criticism that helped to develop these movements in relation to literary traditions, see especially Roland Barthes, 'The Death of the Author'; Jacques Derrida, *Of Grammatology* (1967); Michel Foucault, 'What is an Author?' (1969); Fredric Jameson, *The Political Unconscious* (1981) and Judith Butler, *Gender Trouble* (1990).

16 Bloom pits relativism against universal and essentialized forms of epistemology and blames popular music and radical movements of the 1960s for the rise of relativism. (see Bloom 1988).

17 See for example Margaret W. Ferguson, Maureen Quilligan and Nancy J. Vickers, eds.

18 The *Early Modern Englishwoman: A Facsimile Library of Essential Works* series continues to expand, adding volumes devoted to lesser known writers such as Anna Hume and Elizabeth Cellier as well as genres such as 'Mothers' Advice Books' and 'Writing on Medicine'. Other recent anthologies of early modern women's writing include *Early Modern Women Poets* (Stevenson and Davidson, 2001) as well as *Major Women Writers of Seventeenth-Century England* (Fitzmaurice et al., 1997) and *Women Writers in Renaissance England* (Martin 1997).

19 See for example the following collections of critical essays on women writing in the early modern period: Benson and Kirkham, eds., (2005); Chedgzoy, Hansen, Trill, eds., (1997); Haselkorn, Travitsky, eds., (1990) and Ostovich, Silcox and Roebuck, eds., (1999).

20 See for example the following recent scholarship: Herman, ed., (2002); Bell, (2004); Szonyi, (2005).

21 Students and instructors can find a wealth of online resources that accompany the *Norton Anthology of English Literature* at the following website: http://www.wwnorton.com/college/english/nael/

22 While many large research institutions provide access to the Early English Books Online database (http://eebo.chadwyck.com/home) and many other online database resources, smaller and less financially powerful institutions often lack these kinds of resources.

23 See the annotated bibliography at the end of this volume for a fuller description of these resources.

Chapter 8

1 From the 'The Supper of the Lorde and holy Communion, commonly called the Masse' in the 1549 *Book of Common Prayer*, at http://justus.anglican.org/resources/bcp/1549/Communion_1549.htm, accessed 16 April 2008. This phraseology remains constant in 1552, 1559 and 1662, though in the Elizabethan BCP from 1549 'catholike' is printed with a small 'c'.

2 John Milton, *Paradise Lost*, VII, 31, Alastair Fowler, editor (London: Longman, 1968). See Simpson, 2007 for a cogent reconsideration of Protestantism's liberal reputation.

Digital Resources

Introduction

The bibliography of works that follows below may seem daunting to the student embarking on a study of English Renaissance Literature for the first time. But it is always worth remembering that the first place to begin is with the literature itself: the more you read in the primary texts of the period, the better you will understand both the period itself and the individual primary texts that you are studying. In the case of drama, you will also benefit enormously from attending productions of the plays, and/or from watching productions of them on film, and many university libraries are now well stocked with different filmic productions of plays from the period: Shakespeare, of course – but there exist also films of other early modern dramas, such as *The Changeling*, *Volpone* and *'Tis Pity She's a Whore*.

Insofar as secondary literature is concerned, you will find that there is a wealth of introductory material to choose from. Compendiums of essays on individual texts (such as, for example, the Macmillan New Casebooks) will often enable you to grasp, quite efficiently, a sample of the most influential essays on a given topic; and introductory surveys of specific genres are also easy to come by. Michael Mangan's *Preface to Shakespearean Comedy*, for example, John Drakakis' volume on *Tragedy*, or Terry Gifford's New Critical Idiom volume on *Pastoral* are just three examples of the kind of introductory material you might seek out to give you a mental map of a particular genre (Mangan 1996, Drakakis 1998, Gifford 1999). For a more in-depth understanding of the range of critical approaches to early modern literature you could do worse than begin by browsing through the volumes covered by Orchard in Chapter Four of this volume, all of which have been seminal texts of scholarship in this period.

Digital Resources

The Richard Brome Project
This project is focused on one artist, Richard Brome. It is intended to be an online anthology of his works and guide to its performance. The creation of this website is aimed primarily at scholars of drama and theatre. The site seeks to combine dramatic theoretical knowledge with practical advice for the performance of the works of Richard Brome.

Brown University's Women Writers Online
One of the earliest digital resources of its kind, this helpful archive focuses on women writers of the pre-Victorian era, making lesser known works more accessible to the public and more visible in the literary world.

Digital Scriptorium [http://scriptorium.columbia.edu]
An image database of Medieval and Renaissance manuscripts.

EEBO, Early English Books Online
Early English Books Online is a compilation of early modern works from the first printed English book to texts from the time of Shakespeare and Spenser. EEBO is useful for research in the fields of literature, history, philosophy, linguistics, theology and the arts and sciences of the times. This resource documents the transformation of the literary culture across the varying social classes. EEBO contains roughly one hundred thousand works from the microfilm, *Pollard and Redgrave Short Title Catalogue*.

Hamlet on the Ramparts [http/shea.mit.edu/ramparts]
A website designed and maintained by the MIT Shakespeare Project in collaboration with the Folger Shakespeare library. It provides access to a collection of texts, images and films relating to Hamlet's first encounter with the ghost.

The Internet Renaissance Band [http://www.curtisclark.org/emusic]
Excellent site, where you can listen to the music that might have accompanied dramatic productions or other early modern festivities.

Project Luminarium
Project Luminarium is an anthology of English literature, and houses a separate database designed to give historical context for the people, places and events described therein. Contents are mainly primary, but secondary sources are searchable to afford the reader contextual insights into the works.

Renaissance Literature: Happenings and Cavortings in the Early Modern World [http://earlymodern-lit.blogspot.com]
This will mainly be of interest to graduate students and to academics: the blog provides notice of forthcoming conferences, as well as calls for papers and so forth.

Representative Poetry Online [http://rpo.library.utoronto.ca/display]
A University of Toronto website which reproduces a number of early modern poems and includes various search facilities such as an extensive glossary of literary terms.

VOS, Voice of the Shuttle
Voice of the Shuttle is a dynamic database that users can contribute to on a wide range of topics ranging from general humanities research, to science and technology, to dance and music. Users with accounts have some editorial privileges over submissions they have made, and there is a central team of vetting staff maintained by the University of California at Santa Barbara to monitor submission accuracy. This is a more general research tool usable by students of more diverse concentrations.

Works Cited

Abbagnano, Nicola. 'Renaissance Humanism'. 1973. *The Dictionary of the History of Ideas*. Academic Publishers, 2005.

Achinstein, Sharon. *Literature and Dissent in Milton's England*. Cambridge: Cambridge University Press, 2003.

Addison, Joseph. *The Spectator*. Edited by Donald Bonds. 5 vols. Oxford: Clarendon Press, 1965.

Aers, David. ' "A Whisper in the Ear of Early Modernists" or, Reflections on Literary Critics, Writing the "History of the Subject" '. In *Culture and History 1350–1600: Essays on English Communities, Identities and Writing*, edited by David Aers. Detroit: Wayne State University Press, 1992.

Aeschylus. *Oresteia*. Translated by Hugh Lloyd-Jones. Berkeley: University of California Press, 1993.

Agnew, Jean-Christophe. *Worlds Apart: The Market and the Theater in Anglo-American Thought, 1550–1750*. Cambridge. Cambridge University Press, 28 October 1988.

Alexander, Peter, ed. *Academy Lectures*. Oxford: Oxford University Press, 1963, 201–18.

Alfar, Christina León. 'Looking for Goneril and Regan'. *Privacy, Domesticity, and Women in Early Modern England*. Ed. Corinne S. Abate. Aldershot: Ashgate, 2003. 167–98.

Alighieri, Dante. *The Divine Comedy*. Edited by C. H. Grandgent. New York: Vintage Books, 1959.

Anderson, Benedict. *Imagined Communities: Reflections on the Origin and Spread of Nationalism*. 2nd ed. London: Verso, 2006.

Arden of Faversham. London: Methuen Drama, 2007.

Ariosto and Euripedes. *Supposes; and, Jocasta*. Translated by George Gascoigne. Boston: D.C. Heath, 1906.

Armstrong, N. and L. Tennenhouse. *The Imaginary Puritan: Literature, Intellectual Labor, and the Origins of Personal Life*. Berkeley: University of California Press, 1992.

Arnold, Matthew. *Essays in Criticism*. Edited by S. R. Littlewood. London: Macmillan, 1958.

Ashcroft, Bill, Gareth Griffiths and Helen Tiffin. *Key Concepts in Post-Colonial Studies*. New York: Routledge, 1995.

Ashton, John, ed. *The Long Nos'd Lass. Humour, Wit and Satire of the Seventeenth Century*. Whitefish, Montana: Kessinger Publishing, LLC, 2006.

Ashton, Robert. *The English Civil War: Conservatism and Revolution*. London: Weidenfeld and Nicholson, 1978. 30–31.Bach, Rebecca Ann. *Colonial Transformations: The Cultural Production of the New Atlantic World, 1580–1640*. London: Palgrave, 2000.

Askew, Anne and Elaine V. Beilin, ed. *Examinations of Anne Askew: Women Writers in English 1350–1850*. New York: Oxford University Press, 1996.

Atchity, K. K., *The Renaissance Reader*. New York: HarperCollins, 1996.

Axton, Marie, ed. *Three Tudor Classical Interludes: Thersites, Jacke Jugeler, Horestes.* Woodbridge: D.S. Brewer, 1982.

Bach, Rebecca Ann. *Colonial Transformations: The Cultural Production of the New Atlantic World, 1580–1640.* London: Palgrave, 2000.

Bacon, Francis. *The New Atlantis.* London, 1627.

—— . *The Advancement of Learning.* Cont. Stephen Jay Gould. New York: Modern Library, 2001.

Baker, David, J and Willy Maley, eds. *British Identities and English Renaissance Literature.* Cambridge: Cambridge University Press, 2002.

Bakhtin, Mikhail. *Rabelais and His World.* Translated by Helene Iswolsky. Cambridge, MA: MIT Press, 1968.

—— . *Problems of Dostoevski's Poetics.* Leningrad, 1929; revised 1963. Trans. R. W. Rotsel. Ann Arbor: Ardis, 1973.

Baldick, Chris. *The Concise Oxford Dictionary of Literary Terms.* Oxford: Oxford University Press, 2001.

Baldwin, William, William A. Ringler and Michael Flachmann. *Beware the Cat: The First English Novel* (c. 1554, printed 1570). 1st Ed. San Marino, CA: Huntington Library Press, 1995.

Bale, John and Barry B. Adams. *King Johan.* 1538. Cont. Barry B. Adams. San Marino, CA: Huntington Library, 1969.

Barbour, Richmond. *Before Orientalism.* New York: Cambridge University Press, 2003.

Barrell, John. *Poetry, Language, and Politics.* Manchester: Manchester University Press, 1988.

Bartels, Emily C. 'The Double Vision of the East: Imperialist Self-Construction in Marlowe's *Tamburlaine, Part One'.* In *Renaissance Drama in an Age of Colonization,* edited by Mary Beth Rose, 3–23. Evanston: Northwestern University Press, 1992.

Barthelemy, Anthony Gerald. *Black Face, Maligned Race: The Representation of Blacks in English Drama from Shakespeare to Southerne.* Baton Rouge: Louisiana University Press, 1987.

Barthes, Roland. 'Death of the Author'. In *Image-Music-Text.* Translated by Stephen Heath. New York: Hill and Wang, 1978.

Beaumont, Francis. *The Knight of the Burning Pestle.* 1607. New Mermaids Edition. London: Bedford, 1996.

Beaumont, Francis and John Fletcher. *Comedies and Tragedies Written by Francis Beaumont and John Fletcher Gentlemen.* London, 1647.

Beidler, Philip and Gary Taylor, eds. *Writing Race across the Atlantic World: Medieval to Modern.* London: Palgrave, 2005.

Beilin, Elaine V. Redeeming Eve: *Women Writers of the English Renaissance,* Princeton, NJ: Princeton University Press, 1990.

Bell, Ilona. 'Elizabeth Tudor: Poet'. *Explorations in Renaissance Culture* 30, no. 1 (2004): 1–22. Bellow, 1991.

Belsey, Catherine. *The Subject of Tragedy: Identity and Difference in Renaissance Drama.* London: Methuen, 1985.

—— . *John Milton: Language, Gender, Power.* Oxford: Oxford University Press, 1988.

—— . 'Desire's Excess and the English Renaissance Theatre: *Edward II, Troilus and Cressida, Othello'. Erotic Politics: The Dynamics of Desire in the Renaissance Theatre.* Edited by Susan Zimmerman. London: Routledge, 1992.

Benedict, Barbara M. *Making the Modern Reader: Cultural Mediation in Early Modern Literary Anthologies.* Princeton, NJ: Princeton University Press, 1996.

Benson, Pamela Joseph and Victoria Kirkham, eds. *Strong Voices, Weak History: Early Women Writers in England, France, and Italy.* Ann Arbor: University of Michigan Press, 2005.

Berek, P. 'The Jew as Renaissance Man'. *Renaissance Quarterly* 51, no. 1 (1998): 128–62.

Best, S. *The Politics of Historical Vision: Marx, Foucault, Habermas*. New York & London: Guilford Press, 1995.

Bloom, Allan. *The Closing of the American Mind*. New York: Simon and Schuster, 1988.

Bloom, Harold. 'The Breaking of Form'. *Deconstruction and Criticism*. Edited by G. Hartman. New York: Continuum, 1979, 1–37.

——. *The Western Canon: The Books and Schools of the Ages*. New York: Riverhead, 1994.

——. *The Anxiety of Influence: A Theory of Poetry*. New York and London: Oxford University Press, 1973; rev. intro. 1997.

——. *Shakespeare: The Invention of the Human*. New York: Riverhead, 1998.

Boas, F. S. *Shakespeare and His Predecessors*. New York: Greenwood Press, 1969.

Boccaccio, Giovanni. *L'Ameto*. Edited by Judith Serafini-Sauli Powers. 1st ed. New York: Garland, 1985.

——. *The Decameron*. c. 1350. Edited by G. H. McWilliam. 2nd ed. London: Penguin Classics, 2003.

Book of Common Prayer. London, 1549.

Bowra, C. *From Virgil to Milton*. London: Macmillan, 1945.

Bradley, A. *Oxford Lectures on Poetry*. London: Macmillan, 1909.

——. *Shakespearean Tragedy*. 1904. India: Atlantic Publishers & Distributors, 2008.

Bradshaw, Brendan, Andrew Hadfield and Willy Maley, eds. *Representing Ireland. Literature and the Origins of Conflict, 1534–1660*. Cambridge: Cambridge University Press, 1993.

Bradshawe, Graham. *Misrepresentations: Shakespeare and the Materialists*. Ithaca, NY: Cornell University Press, 1993.

Brannigan, John. *New Historicism and Cultural Materialism*. London: Palgrave, 1988.

Bray, Alan. *Homosexuality in Renaissance England*. London: Gay Men's Press, 1982.

——. *Homosexuality in Renaissance England*. New York: Columbia University Press, 1995.

Bredbeck, Gregory W. *Sodomy and Interpretation: Marlowe to Milton*. Ithaca, NY: Cornell University Press, 1991.

Bretzius, Stephen. *Shakespeare in Theory: The Postmodern Academy and the Early Modern Theater*. Ann Arbor: University of Michigan Press, 1997.

Brink, Jean R. and William F. Gentrup, eds. *Renaissance Culture in Context: Theory and Practice*. Aldershot, UK: Scolar Press, 1993.

Bristol, Michael D. *Carnival and Theater: Plebeian Culture and the Structure of Authority in Renaissance England*. London: Routledge, September 1989.

Brome, Richard. *The Antipodes*. 1636. Edited by David Scott Kastan and Richard Proudfoot. London: Nick Hern Books, 2000.

Brooks, Cleanth. *The Well-Wrought Urn: Studies in the Structure of Poetry*. 1947. New York: Harvest Books, 1956.

Brown, Pamela Allen. *Better a Shrew than a Sheep: Women, Drama, and the Culture of Jest in Early Modern England*, New York, Columbia University Press, 1998.

Brown, Paul. '"This Thing of Darkness I Acknowledge Mine': *The Tempest* and the Discourse of Colonialism". Ed. Jonathan Dollimore and Alan Sinfield. Manchester University Pres, 1985. 48–71.

Browne, William. 'Britania's Pastorals'. *Original Poems*. London, 1613.

——. 'The Shepherd's Pipe'. 1614. London: Imprinted at the Clerk's Private Press, 1914.

Bruce, Susan, ed. *Shakespeare: King Lear*. New York. Columbia University Press, 1998.

——. ed. *Three Early Modern Utopias*. Oxford: Oxford University Press, 1999.

Bullough, G. *Narrative and Dramatic Sources of Shakespeare*. London: Routledge; New York: Columbia University Press.

Bunyan, John. *Pilgrim's Progress*. London: William Collins, Sons & Co., 1678.

Burckhardt, Jacob. *The Civilization of the Renaissance in Italy*. Translated by S. G. Middlemore. Harmondsworth: Penguin Books, 1990.

Burton, Jonathan. *Traffic and Turning: Islam and English Drama, 1579–1624*. Newark: University of Delaware Press, 2005.

Burton, Rosemary. *Pudentius Psychomachia/Commentary and Text (Bryn Mawr Latin Commentary Series)*. Bryn Mawr, PA: Bryn Mawr Commentaries, 1989.

Butler, Judith. *Gender Trouble: Feminism and the Subversion of Identity*. New York: Routledge Classics, 2006.

Callaghan, Dympna. *A Feminist Companion to Shakespeare*. Oxford: Wiley-Blackwell, 2000.

Camden, William. *Remaines concerning Britaine their languages*, 1637.

Campbell, J. *The Hero With a Thousand Faces*. Princeton: Princeton University Press, 1949.

Campbell, Lily B, ed. *The Mirror for Magistrates*. Cambridge: Cambridge University Press, 1938.

Carew, Thomas. 'To Saxham'. In *The Poems of Thomas Carew*, edited by Arthur Vincent, 36–38. London: Routledge, 2001.

Carey, Elizabeth. *Tragedy of Miriam: Queen of Jewry*. 1613. Calgary: Broadview Press, 2000.

Carey, John. *John Donne: Life, Mind and Art*. New York: Oxford University Press, 1981.

Cassirer, E., P. O. Kristeller and J. H. Randall, Jr. *The Renaissance Philosophy of Man*. Chicago: University of Chicago Press, 1948.

Castiglione, Baldassare. *The Courtier of Count Baldessar Castilio . . . Done into English by Castilio*. London: Wyllyam Seres, 1561.

Cavendish, Margaret. 'True Relation of My Birth, Breeding, and Life'. 1656. *Paper Bodies: A Margaret Cavendish Reader*. Peterborough, Ontario: Broadview Press, 2000.

Cawood, John. *The Ecologues of Alexander Barclay from the Original Edition*. Oxford: Oxford University Press, 1961.

Chalmers, Hero. *Royalist Women Writers, 1650–1689*. Oxford: Oxford University Press, 2004.

Chamberlain, John. *Letters*. Edited by N.E. McClure, 3 vols. Philadelphia: American Philosophical Society, 1939.

Chambers, E. K. *The Elizabethan Stage*. 4 vols. Oxford: Clarendon Press, 1923.

Chapman, George. *All Fools* (*c.* 1604). Edited by Frank Manley. Lincoln: University of Nebraska Press, 1968.

Chapman, George. *An Humorous Day's Mirth*. 1597. Edited by Henry Willis Wells. London: Malone Society, 1937.

——. *Conspiracy and Tragedy of Charles Duke of Byron* (1608). Edited by John Margeson. Manchester University Press, 1990.

——. *Bussy D' Ambois* (*c.* 1604). Edited by Nicholas Brooke. Manchester: Manchester University Press, 1999.

Chaucer, Geoffrey. 'Tale of Sir Thopas'. In *Chaucer: Tale of Sir Thopas [and] Monk's Tale*, edited by A. J. Wyatt. London: University Tutorial Press, 1948.

Chedgzoy, Kate, Melanie Hanson and Suzanne Trill, eds. *Voicing Women: Gender and Sexuality in Early Modern Writing*. Pittsburgh: Duquesne University Press, 1988.

——. *Voicing Women: Gender and Sexuality in Early Modern Writing*. Pittsburgh: Duquesne University Press, 1997.

Chettle, Henry. *Hoffman; A Revenge for a Father*. Edited by Henry Barrett-Lennard. London: Thomas Hailes Lacy, 1852.

Cicero. *Cicero: Rhetorica ad Herennium*. Translated by Harry Caplan. Cambridge: Harvard University Press, 1954.

Clark, Donald Lehman. *Milton at St. Paul's School: A Study of Ancient Rhetoric in Renaissance Education*. New York: Columbia University Press, 1948.

Clegg, Cyndi. *Press Censorship in Jacobean England*. Cambridge: Cambridge University Press, 2001.

Clifford, Anne. 'Diaries' (1616–19). In *The Diaries of Lady Anne Clifford*, edited by D. J. H. Clifford. Stroud, Gloucestershire: Sutton Publishing, 2003.

Clowes, W. *A Profitable and Necessarie Book of Obseruations, for All Those that Are Burned with the Flame of Gun powder*. London, 1596.

Cohen, Adam Max. *Shakespeare and Technology: Dramatizing Early Modern Technological Revolutions*. New York: Palgrave, 2006.

Coleridge, S. *Biographia Literaria*. Princeton: Princeton University Press, 1983.

Collier, John Payne. ed. *The Adoration of the Shepherds. Five Miracle Plays: Or Scriptural Dramas*. 1836. Whitefish, Montana: Kessinger Publishing, LLC, 2008.

Comensoli, Vivian and Paul Stephens, eds. *Discontinuities: New Essays on Renaissance Literature and Criticism*. Toronto: University of Toronto Press, 1998.

Congreve, William. *Incognita; or Love and Duty Reconcil'd*. Edited by Herbert Francis Brett Brett-Smith. Oxford: B. Blackwell, 1922.

—— . *Judgment of Paris*. 1701. Rewritten by John Weldon. Edited by David W. Music. Madison: A-R Editions, 1999.

—— . *Incognita or Love and Duty Reconciled*. New York: Kessinger Publishing, 2004.

Constable, Henry. 'Diana'. 1594. *Diana: The Sonnets and Other Poems of Henry Constable*. London : [s.n.], 1859.

Corns, Thomas N. *Uncloistered Virtue: English Political Literature, 1640–1660*. Oxford: Oxford University Press, 1992.

Cowley, Abraham. 'Davideis'. 1656. *Davideis, a Sacred Poem of the Troubles of David. In Four Books*. London, 1707.

Craik, K. *Reading Sensations in Early Modern England*. Basingstroke and New York: Palgrave Macmillan, 2007.

Crane, Mary Thomas. 'Women and the Early Modern Canon: Recent Editions of Works by English Women, 1500–1660'. *Renaissance Quarterly* 51(1998): 942–56.

Crowley, S. *A Teacher's Introduction to Deconstruction*. Urbana: NCTE, 1989.

Crystal, David, ed. *A Dictionary of the English Language*. London: Penguin Classics, 2007.

Culler, J. 'Literary Theory'. In *Introduction to Scholarship in Modern Languages and Literatures*, edited by J. Gibaldi. New York: MLA, 1992, 201–35.

Daalder, Joost and Anthony Telford More. ' "There's Scarce a Thing But is Both Loved and Loathe": *The Changeling* I.i 91–129'. *English Studies* 80 (1999): 499–509.

Daborne, Robert. *A Christian Turn'd Turk*. New York: Da Capo Press, 1973.

Daniel, Samuel. *Delia*. 1592. Edited by Henry Constable. London: Trübner and Co., 1896.

—— . *Civil Wars*. 1595. Edited by Laurence Anthony Michel. New Haven: Yale University Press, 1958.

—— . *The Tragedy of Philotas*. 1604. Edited by Laurence Michel. Hamden: Archon Books, 1970.

Davenant, William. *Salmacia Spoilia: A Masque*. London: Thomas Wilkey, 1639.

Davies, Stevie. *The Feminine Reclaimed: The Idea of Woman in Spenser, Shakespeare, and Milton*. Lexington: University of Kentucky Press, 1985.

Davison, Francis. *The Dialogue between the Squire, Proteus Amprhirite and Thamesis. Forming Part of a Masque Performed at Grey's Inn 1594*. London, 1688.

Daybell, James. *Women Letter Writers in Tudor England*. Oxford: Oxford University Press, 2006.

De Cervantes, Miguel. *Don Quixote*. Translated by Edith Grossman. New York: Harper Perennial, 2005.

de Lorris, Gilliaume. *Roman de la Rose*. Paris: Librairie Honore Champion, 1970.

Degenhardt, Jane Hwang. 'Catholic Martyrdom in Dekker and Massinger's *The Virgin Martir* and the Early Modern Threat of "Turning Turk" '. *ELH* 73, no. 1 (2006): 83–116.

Dekker, Thomas. *Newes from Graves-end: The Plague Pamphlets of Thomas Dekker*. Oxford: Clarendon Press, 1925.

——. *Wonderfull Yeare: The Plague Pamphlets of Thomas Dekker*. Oxford: Clarendon Press, 1925.

——. 'The Dramatic Works of Thomas Dekker, Volume II: *The Honest Whore. The Magnificent Entertainment Given to King James. Westward Ho. Northward Ho.*' In *The Whore of Babylon*, edited by Fredson Bowerd Thomas. Cambridge: Cambridge University Press, 1955.

——. *The Shoemaker's Holiday*. London: Methuen Drama, 2007.

Deloney, Thomas. *The Gentle Craft*. Edited by Simon Barker. Farnham, Surrey: Ashgate, 2007.

——. *The Pleasant History Of John Winchcomb: In His Younger Years Called Jack Of Newberie, The Famous and Worthy Clothier Of England*. Whitefish, Montana: Kessinger Publishing, LLC, 2007.

Deresiewicz, W. 'The business of theory'. *The Nation* 16 Feb 2004, 1–3.

Derrida, Jacques. *Of Grammatology*. Translated by Gayatri Chakravorty Spivak. Baltimore: Johns Hopkins University Press, 1976.

DiGangi, Mario. *The Homoerotics of Early Modern Drama*. New York and Cambridge: Cambridge University Press, 1997.

Dionne, Craig and Steve Mentz, eds. *Rogues and Early Modern English Culture*. Ann Arbor: University of Michigan Press, 2004.

Dolan, F. E. *The Taming of the Shrew: Texts and Contexts*. Boston and New York: Bedford, 1996.

Dollimore, Jonathan. *Radical Tragedy: Religion, Ideology and Power in the Drama of Shakespeare and his Contemporaries*, Chicago: Chicago University Press, 1984.

——. *Sexual Dissidence: Augustine to Wilde, Freud to Foucault*. Oxford: Oxford University Press, 2001.

Dollimore, Jonathan and Alan Sinfield, eds. *Political Shakespeare: Essays in Cultural Materialism*. Manchester: Manchester University Press, 1985.

——. *Political Shakespeare: Essays in Cultural Materialism*. Manchester: Manchester University Press, 1994.

Donne, John. *The Sermons of John Donne*. 10 vols. Edited by George R. Potter and Evelyn M. Simpson. Berkeley: University of California Press, 1953–1961.

——. *The Complete English Poems*. Edited by A. J. Smith. London: Penguin Classics, 1996.

——. *Complete English Poems*. Ed. C. A. Patrides. London: J. M. Dent, 2001.

——. *Songs and Sonnets: The Complete Poetry and Selected Prose of John Donne*. New York: The Modern Library, 2001.

Doob, Penelope. *The Idea of the Labyrinth from Classical Antiquity through the Middle Ages*. Ithaca, New York: Cornell University Press, 1992.

Drakakis, John and Naomi Liebler, eds. *Tragedy*. Harlow: Longman, 1998.

Drayton, Michael. *Eclogues: The Complete Works of Michael Drayton, Now First Collected*. Charleston, South Carolina: BookSurge Publishing, 2001.

——. *England's Heroicall Epistles: The Complete Works of Michael Drayton, Now First Collected*. Charleston, South Carolina: BookSurge Publishing, 2001.

——. *Idea's Mirror. The Complete Works of Michael Drayton, Now First Collected*. Charleston, South Carolina: BookSurge Publishing, 2001.

Dryden, John. *Absalom and Achitophel*. Whitefish, Montana : Kessinger Publishing, LLC, 2004.

Eagleton, Terry. *Literary Theory: An Introduction*. Minneapolis: University of Minnesota Press, 1983.

—— . *William Shakespeare*. 1986. Oxford: Blackwell, 2000.

Edward, Richard. *Damon and Pythias*. New York: Oxford University Press, 1957.

Eliot, T. S. 'Tradition and the Individual Talent'. *The Sacred Wood: Essays on Poetry and Criticism*. New York: Faber & Faber, 1997.

Elizabeth I. *Collected Works*. Edited by Leah Marcus, Janel M. Mueller and Mary Beth Rose. Chicago: University of Chicago Press, 2000.

Empson, W. *Some Versions of Pastoral*. New York: New Directions, 1974.

Enterline, Lynne. *The Tears of Narcissus: Melancholia and Masculinity in Early Modern Writing*. Stanford: Stanford University Press, 1995.

Erasmus, Desiderius. *De Utraque Verborem Ac Rerum Copia*. Paris: Badius, 1512.

—— . *De Copia. Collected works of Erasmus*. Toronto: University of Toronto Press, 1978.

—— . *The Praise of Folly and Other Writings*. Edited by Robert M. Adams. New York: W. W. Norton, 1989.

Erickson, Peter. 'The Two Renaissances and Shakespeare's Canonical Position'. *Kenyon Review* 14, no. 2 (1992): 56–70.

Erickson, Peter and Clark Hulse, eds. *Early Modern Visual Culture: Representation, Race, and Empire in Renaissance England*. Philadelphia: University of Pennsylvania Press, 2000.

Euripides. *Iphigenia at Aulis*. Translated by Lady Lumley (Prepared by Harold H. Child). London: Malone Society Reprints, 1909.

Everyman and The Second Sheperds' Play – Literary Touchstone Classic. Clayton, Delaware: Prestwick House, 2007.

Farmer, John S., ed. *Hyckescorner. Six Anonymous Plays: 1510–1537*. Edited by Montana Whitefish: Kessinger Publishing, LLC, 2008.

Ferguson, M., M. Quilligan and N. Vickers. *Rewriting the Renaissance: The Discourses of Sexual Difference in Early Modern Europe*. Chicago: Chicago University Press, 1986.

Ferguson, Margaret W., A. R. Buck and Nancy E. Wright. *The Lawes Resolutions of Womens Rights: Or the Lawes Provision for Woemen*. Clark, New Jersey: Law Book Exchange, 2005.

Ferguson, Margaret W., Maureen Quilligan and Nancy J. Vickers, eds. *Rewriting the Renaissance: the Discourses of Sexual Difference in Early Modern England*. Chicago: University of Chicago Press, 1986.

Finucci, Valeria and Regina Shwartz, eds. *Desire in the Renaissance: Psychoanalysis and Literature*. Princeton: Princeton University Press, 1994.

Fish, Stanley. *Self-Consuming Artifacts*. Berkeley: University of California Press, 1972.

—— . 'Interpreting the *Variorum*', *Critical Inquiry* 2, no. 3 (1976): 465–85.

—— . *Self-Consuming Artifacts*. Pittsburgh: Duquesne University Press, 1998.

Fisher, Joshua B. ' "He is turned a ballad-maker": Ballad Appropriations in Early Modern England'. *Early Modern Literary Studies* 9, no. 2 (2003): 3.1–22.

Fitzmaurice, James, Carol Barish, Eugene Cunnar and Nancy Gutierrez, eds. *Major Women Writers of Seventeenth-Century England*. Ann Arbor: University of Michigan Press, 1997.

Fletcher, John. *Bonduca: The Dramatic Works in the Beaumont and Fletcher Canon*. New York: Cambridge University Press, 2008.

—— . *Faithful Shepherdess: The Dramatic Works in the Beaumont and Fletcher Canon*. New York: Cambridge University Press, 2008.

Fletcher, John and Francis Beaumont. *The Maid's Tragedy: The Dramatic Works in the Beaumont and Fletcher Canon*. New York: Cambridge University Press, 2008.

Fletcher, John and Philip Massinger. *Sir John Van Olden Barnavelt*. British Library, MS Add. 18653, fol. 5v.

—— . *The Elder Brother: The Dramatic Works in the Beaumont and Fletcher Canon*. New York: Cambridge University Press, 2008.

—— . *A King and No King: The Dramatic Works in the Beaumont and Fletcher Canon*. New York: Cambridge University Press, 2008.

—— . *Philaster: The Dramatic Works in the Beaumont and Fletcher Canon*. New York: Cambridge University Press, 2008.

Ford, Emanuel. *Ornatus and Artesia. Shorter Novels: Seventeenth Century: Ornatus and Artesia – Oroonoko Isle of Pines – Incognita*. London: J. M. Dent and Sons, 1930.

Ford, John. *'Tis Pity She's a Whore. 'Tis Pity She's a Whore and Other Plays*. Edited by Marion Lomax. New York: Oxford University Press, 2008.

Foucault, Michel. 'What is an Author?' *Language, Counter Memory, Practice*. Edited by. Donald Bouchard. Ithaca: Cornell University Press, 1980, 113–38.

—— . *Archaeology of Knowledge*. New York: Pantheon, 1982.

—— . *The History of Sexuality*. Colchester, Essex: Vintage, 1990.

Fox, Adam. *Oral and Literate Culture in England 1500–1700*. Oxford: Oxford University Press, 2002.

Foxe, John. *Foxe's Book of Martyrs*. London, 1684.

Fraser, D., H. Hibbard and M. J. Lewine. *Essays in the History of Art Presented to Rudolf Wittkower*. London: Phaidon, 1967.

Fraser, R. A. and N. Rabkin. *Drama of the Renaissance II: The Stuart Period*. New York: MacMillan, 1976.

Fraser, R. A. and N. Rabkin, eds. 'Gammer Gurton's Needle. 1566'. In *Drama of the English Renaissance I: The Tudor Period*, 35–60. New York: Macmillan Publishing, 1976.

French, Marilyn. *Shakespeare's Division of Experience*. New York: Ballantine Books, 1983.

Freud, Sigmund. *The Interpretation of Dreams*. 1900. Translated by James Strachey. New York: Avon, 1965.

—— . *Three Essays on the Theory of Sexuality*. New York: Basic Books, 2000.

Frey, S. 'Of Chastity and Violence: Elizabeth I and Edmund Spenser in the House of Busirane'. *Signs* 20, no. 1 (1994): 49–78.

Frye, Northrop. *Anatomy of Criticism: Four Essays*. Princeton: Princeton University Press, 1957.

Frye, Susan. *Elizabeth I: The Competition for Representation*. Oxford University Press, 1996.

Fuchs, Barbara. *Mimesis and Empire: The New World, Islam, and European Identities*. Cambridge: Cambridge University Press, 2001.

Fulwell, Ulpian. *The Dramatic Writings of Ulpian Fulwell Comprising Like Will to Like – Note-Book and Word-List*. Edited by J. S. Farmer. London: Early English Dramatists, 1905.

Fumerton, Patricia and Simon Hunt, eds. *Renaissance Culture and the Everyday*. Philadelphia: University of Pennsylvania Press, 1998.

Furnivall, Frederick James and Alfred W. Pollard, ed. *The Macro Plays: Mankind; Wisdom; The Castle of Perseverance*. Whitefish, Montana: Kessinger Publishing, LLC, 2008.

Gallagher, Susan VanZanten. 'Contingencies and Intersections: The Formation of Pedagogical Canons'. Pedagogy 1, no. 1 (2001): 53–67.

Gilman, Ernest. '"To adore, or scorne an image": Donne and the Iconoclastic Controversy', in *John Donne Journal* 5 (1986): 63–100.

Glynne Wickham, Herbert Berry and William Ingram, eds. 'A Funeral Elegy on the Death of the Famous Actor Richard Burbage Who Died on Saturday in Lent the

13th of March 1618'. *English Professional Theatre, 1530–1660*. New York: Cambridge University Press, 2000.

Godwin, Francis. *The Man in the Moone: Or, A Discourse of a Voyage Thither*. New York: Da Capo Press, 1972.

Goldberg, Jonathan. *Voice Terminal Echo: Postmodernism and English Renaissance Texts*. New York and London: Methuen, 1986.

——. *Sodometries: Renaissance Texts, Modern Sexualities*. Palo Alto: Stanford University Press, 1992.

——. *Queering the Renaissance*. Durham: Duke University Press, 1994.

——. ed. *Queering the Renaissance*. Series Q. Durham, NC and London: Duke University Press, 1994.

Good, G. 'Presentism: Postmodernism, Poststructuralism, Postcolonialism'. In *Theory's Empire: An Anthology of Dissent*, edited by D. Patai and W. Corral, 287–97. New York: Columbia University Press, 2005.

Gosson, Stephen. *The School of Abuse*. London, 1579.

Grabes, Herbert, ed. *Writing the Early Modern English Nation: The Transformation of National Identity in Sixteenth and Seventeenth-Century England*. Amsterdam: Rodopi, 2001.

Grady, Hugh and Terrence Hawkes, eds. *Presentist Shakespeares*. Abingdon, Oxfordshire: Routledge, 2007.

Graham, Elspeth. *Her Own Life: Autobiographical Writings by Seventeenth-Century Englishwomen*. Edited by Helen Wilcox, Elaine Hobby, Hilary Hind and Elspeth Graham. London: Routledge, 1989.

Greenblatt, Stephen. *Renaissance Self-fashioning: From More to Shakespeare*. Chicago and London: University of Chicago Press, 1980.

——. *Renaissance Self-Fashioning: From More to Shakespeare*. Chicago: University of Chicago Press, 1980.

——. *Shakespearean Negotiations: The Circulation of Social Energy in Renaissance England*. Berkeley: University of California Press, 1988.

——. 'Learning to Curse'. *Learning to Curse: Essays in Early Modern Culture*. London and New York: Routledge, 1990, 16–39.

——. 'The Death of Hamnet and the Making of Hamlet'. *New York Review of Books* 51 (2001).

——. *Will in the World: How Shakespeare Became Shakespeare*. New York: W.W. Norton & Company, 2004.

——. ed. *The Norton Anthology of English Literature*. 8th ed. New York: W. W. Norton, 2006.

Greenblatt, Stephen and Giles B. Gunn. *Redrawing the Boundaries: The Transformation of English and American Literary Studies*. New York: Modern Language Association of America, 1992.

——. *Redrawing the Boundaries: The Transformation of English and American Literary Studies*. New York: MLA, 1992.

Greene, Robert. *Adaptation of Ariosto's The Historie of Orlando Furiosto*. London, 1592.

——. *Pandosto, or, The Historie of Dorastus and Fawnia*. New Rochelle: Elston Press, 1902.

——. *The Scottish History of James IV*. Edited by J. A. Lavin. London: Benn, 1967.

——. *Menaphon: Camillas Alarum to Slumbering Euphues, Euphues His Censure to Philautus*. New York: Classic Books, 2001.

Greenfeld, Liah. *Nationalism: Five Roads to Modernism*. Cambridge: Harvard University Press, 1993.

Greville, Fulke. *The Tragedy of Mustapha*. Edited by Baron Brooke. London: Nathaniel Butter, 1609.

——— . *Alaham*. 1600. Edited by Baron Brooke. London: E.P., 1613.

Guardati, Tommaso. *Ill Novellino*. 1467. Edited by Salernitano Masuccio. Napoli: Antonio Morano, 1877.

Guarini, Battista. *Compendio della poesia tragicomica, tratto dai duo Verati, per opera dell'Autore del Pastor Fido, con la giunta di molte cose spettanti all'arte*. Venetia, 1603.

Guillory, John. *Cultural Capital: The Problem of Literary Canon Formation*. Chicago: University of Chicago Press, 1993.

Guy-Bray, Stephen. *Homoerotic Space: The Poetics of Loss in Renaissance Literature*. Toronto: University of Toronto Press, 2002.

Haaker, Ann. 'The Plague, the Theater and the Poet'. *Renaissance Drama* 1(1968): 283–306.

Hadfield, Andrew. *Literature, Politics, and National Identity: Reformation to Renaissance*. New York: Cambridge University Press, 1994.

Haec Vir: Or the Womanish Man. London, 1620.

Hakluyt, Richard. *Principal Navigations: The Principal Navigations, Voyages, Traffiques & Discoveries of the English Nation Made by Sea or Over-Land to the Remote and Farthest Distant Quarters of the Earth at Any Time within the Compasse of These 1600 Yeeres*. Glasgow: J. MacLehose and Sons, 1903–05.

Hall, Edward. Hall's Chronicle; containing the history of England, during the reign of Henry the Fourth, and the succeeding monarchs, to the end of the reign of Henry the Eighth, in which are particularly described the manners and customs of those periods. c. 1540. New York: AMS Press, 1965.

Hall, Kim. *Things of Darkness: Economies of Race and Gender in Early Modern England*. Ithaca, NY: Cornell University Press, 1995.

Halpern, Richard. *The Poetics of Primitive Accumulation: English Renaissance Culture and the Genealogy of Capital*. Ithaca: Cornell University Press, 1991.

——— . *Shakespeare's Perfume: Sodomy and Sublimity in the Sonnets, Wilde, Freud, and Lacan*, Philadelphia: University of Pennsylvania Press, 2002.

Hamilton, A. C., ed. *The Spenser Encyclopedia*. Toronto: University of Toronto Press, 1990.

Hardison, O. *The Enduring Monument: A Study of the Idea of Praise in Renaissance Literary Theory and Practice*. Chapel Hill: University of North Carolina Press, 1962.

Harrier, Richard, ed. *The Canon of Sir Thomas Wyatt's Poetry*. Cambridge, Mass.: Harvard University Press, 1975.

Harrington, John. *Lodovico Ariosto's Orlando Furioso*. London, 1634.

Haselkorn, Anne M. and Betty S. Travitsky, eds. *The Renaissance Englishwoman in Print: Counterbalancing the Canon*. Amherst: University of Massachusetts Press, 1990.

Healy, Thomas. *New Latitudes: Theory and Renaissance English Literature*. London: Hodder & Stoughton, 1992.

Helgerson, Richard. *Forms of Nationhood: The Elizabethan Writing of England*. Chicago: University of Chicago Press, 1994.

Hendricks, Margo and Patricia Parker, eds. *Writing, 'Race' and Writing in the Early Modern Period*. London: Routledge, 1994.

Henry; John Heywood, Nicholas Udall, 'Mr. S. Mr. Of Art', George Gascoigne. *Five Pre-Shakespearean Comedies: Fulgens and Lucrece, The Four P. P., Ralph Roister Doister, Gammer Gurton's Needle, Supposes*. New York: Oxford University Press, 1958.

Henslowe, Phillip. *Henslowe's Diary: Edited with Supplementary Material, Introduction and Notes*. Ed. R. A. Foakes and R. T. Rickert. Cambridge: Cambridge University Press, 1961. 266. Print.

——— . *Henslowe's Diary*. Edited by R. A. Foakes & R. T. Rickert. Cambridge and New York: Cambridge University Press, 2002.

Hentschell, Roze. 'Teaching in Context/Reading on the Margins: Renaissance "Non-Canonical" Literature on the Undergraduate Syllabus'. *Working Papers on the Web* 4 (Sept. 2002): no pagination, http://extra.shu.ac.uk/wpw/renaissance/hentschell.htm

Herbert, George. *The Temple*. Edited by Henry L. Carrigan. Brewster: Paraclete Press, 2001.

Herman, P. (2005), *Destabilizing Milton: 'Paradise Lost' and the Poetics of Incertitude*. New York: Palgrave.

Herman, Peter, ed. *Reading Monarchs Writing: The Poetry of Henry VIII, Mary Stuart, Elizabeth I, and James VI/I*. Tempe: Arizona Center for Medieval and Renaissance Studies, 2002.

Herman, Peter C. *Destabilizing Milton: 'Paradise Lost' and the Poetics of Incertitude*. New York: Palgrave Macmillan, 2005.

Herrnstein-Smith, Barbara. *Contingencies of Value: Alternative Perspectives for Critical Theory*. Cambridge, MA: Harvard University Press, 1988.

—— . *A Woman Killed with Kindness*. Menston: Scolar Press, 1971.

Heywood, John. *The Plays of John Heywood (Tudor Interludes)*. Edited by Richard Axton and Peter Happe. Woodbridge, Suffolk: D. S. Brewer, 1991.

Heywood, Thomas. *If You Know Not Me You Know Nobody*. London, 1604.

—— . *Thomas Heywood's The Four Prentices of London: A Critical Old Spelling Edition*. Edited by *Mary Ann Weber Gasior*. New York: Garland Publishing, 1980.

—— . *The Wise Woman of Hogsdon*. Edited by Sonia Massai. London: Routledge, 2002.

Hic Mulier or, The Man-woman. London, 1620.

Hill, Christopher. *The Intellectual Origins of the English Revolution – Revisited*. Oxford: Clarendon Press; New York: Oxford University Press, 1997.

—— . *Milton and the English Revolution*. London: Faber and Faber, 1977.

History Through Literature: About the Hero's Journey Project. University of California at Berkeley, http://ias.berkeley.edu/orias/hero/about.html accessed 10 Aug 2007.

Hoby, Thomas and Baldassarre Castiglione. *The Courtyer of Count Baldessar Castilio*. London: Wyllyam Seres, 1561.

Hoby, Margaret. *The Private Life of an Elizabethan Lady: The Diary of Lady Mary Hoby, 1599–1605*. Stroud, Gloucestershire: Sutton Publishing, 1998.

Hogdon, Barbara. 'Race-ing Othello; Re-Engendering White-Out'. In *Shakespeare, the Movie: Popularizing the Plays on Film, TV, and Video*, edited by Lynda E. Boose and Richard Burt. London: Routledge, 1997.

Holland, N. *The Dynamics of Literary Response*. New York: Oxford University Press, 1968.

—— . *5 Readers Reading*. New Haven: Yale University Pess, 1975.

Hollander, Robert. *Dante: A Life in Works*. Ann Arbor: University of Michigan, 2001.

Hooker, Richard. *Of the Laws of Ecclesiastical Polity*. Edited by R. W. Church. Oxford: Clarendon Press, 1868.

Horace: His Arte of Poetrie, Pistles, and Satyrs. Translated by Thomas Drant. Ann Arbor, Michigan: Caravan Books, 1999.

Howard, Henry. *Songes and Sonettes*. London: Apud Richardum Tottel, 1557.

Hugo, Victor. *Ruy Blas*. 1838. Edited by Herbert F. Collins. New York: St. Martin's Press, 1966.

—— . *Hernani*. 1830. Edited by Newton Crosland. New York: H. Fertig, 2005.

Hulme, Peter, and William H. Sherman, eds. *"The Tempest" and Its Travels*. Philadelphia: University of Pennsylvania Press, 2000.

Hutson, Lorna. *Thomas Nashe in Context*. Oxford: Clarendon Press, 1989.

Hyman, Wendy. 'Authorial Self-Consciousness in Nashe's *the Vnfortvnate Traveller'*. *Studies in English Literature 1500–1900*, 45.1 (2005): 23–41.

Ingham, Patricia Clare and Michelle R. Warren. eds. *Postcolonial Moves: Medieval through Modern*. London: Palgrave, 2003.

Iyengar, Sujata. *Shades of Difference: Mythologies of Skin Color in Early Modern England*. Philadelphia: University of Pennsylvania Press, 2005.

James VI. *Daemonologie*. 1597. Edinburgh: Robert Walde-graue, 1597.

—— . *Basilikon Doron*. 1599. Edited by Charles Howard McIlwain. Cambridge, MA: Harvard University Press, 1918.

James, Henry. *The Siege of London: The Pension Beaurepas: And the Point of View*. 1883. Whitefish, Montana: Kessinger Publishing, LLC, 2008.

Jameson, A. *Shakespeare's Heroines: Characteristics of Women, Moral, Poetical, Historical*. 1889. New York: AMS Press, 1967.

Jameson, Fredric. *The Political Unconscious: Narrative as a Socially Symbolic Act*. Ithaca: Cornell University Press, 1982.

Januensis, Johannes. *Catholicon*. 1286.

Jardine, Lisa. *Still Harping on Daughters: Women and Drama in the Age of Shakespeare*. Totowa: Barnes & Noble, 1983.

—— . *Still Harping on Daughters: Women and Drama in the Age of Shakespeare*, 2nd ed. New York: Columbia University Press, 1989.

Jocelin, Elizabeth. *The Mothers Legacy to Her Unborn Childe*. 1624. Edited by *Jean LeDrew Metcalfe*. Toronto and Buffalo: University of Toronto Press, 2000.

Johns, Adrian. *The Nature of the Book*. Chicago: University of Chicago Press, 1998.

Johnson, Samuel. *A Dictionary of the English Language*. Edited by John Walker and Robert S Jameson. London: W. Pickering, 1850.

—— . *The Lives of the Poets*. New York: Oxford University Press, 2006.

Johnstone, Nathan. *The Devil and Demonism in Early Modern England*. Cambridge: Cambridge University Press, 2006.

Jones, Ann Rosalind. 'Inside the Outsider: Nashe's *Unfortunate Traveller* and Bakhtin's Polyphonic Novel'. *English Literary History* 50.1 (1983): 61–81.

Jones, Eldred. *Othello's Countrymen: The African in English Renaissance Drama*. London: The University College of Sierra Leone by Oxford University Press, 1965.

Jones, Ernest. 'The Oedipus complex as an explanation of Hamlet's mystery: a study in motive'. *The American Journal of Psychology* 21, no. 1 (1910): 72–113.

—— . *Hamlet and Oedipus*. New York: Norton, 1949.

Jonson, Ben, George Chapman and John Marston. *Eastward Ho!* Edited by R. W. Van Fossen. Manchester: Manchester University Press, 1999.

Jonson, Ben. *Catiline, His Conspiracy*. London: Walter Burre, 1611.

—— . *The Workes of Benjamin Jonson*. London: William Stansby, 1616.

—— . *Timber or Discoveries: Made Upon Men and Matter*. In *The Workes of Benjamin Jonson. The Second Volume*. Vol. 3. London, 1640.

—— . *The Sad Shepherd: or, A Tale of Robin Hood*. Edited by F. G. Waldron and Peter Whalley. London, C. Dilly, 1783.

—— . *The Devil is an Ass*. 1616. New York: H. Holt and Co., 1905.

—— . *The Magnetic Lady; or Humors Reconciled*. Edited by Harvey Whitefield Peck. New York: H. Holt, 1914.

—— . *Every Man Out of His Humour, 1600*. Edited by F. P. Wilson; W. W. Greg. London: Malone Society at Oxford University Press, 1920.

—— . *Epigrams, The Forest, Underwoods*. Edited by Hoyt Hopewell Hudson. New York: Columbia University Press, 1936.

—— . *The Poetaster, or His Arraignment*. 1601. Edited by George A. E. Parfitt. Nottingham, Nottinghamshire: Nottingham Drama Texts, 1979.

——— . *Sejanus His Fall*. 1603. Edited by Philip J. Ayres. New York: St. Martin's Press, 1990.

——— . *Hymenai*. Cambridge, England: Chadwyck-Healey, 1994.

——— . *Masque of Blacknesse*. Cambridge, England: Chadwyck-Healey, 1994.

——— . *The masque of queens celebrated from the house of Fame by the Queene of Great Britaine, with her ladies at White-Hall, Febr. 2, 1609*. Cambridge: Chadwyck-Healey, 1995.

——— . *Four Comedies*. Edited by Helen Ostovich. London and New York: Longman, 1997.

——— . *Irish Masque*. Cambridge, England: Chadwyck-Healey, 1997.

——— . *Volpone*. Edited by Brian Parker and David Bevington. Manchester: Manchester University Press, 1999.

——— . 'To Penshurst'. 1616. *The Works of Ben Jonson Volume 3*. NY: Adamant Media Corporation, 2007.

——— . *The Alchemist, and other plays: Volpone, or The Fox; Epicene, or The Silent Woman; The Alchemist; Bartholomew Fair*. Edited by Gordon Campbell. Oxford: Oxford University Press, 2008.

——— . 'To My Book-seller' (*Literature Online* http://gateway.proquest.com/openurl?ctx_ver=Z39.88-2003&xri:pqil:res_ver=0.2&res_id=xri:lion&rft_id=xri:lion:ft:po:Z300405976:3)

Jordan, C., C. Carroll and D. Damrosch. *The Longman Anthology of British Literature, Third Edition, Volume 1B*. New York: Longman. 2006.

Joseph, M. *Shakespeare's Use of the Arts of Language*. New York: Columbia University Press, 1947.

Kahn, V. *Machiavellian Rhetoric: From the Counter-Reformation to Milton*. Princeton: Princeton University Press, 1994.

Kant, Immanuel. *Critique of Judgment*. 1790. Translated by James Creed Meredith. New York: Oxford University Press, 1978.

Kelly-Gadol, Joan. 'Did Women Have a Renaissance?' In *Becoming Visible: Women in European History*, edited by Renate Bridenthal and Claudia Koonz, 137–64. Boston: Houghton Mifflin, 1977.

Kelsey, Lin. 'Spenser, Ralegh, and the Language of Allegory'. *Spenser Studies: A Renaissance Poetry Annual*. 42 (2003): 183–213.

Kermode, Frank. *John Donne*. London: Longmans, Green & Co, 1957.

——— . *Pleasure and Change: The Aesthetics of Canon*. Oxford: Oxford University Press, 2004.

Kernan, Alvin. *The Death of Literature*. New Haven: Yale University Press, 1992.

Kerrigan, William. *The Prophetic Milton*. Charlottesville: University Press of Virginia, 1974.

Kinney, Arthur. *Rogues, Vagabonds, and Sturdy Beggars*. Amherst: University of Massachusetts Press, 1990.

Kinsey, Alfred, C. Wardell, P. Pompey and Clyde Martin. *Sexual Behaviour in the Human Malc*. 1948. Bloomington, IN: Indiana University Press, 1998.

Kittredge, G. *The Complete Works of Shakespeare*. New York: Grolier, 1958.

Knight, G. Wilson. *The Wheel of Fire: Essays in Interpretation of Shakespeare's Sombre Tragedies*. London: Oxford University Press, 1930.

——— . *The Imperial Theme: Further Interpretations of Shakespeare's Tragedies Including the Roman Plays*. London: Oxford University Press, 1931.

Knight, Stephen and Thomas Ohlgren, eds. *Robin Hood and Other Outlaw Tales*. Kalamazoo, Michigan: Published for TEAMS by Medieval Institute Publications, Western Michigan University, 2000.

Knights, L. 'How Many Children Had Lady Macbeth? An essay in the Theory and

Practice of Shakespeare criticism'. *Explorations: Essays in Criticism Mainly on the Literature of the Seventeenth Century*. London: Chatto, 1946. 1–39.

Knox, John. *The First Blast of the Trumpet against the Monstrous Regiment of Women*. Geneva, 1558.

Kranidas, T. *The Fierce Equation: A Study of Milton's Decorum*. The Hague: Mouton, 1965.

—— . *Milton and the Rhetoric of Zeal*. Pittsburgh: Duquesne University Press, 2005.

Krontiris, Tina. *Oppositional Voices: Women as Writers and Translators of Literature in the English Renaissance*. London: Routledge, 1992.

Kumar, Krishan. *The Making of English National Identity*. Cambridge: Cambridge University Press, 2003.

Kyd, Thomas. *The Spanish Tragedy*. London: Methuen Drama, 2007.

Langland, William. *Piers Plowman by William Langland: A New Annotated Edition of the C-Text (UEP Exeter Medieval Texts and Studies)*. Edited by Derek Pearsall. Exeter: University of Exeter Press, 2008.

Lanham, Richard. *The Motives of Eloquence: Literary Rhetoric in the Renaissance*. Chicago: University of Chicago Press, 1976.

Lanyer, Aemilia. *The Poems of Aemilia Lanyer: Salve Deus Rex Judaeorum (Women Writers in English 1350–1850)*. New York: Oxford University Press, 1993.

Leavis, F. R. *Revaluation: Tradition and Development in English Poetry*. New York: Norton, 1963.

Lee, Maurice, Jr. *Great Britain's Solomon: James VI and I in His Three Kingdoms*. Urbana-Champaign: University of Illinois Press, 1990.

Leftow, Brian and Brian Davies, eds. *Aquinas: Summa Theologiae*. Cambridge: Cambridge University Press, 2006.

Leigh, Dorothy. *The Mothers Blessing or the godly Counsell of a Gentle-Woman, Not Long Since Deceased, Left Behind for Her Children*. London, 1616.

Lenz, C., G. Greene and C. Neely, eds. *The Woman's Part: Feminist Criticism of Shakespeare*. Urbana-Champaign: University of Illinois Press, 1980.

Lester, G. A., ed. *Three Late Medieval Morality Plays: Mankind, Everyman, Mundus et Infans*. London: Methuen Drama, 2007.

Lewalski, Barbara K. *Writing Women in Jacobean England*, Cambridge, MA: Harvard University Press, 1993

—— . 'Old Renaissance Canons, New Women's Texts: Some Jacobean Examples'. *Proceedings of the American Philosophical Society*. 138, no. 3 (1994): 397–406.

Lewis, C. S. *English Literature in the Sixteenth Century Excluding Drama*, Oxford: Clarendon Press, 1954.

—— . 'Hamlet: The Prince or the Poem?' 1942. In *Studies in Shakespeare: British Academy Lectures*, edited by Peter Alexander, 201–18. Oxford: Oxford University Press, 1963.

—— . *The Allegory of Love: A Study in Medieval Tradition*. Oxford: Oxford University; Lewistown, NY: The Edwin Mellen Press, 1975.

Link, Eric Carl. 'Canon Formation and Marginality.' *Essays in Arts and Sciences* XXVIII (October 1999): 17–33.

Loades, D. M. *Politics and Nation: England, 1450–1660*. Oxford and Malden: Blackwell Publishers, 1999.

Lodge, Thomas. *Scillae's Metamorphosis*. London, 1589.

—— . *Phillis*. London, 1593.

—— . *A Fig for Momus*. London, 1595.

—— . *Rosalynde*. Edited by Brian Nellist. New York: Columbia University Press, 1998.

Loomba, Ania. *Gender, Race, Renaissance Drama*. Manchester: Manchester University Press, 1989.

——— . 'Shakespeare and Cultural Difference'. In *Alternative Shakespeares, Vol. 2*, edited by Terrence Hawkes, 164–91. London and New York: Routledge, 1996.

——— . *Colonialism and Postcolonialism*. London, New York: Routledge, 1998.

——— . *Shakespeare, Race, and Colonialism*, Oxford: Oxford University Press, 2002.

Lydgate, John. *Fall of Princes*. 4 vols. Edited by H. Bergen. Washington: Carnegie Institute, 1923.

Lyly, John. *The Complete Works of John Lyly: Euphues and His England; The Plays V2*. Whitefish, Montana: Kessinger Publishing, LLC, 2007.

Lyne, Raphael. *Ovid's Changing Worlds: English Metamorphoses 1567–1632*. Oxford: Oxford University Press, 2001.

MacCallum, M. Shakespeare. *Roman Plays and Their Background*. London: Macmillan, 1910.

Maley, Willy. *Salvaging Spenser: Colonialism, Culture and Identity*. New York: St. Martin's, 1997.

——— . *Nation, State, and Empire in English Renaissance Literature: Shakespeare to Milton*, London: Palgrave, 2003.

——— . *Nation, State and Empire in English Renaissance Literature: Shakespeare to Milton*. New York and Basingstoke: Palgrave/St. Martin's Press, 2003.

Malory, Thomas. *Le Morte D'Arthur: The Winchester Manuscript*. Edited by Helen Cooper. New York: Oxford University Press, 2008.

Mangan, Michael. *A Preface to Shakespeare's Comedies*. London: Longman, 1996.

Mannoni, O. *Psychologie de la colonisation*. Paris: Seuil, 1950.

Marchitell, Howard. 'Desire and domination in *Volpone*'. *Studies in English Literature* 31, no. 2 (1991): 287–308.

Marcus, L. *The Politics of Mirth: Jonson, Herrick, Milton, Marvell, and the Defense of Old Holiday Pastimes*. Chicago and London: University of Chicago Press, 1989.

——— . *Puzzling Shakespeare: Local Reading and Its Discontents*. Berkeley: University of California Press, 1990.

Marcus, Leah S., Janel Mueller and Mary Beth Rose, eds. *Elizabeth I: The Collected Works*. Chicago: University of Chicago Press, 2000.

Marlowe, Christopher. *Doctor Faustus: A- and B-texts (1604, 1616)*. Ed. David Bevington and Eric Rasmussen. Manchester: Manchester University Press, 1993.

——— . *Dr Faustus: Based on the A Text*. Ed. Roma Gill. 2nd ed., reprinted. Manchester: Manchester University Press, 2002.

——— . *Christopher Marlowe: The Complete Plays*. Edited by Frank Romany and Robert Lindsey. NY: Penguin, 2003.

——— . *The Complete Poems and Translations*. Ed. Stephen Orgel. New York: Penguin, 2007.

Marotti, A. F. *Manuscript, Print, and the English Renaissance Lyric*. Ithaca: Cornell University Press, 1995.

Marston, John. *The Scourge of Villanie, 1599*. Edinburgh: Edinburgh University Press, 1966.

——— . *The Malcontent and Other Plays*. Edited by Keith Sturgass. Oxford: Oxford University Press, 1997.

Martin, Randall, ed. *Women Writers in Renaissance England*. New York: Longman, 1997.

Marvell, Andrew. 'Upon Appleton House'. In *The Complete Poems*, edited by Elizabeth Story, 75–99. Donno: Penguin, 2005.

Massinger, Philip. *The Virgin Martyr*. London: James Burns, 1845.

——— . *The Renegado: Three Turk Plays from Early Modern England*. Edited by Daniel Vitkus. New York: Columbia University Press, 2000, 241–339.

——. *The Plays of Philip Massinger*. Edited by William Gifford. Whitefish, Montana: Kessinger Publishing, LLC, 2007.

Matar, Nabil. *Islam in Britain 1558–1685*. Cambridge: Cambridge University Press, 1998.

——. *Turks, Moors, and Englishmen in the Age of Discovery*. New York: Columbia University Press, 1999.

Maus, Katherine Eisaman. *Inwardness and Theater in the English Renaissance*. Chicago: University of Chicago Press, 1995.

McCabe, Richard. *Spenser's Monstrous Regiment: Elizabethan Ireland and the Poetics of Difference*. Oxford: Oxford University Press, 2002.

McClure, Norman Egbert, ed. *The Letters of John Chamberlain*. 2 vols. Philadelphia: The American Philosophical Society, 1939.

McEachern, Claire. *The Poetics of English Nationhood 1590–1612*. Cambridge: Cambridge University Press, 1996.

McGrath, L. *Subjectivity and Women's Poetry in Early Modern England: 'Why on the ridge should she desire to go?'* Aldershot, UK and Burlington, VT: Ashgate, 2002.

McLuskie, Kathleen. 'The Patriarchal Bard: Feminist Criticism and Shakespeare'. *Political Shakespeare*. Ed. Jonathan Dollimore and Alan Sinfield. Manchester University Press, 1985. 88–108.

——. *Renaissance Dramatists (Feminist Readings)*. Atlantic Heights, NJ: Humanities Press, 1989.

McLuskie, K. and D. Bevington, eds. *Plays on Women*. Manchester: Manchester University Press, 1999.

Medwall, Henry. *Fulgens and Lucrece: A Fifteenth-Century Secular Play*. Edited by F. S. Boas and A. W. Reed. Oxford: Oxford University Press, 1926.

Mendelson, Sara. *The Mental World of Stuart Women: Three Studies*, Manchester: Harvester Press, 1987.

Mendle, Michael. 'De Facto Freedom, De Facto Authority: Press and Parliament, 1640–1643'. *The Historical Journal* 38 (1995): 307–32.

Meres, Francis. *Palladis Tamia*. 1598. London, Methuen Drama, 2007.

Middleton, Thomas. *The Collected Works*. Edited by Gary Taylor and John Lavagnino. New York: Oxford University Press, 2008.

Mildmay, Grace, Lady. *The Diary of Lady Mildmay* [electronic resource]: reproduced from the original manuscript held at Northampton Central Library. Wakefield: Microform Academic Publishers, 2005.

Miller, Naomi J. Changing the Subject. *Mary Wroth and Figurations of Gender in Early Modern England*. Lexington: University Press of Kentucky, 1996.

Millett, Kate. *Sexual Politics*. Urbana-Champaign: University of Illinois Press, 2000.

Mills, James, ed. *Account Roll of the Priory of the Holy Trinity, Dublin 1337–1346 with the Middle English Moral Play 'The Pride of Life'*. Dublin: The Royal Society of Antiquaries of Ireland, 1891.

Milner, A. *John Milton and the English Revolution: A Study in the Sociology of Literature*. Totowa, NJ: Barnes and Noble, 1981.

Milton, John. *Paradise Lost*. Edited by Alastair Fowler. London: Longman, 1968.

——. *The Major Works*. Edited by Stephen Orgel and Jonathan Goldberg. New York: Oxford University Press, 2008.

Montemayor, Jorge de. *Diana*. 1560. Translated by B. Yong. Edited by J. Kennedy. Oxford: Oxford University Press, 1968.

Montrose, Louis. *The Purpose of Playing: Shakespeare and the Cultural Politics of the Elizabethan Theater*. Chicago: University of Chicago Press, 1997.

More, Thomas. *Utopia*. (Norton Critical Editions). Translated by Robert M. Adams. 2nd ed. New York: W. W. Norton, 1991.

Murphy, Arthur, ed. *The Works of Samuel Johnson, LL.D.* Published by Alexander Blake, 1840.

Nanda, M. *Prophets Facing Backward: Postmodern Critiques of Science and Hindu Nationalism in India.* New Brunswick, NJ: Rutgers University Pess, 2003.

Nashe, Thomas. *The Unfortunate Traveler; or, The Life of Jack Wilton.* New York: Greenberg, 1926.

——. *Pierce Penniless, his supplication to the devil . . . and selected writings.* Edited by Stanley W Wells. London: E. Arnold, 1964.

——. *The Unfortunate Traveller and Other Works.* Ed. J. B. Steane. Harmondsworth: Penguin, 1972.

——. *The Works of Thomas Nashe* (1908). Edited by Ronald B. McKerrow. Whitefish, Montana: Kessinger LLC, 2008.

Neely, C. 'Constructing the Subject: Feminist Practice and the New Renaissance Discourses'. *English Literary Renaissance* 18 (1988): 5–18.

Nevitt, Marcus. *Women and the Pamphlet Culture of Revolutionary England, 1640–1660.* Aldershot, UK: Ashgate, 2006.

Newton, Thomas and Caelius Agostino Curio. *A Notable History of the Saracens.* London: Veale, 1575.

Nicholl, Charles. 'Nashe, Thomas (bap. 1567, d. c.1601)'. *Oxford Dictionary of Biography.* London: Oxford University Press, 2004.

Nicholls, Andrew. *The Jacobean Union: A Reconsideration of British Civil Policies Under the Early Stuarts.* Westport, CT.: Greenwood Press, 1999.

Norbrook, David and H. R. Woudhuysen, eds. *The Penguin Book of Renaissance Verse.* New York: Penguin, 1993.

Norton, Thomas and Thomas Sackville. *Gorboduc, or Ferrex and Porrex.* Whitefish, Montana : Kessinger Publishing, LLC, 2009.

O'Connor, E. 'Preface for a Post-Postcolonial Criticism'. In *Theory's Empire: An Anthology of Dissent*, edited by D. Patai and W. Corral, 297–312. New York: Columbia University Press, 2005.

Orgel, Stephen. 'Prospero's Wife'. In *Rewriting the Renaissance: The Discourse of Sexual Difference in Early Modern Europe*, edited by M. Ferguson, M. Quilligan and N. Vickers, 50–64. Chicago: University of Chicago Press, 1986.

Ostovich, Helen, Mary V. Silcox and Graham Roebuck, eds. *Other Voices, Other Views: Expanding the Canon in English Renaissance Studies.* Newark: University of Delaware Press, 1999.

Parker, Kenneth, ed. *Early Modern Tales of Orient: A Critical Anthology.* New York: Routledge, 1999.

Parker, Patricia, and David Quint, eds. *Literary Theory / Renaissance Text.* Baltimore: Johns Hopkins University Press, 1986.

Parr, Anthony, ed. *Three Renaissance Travel Plays.* New York: Manchester University Press, 1995.

Paster, Gail Kern. *Humoring the Body: Emotions and the Shakespearean Stage.* Chicago: University of Chicago Press, 2004

Patterson, Annabel. 'Historical Scholarship'. In *Introduction to Scholarship in Modern Languages and Literatures*, edited by J. Gibaldi, 183–201. New York: MLA, 1992.

——. *Reading Holinshed's Chronicles.* Chicago and London: University of Chicago Press, 1994.

Patterson, Lee. 'On the Margin: Postmodernism, Ironic History, and Medieval Studies'. *Speculum* 65 (1990): 1.

——. *Chaucer and the Subject of History.* London: Routledge, 1991.

Peele, George and Anello Paulilli. *The Araygnement of Paris.* London: Henrie Marsh Anno, 1584.

Pepys, Samuel. *The Diary (1661)*. Edited by Robert Latham and William Matthews. Bell & Hyman: London, 1973.

Peterson, R. *Imitation and Praise in the Poetry of Ben Jonson*. New Haven: Yale University Press, 1982.

Plautus. *Plautus: Amphitruo (Cambridge Greek and Latin Classics)*. Edited by David M. Christenson. New York: Cambridge University Press, 2000.

Poole, Kristen. ' "The Fittest Closet for All Goodness": Authorial Strategies of Jacobean Mothers' Manuals'. *SEL* 35, no. 1 (1995): 69–88.

Pooley, Roger. *English Prose of the Seventeenth Century 1590–1700*. Harlow: Longman, 1992.

Powell, J. Enoch. *Reflections of a Statesman: The Writings and Speeches of Enoch Powell*. London: Bellew Publishers, 1991.

Powell, R. *Shakespeare and the Critics' Debate*. New York: Rowman and Littlefield, 1980.

Pratt, Mary Louise. *Imperial Eyes: Studies in Travel Writing and Transculturation*. London & New York: Routledge, 1992.

Preston, Thomas. *A Critical Edition of Thomas Preston's Cambises*. Edited by Robert Carl Johnson. Lewistown, NY: The Edwin Mellen Press, 1975.

Prynne, William. *Histriomastix*. London, 1633.

Puttenham, George. *The Art of English Poesy*. Edited by Frank Whigham and Wayne A. Rebhorn. Ithaca, NY: Cornell University Press, 2007.

Raffel, Burton, trans. *Sir Gawain and the Green Knight*. New York: Signet Classics, 2001.

Ralegh, Walter. *The Epistle to Martin Mar-Sixtus*. London, 1591.

Ralegh, Walter. *The Discovery of Guiana and the Journal of the Second Voyage Thereto*. Whitefish, Montana: Kessinger Publishing, LLC, 2007.

Rathmell, J. C. A., ed. *The Psalms of Sir Philip Sidney and the Countess of Pembroke*. New York: New York University Press, 1963.

Rawlings, Charles. *An Ancient Love Song: Lusty Juventis*. London: J. Williams, 1899.

Rees, Christine. *Utopian Imagination and Eighteenth-Century Fiction*. London: Longman, 1995.

Resch, R. *Althusser and the Renewal of Marxist Social Theory*. Berkeley: University of California Press, 1992.

Rhodes, Neil. *Elizabethan Grotesque*. London: Routledge & Kegan Paul, 1980.

Richards, I. A. *Practical Criticism*. Kegan Paul, Trench, Trubner: London, 1929.

Ringrose, Chris. 'Productivity: Literary Value and Curriculum'. Working Papers on the Web, 2 (Nov. 2001): no pagination, http://extra.shu.ac.uk/wpw/value/ringrose.htm

Roper, William and Anne Manning. *The Household of Sir Thomas More with Roper's Life of Thomas More*. London: J. M. Dent and Sons, 1911.

Rorty, R. *The Consequences of Pragmatism*. Minneapolis: University of Minnesota Press, 1982.

Ross, Trevor. *The Making of the English Literary Canon*. Montreal: McGill-Queens University Press, 1998.

Rowland, S. *Jung: A Feminist Revision*. Cambridge: Polity Press, 2001.

Rowley, Samuel. *When You See Me, You Know Me*. 1605. Whitefish, Montana: Kessinger Publishing, LLC, 2007.

Rowley, William and Thomas Middleton. *A Fair Quarrel*. Edited by Roger Victor Holdsworth. London: Ernest Benn Ltd, 1976.

—— . *The Changeling* (New Mermaids). 3rd ed. Edited by Michael Neill. London: Methuen, 2007.

Said, Edward. *Orientalism*. New York: Vintage, 1978.

Sawday, J. *The Body Emblazoned: Dissection and the Human Body in Renaissance Culture*. New York: Routledge, 1995.

Sawyer, E., ed. *Memorials of Affairs of State in the Reigns of Queen Elizabeth and King James I, 3 vols.* London, 1725.

Schneider, Alison. 'Stanford Revisits the Course that Set Off the Culture Wars'. *Chronicle of Higher Education*, 9 May 1997. http://www.stanford.edu/group/areaone/reference/Chronicle_article.html

Schoenbaum, S. *Shakespeare's Lives.* Oxford: Oxford University Press, 1991.

Schoenfeldt, Michael C. *Prayer and Power: George Herbert and Renaissance Courtship.* Chicago: University of Chicago Press, 1991.

—— . *Bodies and Selves in Early Modern England: Physiology and Inwardness in Spenser, Shakespeare, Herbert, and Milton.* Cambridge: Cambridge University Press, 1999.

Schwarz, K. 'Breaking the Mirror Stage'. *Historicism, Psychoanalysis, and Early Modern Culture.* Edited by C. Mazzio and D. Trevor. New York and London: Routledge, 2000. 272–98.

Schwyzer, Philip and Simon Mealor, eds. *Archipelagic Identities.* Aldershot: Ashgate Press, 2004.

Schwyzer, Philip. *Literature, Nationalism, and Memory in Early Modern England and Wales.* Cambridge: Cambridge University Press, 2004.

Sedgwick, Eve Kosofsky. *Between Men: English Literature and Male Homosocial Desire.* New York: Columbia University Press, 1985.

Seelig, Sharon Cadman. *Autobiography and Gender in Early Modern Literature: Reading Women's Lives, 1600–1680.* Cambridge: Cambridge University Press, 2006.

Shadwell, Thomas. *Bury-Fair: A Critical Edition.* Edited by John C. Ross. New York: Garland Publishing, 1995.

Shakespeare, William and John Fletcher. 'Cardenio'. *The Norton Shakespeare: Based on the Oxford Edition (Second Edition).* New York: W. W. Norton, 2008.

—— . *The Two Noble Kinsmen: The Norton Shakespeare: Based on the Oxford Edition (Second Edition).* New York: W. W. Norton, 2008.

Shakespeare, William. *First Folio (1623): Norton Facsimile.* Edited by Chartlon Hinman. New York: W. W. Norton, 1996.

—— . *Love's Labours Lost.* Edited by H. R. Woudhuysen. Walton on Thames: Thomas Nelson, 1998.

—— . *King Lear: A Parallel Text Edition.* Ed. René Weis. Harlow: Longman, 1998.

—— . *The History of King Lear.* Ed. Stanley Wells. Oxford: Oxford University Press, 2000. 167–98.

—— . *King Lear.* Ed. R. A. Foakes. London: Arden Shakespeare, 2005.

—— . *Hamlet, and Hamlet: The Texts of 1603 and 1623.* Edited by Ann Thompson and Neil Taylor. London: The Arden Shakespeare, 2006.

—— . *The Norton Shakespeare: Based on the Oxford Edition (Second Edition).* Edited by Stephen Greenblatt, Walter Cohen, Jean E. Howard and Katharine Eisaman Maus. New York: W. W. Norton, 2008.

Shapiro, James. *Shakespeare and the Jews.* New York: Columbia University Press, 1996.

Shawcross, John. *John Milton: The Self and the World.* Lexington: University Press of Kentucky, 1993.

Shelley, Percy Bysshe. *The Cenci.* Edited by Cajsa C. Baldini. Kansas City, Missouri: Valancourt Books, 2008.

Shepard, Alan C. *Marlowe's Soldiers: Rhetorics of Masculinity in the Age of the Armada.* Aldershot: Ashgate Publishing, 2002.

Shepard, Alan and Stephen D. Powell, eds. *Fantasies of Troy: Classical Tales and the Social Imaginary in Medieval and Early Modern Europe.* Toronto: Center for Renaissance and Reformation Studies, 2004.

Shirley, James. 'Cupid and Death'. In *The Dramatic Works and Poems of James Shirley,*

Now First Collected: Volume 1. Charleston, South Carolina: BookSurge Publishing 2005.

Shrank, Cathy. *Writing the Nation in Reformation England, 1530–1580*, Oxford: Oxford University Press, 2006.

Sidney, Mary. *The Tragedie of Antoine*. Denver: Aardvark Press, 2000.

Sidney, Philip. *Astrophel and Stella*. Whitefish, Montana: Kessinger Publishing, LLC, 2007.

—— . 'Arcadia'. In *Sir Philip Sidney: The Major Works*, edited by Katherine Duncan-Jones. New York: Oxford University Press, 2009.

—— . 'Defence of Posey'. In *Sir Philip Sidney: The Major Works*, edited by Katherine Duncan-Jones. New York: Oxford University Press, 2009.

—— . 'The Countess of Pembroke's Arcadia'. In *Sir Philip Sidney: The Major Works*, edited by Katherine Duncan-Jones. New York: Oxford University Press, 2009.

Siegel, L. 'Queer Theory, Literature, and the Sexualization of Everything: The Gay science'. In *Theory's Empire: An Anthology of Dissent*, edited by D. Patai and W. Corral, 424–41. New York: Columbia University Press, 2005.

Simpson, James. *Burning to Read: English Fundamentalism and its Reformation Opponents*. Cambridge, MA and London: Harvard University Press, 2007.

Sinfield, Alan. *Cultural Politics: Queer Reading*. London: Routledge, 1994.

—— . *On Sexuality and Power*. New York: Columbia University Press, 2005.

—— . *Shakespeare, Authority, Sexuality: Unfinished Business in Cultural Materialism*. London: Routledge, 2006.

Skelton, John. *Magnificence*. 1519. Edited by Paula Neuss. Manchester, England: Manchester University Press; Baltimore, Maryland: Johns Hopkins University Press, 1980.

Skelton, John. 'Speak, Parrot'. *John Skelton: Selected Poems*. London: Routledge, 2003, 91–107.

Sloan, Thomas O. *Donne, Milton, and the End of Humanist Rhetoric*. Berkeley: University of California Press, 1985.

Smith, Barbara and Ursula Appelt, eds. *Write or Be Written: Early Modern Women Poets and Cultural Constraints*. Aldershot, UK: Ashgate, 2001.

Smith, Barbara Herrnstein. *Contingencies of Value: Alternative Perspectives for Critical Theory*. Cambridge, MA: Harvard University Press, 1988.

Smith, Bruce R. *Homosexual Desire in Shakespeare's England: A Cultural Poetics*. Chicago: Chicago University Press, 1991.

—— . *Homosexual Desire in Shakespeare's England: A Cultural Poetics*. Chicago, London: University Of Chicago Press, 1995.

Smuts, R. Malcolm, ed. 'The Whole Royal and Magnificent Entertainment of King James through the City of London, 15 March 1604, with the Arches of Triumph'. *Thomas Middleton: The Collected Works*. Ed. Gary Taylor and John Lavignino. Oxford: Clarendon Press, 2001. 219–279.

Snook, Edith. *Women, Reading and the Cultural Politics of Early Modern England*. Aldershot, UK: Ashgate, 2005.

Sondergard, Sidney, L. *Sharpening Her Pen: Strategies of Rhetorical Violence by Early Modern English Women Writers*. Selinsgrove: Susquehanna University Presses, 2002.

Speght, Rachel. *A Muzzle for Melastomus*. London, 1617.

Spenser, Edmund. *Colin Clout's Come Home Againe*. Edited by Thomas Creede; William Ponsonby; English Printing Collection (Library of Congress). London: William Ponsonbie, 1595.

—— . *The Shepheardes Calender*. 1579. Edited by H. Oskar Sommer. London: J.C. Nimmo, 1890.

——. ' "Epistle" to *The Shepheardes Calender'*. Edited by William A. Oram, et al. *The Yale Edition of the Shorter Poems of Edmund Spenser*. New Haven and London: Yale University Press, 1989.

——. *The Faerie Queene*. Edited by Thomas P. Roche. London: Penguin, 1997.

——. *The Faerie Queene*. Ed. A. C. Hamilton. Harlow: Longman, 2007.

——. *Amoretti*. 1595. Edited by Teresa Pape. Maidstone: Crescent Moon, 2008.

Spivak, Gayatri. 'Can the subaltern speak?' In *Marxism and the Interpretation of Culture*, edited by Cary Nelson and Lawrence Grossberg, 271–313. Urbana-Champaign: University of Illinois Press, 1988.

Spufford, Margaret. *Small Books and Pleasant Histories: Popular Fiction and Its Readership in Seventeenth-Century England*. Cambridge: Cambridge University Press, 1985.

Spurgeon, C. *Shakespeare's Imagery and What It Tells Us*. Cambridge: Cambridge University Press, 1935.

Stallybrass, P. and A. White. *The Politics and Poetics of Transgression*. Ithaca and London: Cornell University Press, 1986.

Sternhold, Thomas, and John Hopkins. *Complete English Psalter*. London: Daye, 1562.

Stevenson, Jane and Peter Davidson, eds. *Early Modern Women Poets*. Oxford: Oxford University Press, 2001.

Stoller, Robert J. *Sex and Gender: On the Development of Masculinity and Feminity*. London: Hogarth and the Institute of Psycho-Analysis, 1968.

Stone, L. *The Family, Sex and Marriage in England, 1500–1800*. New York: Harper & Row, 1979.

Straznicky, Marta. *Privacy, Playreading, and Women's Closet Drama, 1550–1700*. Cambridge: Cambridge University Press, 2004.

Strier, Richard. *Resistant Structures: Particularity, Radicalism, and Renaissance Texts*. Berkeley: University of California Press, 1997.

Stringer, Gary, ed. *The Variorum Edition of the Poetry of John Donne, Vol. 7, Part I, The Holy Sonnets*. Bloomington: Indiana University Press, 2005.

Stubbes, Philip. *The Anatomie of Abuses*. London, 1583.

Summers, Claude and Ted-Larry Pebworth, eds. *Renaissance Discourses of Desire*. Columbia: University of Missouri Press, 1993.

Summers, Claude, ed. *Homosexuality in Renaissance and Enlightenment England: Literary Representations in Historical Context*. London: Routledge, 1992.

Surrey. *Tottel's Miscellany (1557–1587)*. Cambridge, MA: Harvard University Press, 1929.

Swetnam, Joseph. *The Arraignment of Lewd, Idle, Froward and Unconstant Women*. 1615. Edited by Ester Sowernam. London: J. Smeeton, 1807.

Swift, Jonathan. *A Tale of a Tub and Other Works*. 1704. Edited by *Angus Ross & David Woolley*. Oxford and New York: Oxford University Press, 1999.

Szonyi, György E. 'Cross-Dressing the Tongue: Petrarchist Discourse and Female Voice in Queen Elizabeth's "Sonetto" '. *Hungarian Journal of English and American Studies* 11, no. 1 (2005): 77–91.

Tamar Cham. London, 1602.

Tasso, Torquato. *The Gerusalemme liberata of Tasso*. 1574. Edited by Agostino Isola. Cambridge: F. Archdeacon and F. & F. Merrill, 1786.

Taylor, Gary and John Lavagnino, eds. *Thomas Middleton: The Collected Works*. Oxford: Clarendon, 2007.

Taylor, M. *Shakespeare Criticism in the Twentieth Century*. Oxford: Oxford University Press, 2001.

Taylor, Neil. 'National and racial stereotypes in Shakespeare films'. In *The Cambridge Companion to Shakespeare on Film: Second Edition*, edited by Russell Jackson. New York: Cambridge University Press, 2007.

Taylor, John. 1618. *The Pennilesse Pilgrimage*. London, 1630.

Tennenhouse, L. *Power on Display: The Politics of Shakespeare's Genres*. New York: Methuen, 1986.

Teskey, Gordon, 'Allegory'. *The Spenser Encyclopedia*. Toronto: University of Toronto Press, 1990. 16–22.

Theocritus. *Theocritus: A Selection: Idylls 1, 3, 4, 6, 7, 10, 11 and 13*. Cambridge: Cambridge University Press, 2008.

The Works of Thomas Nashe. Ed. R. B. McKerrow, rev. F. P. Wilson, 5 vols. Oxford: Blackwell, 1958.

'The Wise Man of Westchester'. *The Diary of Philip Henslowe, from 1591 to 1609*. Boston: Adamant Media Corporation, 2002.

Thompson, Ann. 'Are there any women in *King Lear*?', in *The Matter of Difference: Materialist Feminist Criticism of Shakespeare*. Ed. Valerie Wayne. Hemel Hempstead: Harvester Wheatsheaf, 1991. 117–28.

Tillyard, E. M. W. *The Elizabethan World Picture*. New York: Vintage, 1943.

—— . *Shakespeare's History Plays*. London: Chatto, 1944.

Tokson, Elliot.H. *The Popular Image of the Black Man in English Drama, 1550–1688*. Columbia: Columbia University Press, 1970.

Tourneur, Cyril. *The Plays of Cyril Tourneur: The Revenger's Tragedy, the Atheists' Tragedy*. Edited by George Parfitt. Cambridge: Cambridge University Press, 1978.

Traub, Valerie. *The Renaissance of Lesbianism in Early Modern England*. New York: Cambridge University Press, 2002.

Traversi, Derek. An Approach to Shakespeare (1938). Garden City, New York: Anchor Books, 1969.

Travitsky, Betty, Anne Lake Prescott and Patrick Cullen, eds. *The Early Modern Englishwoman: A Facsimile Library of Essential Works*. Multiple Series. Aldershot: Ashgate Press and London: Scolar Press, 2000–2007.

Trill, Suzanne. 'Sixteenth-century women's writing: Mary Sidney's *Psalmes* and the femininity of translation'. *Writing and the English Renaissance*. Ed. William Zunder and Suzanne Trill. London: Longman, 1996. 140–58.

Trill, Suzanne, Kate Chedgzoy, and Melanie Osborne, eds. *Lay By Your Needles, Ladies, Take the Pen*. Oxford: Hodder Arnold, 1998.

Tuve, Rosemond. *Elizabethan and Metaphysical Imagery; Renaissance Poetic and Twentieth-Century Critics*. Chicago: University of Chicago Press, 1947.

—— . *Allegorical Imagery: Some Medieval Books and Their Posterity*. Princeton: Princeton University Press, 1966.

Tyndale, William. *The Obedience of a Christian Man*. 1529. Edited by David Daniell. London; New York: Penguin, 2000.

Udall, Nicholas. *Ralph Roister Doister, the First Regular English Comedy*. 1552. London: Dent, 1928.

—— . *Respublica*. 1533. Edited by W. W. Greg. Cambridge, England: Chadwyck-Healey, 1994.

van Nuis, H. 'Animated Eve Confronting Her Animus: A Jungian Approach to the Division of Labor Debate in Paradise Lost'. *Milton Quarterly* 34, no. 2 (2000): 48–56.

Vaughan, Alden T. and Virginia Mason Vaughan. *Shakespeare's Caliban: A Cultural History*. Cambridge: Cambridge University Press, 1993.

Vaughan, Virginia Mason. *Performing Blackness on English Stages, 1500–1800*. Cambridge: Cambridge University Press, 2005.

Veeser, Aram H, ed. *The New Historicism*. London: Routledge, 1989.

Veeser, Harold Aram. *The New Historicism*. New York: Routledge, 1989.

Vergil. *The Eclogues of Virgil*. Edited by Sir George Osborne Morgan. London: Henry Frowde, University of Oxford, 1897.

Vitkus, Daniel, ed. *Three Turk Plays from Early Modern England.* New York: Columbia University Press, 2000.

Vitkus, Daniel and Nabil Matar, eds. *Piracy, Slavery, and Redemption: Barbary Captivity Narratives from Early Modern England.* New York: Columbia University Press, 2001.

Wall, A. D., ed. *Two Elizabethan Women: Correspondence of Joan and Maria Thynne, 1575–1611.* Wiltshire: Wiltshire Record Society, vol. 38, 1983.

Wall, Wendy. *Staging Domesticity: Household Work and English Identity in Early Modern Drama.* Cambridge: Cambridge University Press, 2002.

Wallace, David. 'Periodizing Women: Mary Ward (1585–1645) and the Premodern Canon'. *Journal of Medieval and Early Modern Studies* 36, no. 2 (2006): 397–453.

Waller, Gary F. *The Sidney Family Romance: Mary Wroth, William Herbert, and the Early Modern Construction of Gender.* Detroit: Wayne State University Press, 1993.

Ward, A. W. and A. R. Waller, eds. *The Cambridge History of English and American Literature.* Vol. 9. New York: Putnam, 1907.

Waswo, Richard. 'Supreme Fictions: Money and Words as Commodifying Signifiers'. In *Fiction and Economy*, edited by Susan Bruce and Valeria Wagner. London: Palgrave Macmillan, 2007.

Watt, Ian. *The Rise of the Novel: Studies in Defoe, Richardson and Fielding.* London: Chatto & Windus, 1957

Watt, Tessa. *Cheap Print and Popular Piety 1550–1640.* Cambridge: Cambridge University Press, 1993.

Webbe, William. *A Discourse of English Poetrie.* London, 1588.

Weber, Max. 'The Protestant Ethic and the Spirit of Capitalism'. 1904. NY: Dover Publications, 2003.

Webster, John. *The Duchess of Malfi: A Tragedy, in Five Acts.* 1614. London: T.H. Lacy, 1860.

—— . *The White Devil.* 1612. Edited by Simon Trussler. London: Nick Hern Books, Stratford, 1996.

Weis, Rene, ed. *King Lear: A Parallel Text Edition.* London: Longman Publishing Group, 1993.

Wellek, René and Austin Warre. *Theory of Literature.* 1942. 3rd ed. New York: Harvest Books, 1984.

Whistler, Charles W. *Havelock the Dane: A legand of Old Grimsby and Lincoln.* Grimsby: Grim and Havelock Association, 2000.

Whitney, Isabella. *Sweet Nosgay, or Pleasant Posye: Contayning a Hundred and Ten Philosophical Flowers.* Ann Arbor: University Microfilms, 1983.

Williams, Raymond. *The Raymond Williams Reader.* Oxford and Malden, MA: Blackwell, 2001.

Wilson, Katherina, ed. *Women Writers of the Renaissance and Reformation.* Athens, GA: University of Georgia Press, 1987

Wilson, Robert. *Three Ladies of London.* Brooklyn, NY: AMS Press, 1970.

Wilson, Scott. *Cultural Materialism: Theory and Practice.* Oxford: Blackwell, 1995.

Wilson, T. *The Art of Rhetorique.* 1553. London. Edited by Peter E. Medine. University Park, PA: Penn State University Press, 1994.

Wilson, Richard. *Christopher Marlowe.* New York: Longman Publishing Company, 1999.

Woods, Susanne and Elizabeth Hagemen, eds. *Women Writers in English 1350–1850.* 14 vols. Oxford: Oxford University Press, 1993–2003.

Woolf, Virginia. A *Room of One's Own* (1929). Edited by Susan Gubar and Mark Hussey. New York: Harvest Books, 2005.

Wroth, Lady Mary. *Pamphilia to Amphilanthus*. Edited by G. F. Waller. Salzburg: Institute for English Language and Literature, 1977.

——. *The Second Part of the Countess of Montgomery's Urania*. Edited by Suzanne Gossett, Janel M. Mueller and Josephine A. Roberts. Binghamton, NY: Medieval And Renaissance Texts and Studies, 1999.

——. *Love's Victory: The Penshurst Manuscript*. Edited by Michael G. Brennan. London: Roxburghe Club, 1988.

——. *The Poems of Lady Mary Wroth*. Edited by Josephine A. Roberts. Baton Rouge, LA: Lousianna State Press, 1992.

——. *The First Part of the Countess of Montgomery's Urania*. Edited by Josephine A. Roberts. Binghamton, NY: Medieval and Renaissance Texts and Studies, 1995.

——. *The Second Part of the Countess of Montgomery's Urania*. Edited by Suzanne Gossett, Janel M. Mueller and Josephine A. Roberts. Binghamton, NY: Medieval And Renaissance Texts and Studies, 1999.

Wyatt, Michael. *The Italian Encounter with Tudor England*. Cambridge: Cambridge University Press, 2005.

Wyatt, Thomas. 'They Flee from Me'. *Selected Poems of Sir Thomas Wyatt*. London: Routledge, 2003. 41.

Wynne-Davies, Marion, ed. *Women Poets of the Renaissance*. London: Routledge, 1999.

Yeats, W.B. *Essays and Introductions*. London: MacMillan, 1921.

Young, R. V. 'Donne, Herbert, and The Postmodern Muse'. *New Perspectives on the Seventeenth-Century Religious Lyric*. Ed. John R. Roberts. Columbia and London: University of Missouri Press, 1994. 168–87.

Zim, Rivkah. *English Metrical Psalms: Poetry as Praise and Prayer 1535–1601*. Cambridge: Cambridge University Press, 1987.

Index